THE CHRISTIAN COLLEGE
IN DEVELOPING INDIA

This is the third and last volume in a series. The following earlier volumes have been published by the Christian Literature Society, Madras :

Richard Dickinson and Nancy Dickinson
Directory of Information on the Christian Colleges of India
1966 (276 pp.)

Richard Dickinson and S. P. Appasamy (eds.)
The Christian Colleges and National Development
1967 (288 pp.)

THE CHRISTIAN COLLEGE

IN DEVELOPING INDIA

A SOCIOLOGICAL INQUIRY

RICHARD D. N. DICKINSON

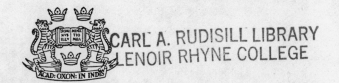

OXFORD UNIVERSITY PRESS

1971

NAVRANG
Oriental Booksellers and Publishers
Inderpuri, DELHI-12 (India)

Oxford University Press, Ely House, London W. 1

GLASGOW NEW YORK TORONTO MELBOURNE WELLINGTON
CAPE TOWN SALISBURY IBADAN NAIROBI DAR ES SALAAM LUSAKA ADDIS ABABA
BOMBAY CALCUTTA MADRAS KARACHI LAHORE DACCA
KUALA LUMPUR SINGAPORE HONG KONG TOKYO
Oxford House, Mount Road, Madras 6

Richard D. N. DICKINSON

Printed in India
by Pyarelal Sah at the Times of India Press, Bombay, India, and published by
John Brown, Oxford University Press, Madras 6

CONTENTS

LIST OF TABLES

LIST OF FIGURES

FOREWORD

History

THE study has grown out of a joint Roman Catholic, World Council of Churches' interest in evaluating the work of churches in 'secular' development activities — health, education and social welfare. Supported by a grant from the Ford Foundation in 1964, the ISS–FERES Project (taking its name from the initials of the two institutions which administered the overall study — the Institute of Social Studies, The Hague, Netherlands and the International Federation of Institutes of Social and Socio-Religious Research, Louvain, Belgium) was directed by Professor Egbert de Vries and Canon François Houtart. The work of the Project was divided into a documentation effort (which included a study of the information system of churches) and six field studies. The field studies were as follows:

Colombia 'Teaching of Development Attitudes in Secondary Education'

Brazil 'The Natal Movement as an Experiment in Community Development'

Cameroun 'Christian Health Services in the Cameroun'

Tanzania 'Primary Education as an Expression of the Churches' Concern for Development'

India 'Christian Higher Education and Indian National Development'

Indonesia 'Christians and Responsible Citizenship in the Indonesian Revolution'

Formulation of the Indian field study began in November 1964, although it was not until one year later that the focus and schedule of the research were finalized. It was first intended that we should concentrate on a description and normative evaluation of the role of Christian colleges in promoting national integration, but it soon became apparent that a broader description of the position and character of Christian colleges in India would be more useful at this juncture. Hopefully the study on Christian colleges and national integration could come later.

Defining the scope

A meeting of Church officials, Christian college principals, other educational leaders, and research technicians was convened in New Delhi in November 1965, to discuss the feasibility and utility of the research design. This meeting endorsed the general scheme, which included the following policy elements.

1. The study would describe the Christian colleges in India today — where they are, who sponsors them, why they were established and what are their current objectives, the religious policy of the institutions, their involvement in nation-building, their participation in community affairs, etc.

2. The study would be information-gathering rather than attempts to substantiate certain hypotheses. This approach was dictated by the paucity of information about the Christian colleges.

3. The study should as far as possible be 'operational' or action research. From the beginning we intended to involve those responsible for Christian higher education in India. This was motivated by a concern both to give a sophisticated interpretation of our findings, situated in actual problems, and to stimulate implementation of the recommended action. Thus, from the beginning two decisions were made which affected the methodology of the study.

(*a*) Despite the difficulties and limitations, it was decided to include all university-level Christian colleges in the study, because we had no adequate basis for selecting certain typical institutions. Further, many colleges would not feel that a study which did not include their particular institution had special relevance for them. Also many of the smaller colleges are frequently omitted from such studies and involvement, and often these are just the ones who most need evaluation.

(*b*) A major part of the study would be a consultation of those primarily responsible for church-sponsored higher education in India. Its purpose would be to discuss the implications of our empirical findings for the future work of Christian colleges in the country. This consultation would give major attention to the empirical, rather than theological, dimensions of Christian colleges today, but it was hoped and intended that fundamental questions of the *raison d'être* would be posed implicitly by those empirical realities. Furthermore, the consultation would, for the first time, bring together people from different parts of the country, various kinds of institutions, and diverse confessional backgrounds, to give varied perspectives and interpretations to common problems. Educators from outside the Christian colleges, from outside of the country, and from outside of the churches would be invited. At one point the question was raised whether it would not be more creative to have a less 'official' representation ! The less pessimistic view of college principals and church officials prevailed, and the optimists' view was ultimately justified in the quality of discussions at the terminal consultation.

4. The study would not seek to compare the work of Christian colleges with that of any other single group of colleges. The purpose of the research was not to make invidious comparisons with non-Christian institutions. Indeed, specific information about other types of colleges was not available. Our purpose was to improve Christian colleges; a comparison with other sponsors promised no significant advantages. We would be primarily concerned, therefore, to measure the performance of Christian colleges against their own capabilities, their own stated objectives, the *general* college situation in the country, good pedagogical theory, standards of education enunciated by the University Grants Commission, and more especially by the Education Commission whose report was due in early 1966.

5. The study would not be primarily historical, nor theoretical. It would be useful to look at the historical evolution of Christian colleges' effort because this would give perspective to their capabilities and about their subtle and sometimes unrecognized (to themselves) directions. To emphasize the historical would be both inconsistent with our primary concern to understand the Christian college as an agent in national development, and might lead to a picture of the role of Christian colleges in the past quite unrelated to the part they might play today. Because most previous discussions of Indian Christian

colleges have stressed philosophical and theological interpretations, it would be sounder to unearth factual and empirical information. This would provide a dimension of information
hitherto not available nor by many considered very important.
This more factual approach could greatly enrich discussions
on the philosophical level. From the beginning we felt assured
that somehow the discussions would gravitate from fact to
theory (which they did). There could never be any danger
of over-emphasizing the raw data. In retrospect we were right,
as more than one person commented after the consultation
was over that it was a shame that all those facts and all those
charts and tables had not been an integral part of the discussions !

6. The study should not be an interpretation and judgment
by 'experts' from the outside. While outside perspective was
to be encouraged, the research was to be a continuous sharing
process endorsed and encouraged by the responsible churches
and colleges. For the sophistication of our interpretation, as
well as for the practical utilization of the results, this was an
important principle in our entire work.

7. This study could not be done either by referring to books,
or exclusively through the mails. Direct, first-hand contacts
were important to create an understanding of what was
intended and to gather the pertinent information. Even by
December 1965, we had been able to develop only a tentative
list of Christian colleges in India (several revisions were later
required) and we had veiy little reliable and current information about those colleges. It became clear that such information
could be procured only at the colleges themselves. Furthermore,
direct support from the churches was imperative. Although we
met with considerable skepticism from the churches at the
beginning, we enjoyed their wholehearted support through
most stages of the study. A measure of their support was their
financial contribution to the consultation, and their own deep
personal involvement in the week-long discussions in Tambaram.

Having received the support of the churches, we formed a
team of interviewers, each responsible for visiting certain

colleges to gather basic information necessary for later stages of our work. A questionnaire of about 250 items was to be filled in for each college. While this was a time-consuming and costly approach, it gave us information and opened up contacts which were of inestimable value in the succeeding work.

Purposes

Positively stated, the goals of the study were the following.

1. We would collect information about the university-level Christian colleges in India, in the light of which those responsible for the colleges could more intelligently develop their own and regional programs. The empirical information gathered would be used to encourage administrators to analyze their colleges' work and to develop their programs for the future.

2. The study sought to promote communication and co-operation among Christian colleges (and eventually other colleges as well), often estranged from one another because of different sponsorship, traditions or purposes. It was hoped that a national organization would be formed to promote communication and co-operation.

3. We hoped to stimulate a critical re-appraisal of the purposes of Christian colleges at this juncture in Indian history. Particular attention would be put on a Christian college's role in developing the community and nation. This re-appraisal of objectives would be both general and particular — general for Christian colleges as a type of institution in the new India of the secular state, and particular with reference to the possible function of individual colleges in particular locales. Further, it would promote new thinking of a college's role in the light of the latest and most comprehensive blue-print for educational reform yet devised for India — the Education Commission Report.

4. The study would promote research and self-study in individual colleges and groups of colleges. Studies on Christian colleges' role in achieving national integration would become a major area of future interest.

5. The study would provide an overall picture of the Christian higher educational effort in India, sharpening the outline of trends, problems, and possibilities — which would assist in planning for the deployment of scarce material and human resources in the future. It was hoped that guidance for strategic action would ensue.

Methodology

The project was divided into five parts.

1. The first was an institutional questionnaire, with questions ranging across the gamut of college life and programs. (This questionnaire was too long to be included in the Appendixes here.) A team of seven young research officers was formed. Each member of this team was assigned between 15 and 20 colleges. Advance letters were sent to the principals, from church officials, the Project office, and the research officer involved — along with a copy of the pre-tested questionnaire. Most questions were answered during research officers' interviews with the principals and various other persons on campus.

This work extended from February through most of July 1966, at which time research officers met for a four-day discussion of their experiences, interpretations and impressions. These sessions gave a lively sense of the situation in most Indian Christian colleges. The anecdotes were priceless! It had been impossible to obtain reliable information on finances, and for statistics five and fifteen years previous. We finally were forced to abandon the time-perspective because most colleges did not have records for 1960-1 and 1950-1. Among other rich information we were now prepared to develop proper samples of teachers and students. Thus we moved into stage two.

2. The first part of stage two was a student-profile questionnaire, for which we selected 2,632 names, hoping for 2,000 responses. Research officers returned to selected colleges and made a random sample from the student rolls. Sometimes these questionnaires were administered to groups with students called together for approximately one hour, to ensure the

availability of the research officer to answer questions about the meaning of questions. More often students took the questionnaires and returned them later to the research officer before his departure from campus. 1,800 students returned their questionnaires.

3. At the same selected colleges, which were very close to the profile of Christian colleges overall in size, type, location, etc., we administered staff (faculty) questionnaires. One thousand teachers were chosen, of which 647 eventually returned questionnaires. Officers encountered considerable reluctance on the part of teachers, especially in Kerala. This reluctance may be partly attributable to teacher agitations in the state just prior to that time, and the continuing uncertainties in the state which surround Kerala colleges. While the sample is not as large as we would have liked, it does provide interesting and useful information.

4. While these questionnaires were being distributed, a third one was being sent to university alumni throughout India. It was not our major interest in this latter questionnaire to compare graduates of Christian and non-Christian colleges, but this aspect of the information proved to be interesting. The main purpose of this alumni survey was to see attitudinal and action indices of concern for, and involvement in, Indian development.

Four universities — two in the North and two in the South — were selected, partly because of the more accessible lists of registered graduates (those who pay a small fee to the University to become eligible to vote in University elections). These lists represented, therefore, a fairly select group of the graduates. On each of the lists, which were all less than three years old, there were between 20,000 and 33,000 names. Two thousand five hundred names were taken at random from the Madras, Kerala and Bombay lists, while only 2,000 were taken from the Calcutta list because the latter was not available after a certain time (which we feel does not at all affect the validity of our sample). Questionnaires were sent out, with postage and envelopes addressed to the Project (which could not have been identified as a church-college project). Questionnaires were originally distributed in September and early October, with reminders sent to all on the list about three weeks later. Respondees were anonymous (although many chose to write in their names). Judging by the second effort, the reminders had boosted the returns from about 32 per cent to 39 per cent. About 12 per cent (1,253) of the questionnaires sent were returned as 'addressee unknown' (showing the unreliability of the university address-lists) and we began processing the returns when we had received 3,200. Only a few came in thereafter, justifying our cut-off point. A copy of this questionnaire, as also '2' and '3' above, is in Appendix 8. Some of the material on the alumni questionnaire is yet to be processed at a later stage. Processing has been done with various sorter-counter Hollerith machines in Madras and New Delhi.

5. The fifth major element of the research itself were position papers prepared for the consultation of principals, and the reports of the discussion groups and speeches at the consultation itself. Most of these have been included in the second volume of this series. About ten papers were prepared in advance of the consultation, and printed for distribution at the meetings. In addition to these various papers, a directory of Christian colleges in India was prepared, based upon the 'institutional' questionnaire (and mountains of follow-up correspondence!) —the first volume of this series.

Explanations and acknowledgements

A few words are in order about the terminology of the tables and figures.

1. Often we refer to the sponsorship of institutions by initials. 'RC' means Roman Catholic; 'RCW' means under the sponsorship of a Roman Catholic Women's Congregation (it does not mean that it is a college for girls, although that is usually the case); 'RCM' refers to institutions under Roman Catholic Men's Orders or Congregations; 'RCD' denotes Roman Catholic Diocesan sponsorship; 'P' means Protestant; 'PS' refers to colleges sponsored by single Protestant denominations; and 'PU' (actually something of a misnomer!) refers to Protestant United efforts, or multi-denominational

sponsorship and 'S' refers to all Syrians who are not in communion with the Roman Catholic Church. The Church of South India and the United Church of North India have been included in this last category. 'NA' means not answered. 'INA' means information not available.

2. Several questions requested ranking, and these are given in the weighted tables. A simple system of weighting was used. When three places were called for (1, 2, 3) the first rank received 3 points, the second 2, and the third 1. Results were put on a scale of 100, which tends to make differences less dramatic, but more solid and reliable. Small differences on the scale of 100 may be quite important, as between 17 and 20 for example. There are justifiable techniques for making differences appear more dramatic, but we have felt that unnecessary here. But we would caution the reader not to be deceived by comparatively small differences on the weighted scale. In most cases of weighted questions, the reader may see the number of first place rankings and the number of no ranks, in addition to the total weighted frequency.

We have naturally avoided using percentage tables to obscure deficient numbers in the samples, preferring to omit a category altogether than to draw unreliable conclusions from too limited data.

3. One additional word of caution is necessary. There may be a tendency to confuse the terminology, in the text and the tables, of (for example) men's colleges — which could mean either colleges run by a men's order, or a college with only male students. Likewise there is a danger of confusing the noun to which the adjective Christian relates in many instances. Usually a 'Christian college graduate' will refer to a graduate of a Christian college (who may not be a Christian), and not to a college graduate who is a Christian. We have tried to avoid these confusions without continually using the same deadening phrase. The sense should be clear if this caution is borne in mind.

Finally, we would like to indulge very briefly in that dangerous game of acknowledgements, with full recognition that many who have been helpful to the success of this large undertaking will not be mentioned, even though they are not forgotten. It is normal to say that without the patience and help of 'my wife and family', this work could not have succeeded. This is certainly true in this case too. There were other indispensable people also: Satya Appasamy, S. P. Appasamy, Sydney Bunker, Father P. Ceyrac, Sheila David, Chandran Devanesen, V. Dharmarajan, J. Edward Dirks, Anthony Fernandez, Gopalakrishnan, Blossom Hamish, Canon François Houtart, George Kalapurakal, the Reverend William Kelley, Father James Keough, Father Theo Mathias, Sister Moira, A.C., Father Jess Montemayor, Suwartik Patel, Angela Reddy, Sadasivan, Hennie van Doren-Schütz, Egbert de Vries, and Ignatius, who nourished tired bodies and revived drooping spirits on many critically important occasions.

RICHARD DICKINSON

Geneva
January 1968

I

A NOTE ON THE CHRISTIAN
COMMUNITY IN INDIA

CHRISTIANITY arrived in India before the colonial powers. Tradition in the Syrian Orthodox community dates the arrival of Christians in India in the first century (with the arrival of the Apostle Thomas). With more certainty Christianity can be positively dated from at least the fourth century, on the Malabar coast. Early Christianity in India was 'Syrian' (using Syriac texts) and possibly was strongly affected by what is perhaps inaccurately called Nestorianism, but Zernov maintains that the Christian community in Malabar probably did not become much involved in those swirling theological disputes of the fourth and fifth centuries.[1] It was only after the arrival of the Portuguese, and later other Western Christians, that the Malabar Christian community was torn asunder time and again by questions of theology and authority. 'The Indian Orthodox considered themselves to be the members of the One, Holy, Catholic and Apostolic Church, and welcomed as their brothers in Christ any visitors from abroad, without enquiring to which of the sections of the divided Church they belonged.'[2]

The arrival of the Portuguese introduced many problems for the Malabar Christian community. Instead of integrating with them, the Portuguese settlement areas were put under bishops of the Latin rite. Under Archbishop Alexis de Menezes, the Synod of Diamper (perhaps canonically invalid) was held at the end of the sixteenth century, at which time the Syrian Orthodox acceded to papal authority. But smouldering discontent persisted and by the 1650s there was open defiance of the Roman Church as symbolized by the zealous Portuguese. There now was a clear division between the Syro-Romans and the Orthodox. When Bishop Mar Gregorius arrived from Syria in 1665, most of the Orthodox in Malabar acknowledged his authority, becoming known popularly as 'Jacobite' Christians (named after Jacob Bardaeus, who revived Syrian Christianity in the Middle East).

Zernov notes that the nineteenth and twentieth centuries have been times of great turbulence in the Malabar Christian communities, largely because of the religious, social and political influences coming from outside, and because some have believed that the church should be reformed.[3] One such influence was the Church Missionary Society (Protestant), after 1836, which led to the formation of a basically Protestant group. Another 'schism', stemming from 1887, led to the creation of the Mar Thoma Church, now numbering almost 350,000. A further division came about between those who accepted the administrative authority of the Jacobite Patriarch in Syria ('Patriarch's Party') and those who wanted more local autonomy ('Catholic's Party'). These were reconciled in 1959, and form a single church of about 750,000 members. The 'last secession from the Malabar community happened in 1930, when one of its leading bishops, Mar Ivanios (d. 1953), left his Church and went over to Rome, taking with him some 30,000 people.'[4]

The Orthodox Church in India is more indigenized than any other branch of Christendom in the country. Despite this there was no attempt until the seventeenth century to translate the Bible into the vernacular ; incomprehensible as it was to the layman, the Syriac text was used for hundreds of years, as was Latin in the West. Syrian Orthodox Christians in India do not seem to have been involved in the great doctrinal disputes of the early church. The faith of the Malabar Church was based not on explicit, formulated teaching but on worship; it is a communion more than a confession. The emphasis upon the family was both a basis for harmony and quarrel, for the Christian community found it difficult to accept into its fellowship those from other groups, and particularly from the lower castes. Despite these firmly held social cleavages, which led more readily to schism than to argument, Zernov contends that there was considerable intellectual tolerance, and that it is not surprising to find the disintegrating effect which Western Christianity had on the Syrian Christian community in India.[5]

Roman Catholicism was introduced in the sixteenth century by the Portuguese and later by the French. Between the sixteenth and nineteenth centuries there were only moderate numbers of converts to Christianity, despite sacrificial efforts by many missionaries, including Francis Xavier, de Nobili and Breschi. But between 1861 and 1911 there was a surging growth of the Catholic Church, reflecting in part the clarification of the Church's administration for the whole of the country (formerly there had been confusion between the role of Portuguese and local bishops). The change in the philosophy of the government toward religious groups, the missionary mood which swept across Europe in the latter half of the nineteenth century, and the development of schools, hospitals, and other social service endeavors by the churches also opened up large new areas of influence, especially among outcaste and tribal groups. Latourette notes that in 1861 there were 1,017,969 Roman Catholics in India, while by 1911 the number had more than doubled.[6] The number of priests, sisters and missionaries also greatly expanded. ' In 1912 India was served by 966 European and 1,142 Indian priests, 440 lay brothers, and 2,778 sisters.'[7] Further, there was during this period a dramatic increase in the number of orders and congregations working within India, many of which were largely indigenous.

Between 1914 and the present the number of Roman Catholics has continued to rise, as have the number of Catholic institutions and programs for social service. Today Roman Catholics number 1·5 per cent of the total population, with approximately 6,616,000 according to the 1964 accounting.[8] Roman Catholics have also greatly expanded their social service institutions, with about 50 new colleges having been founded during this period. The development of indigenous leadership also has been impressive, with more than twice as many Indian as foreign priests in 1961 (4,500 and 2,100 respectively as compared with 3,500 and 2,335 in 1955), and five times as many Indian as foreign nuns (16,000 and 3,000 respectively).[9] This figure represents a sixfold increase in the number of religious sisters in the period from 1921. In 1960 the major seminaries had about 1,800 men preparing for the priesthood, with an additional 1,800 in minor seminaries, leading Bishop Pothacamury to observe that ' vocations to the priesthood and the religious life are steadily on the increase. These figures demonstrate that the Indian Church cannot be regarded as a Western and exotic plant.'[10]

Protestantism's growth in India is also dramatic, covering a shorter time. The East India Company's official opposition to missionary activities was, until 1813, a major factor in restricting the number of Protestant Christians to ' only a few hundred ' in 1814, but by 1914 there were about 1 million Protestants (compared with approximately $2\frac{1}{2}$ million Catholics).[11] Richter puts the figure of Protestant Christians in India at 91,092 in 1851, of which 74,176 were in the Madras Presidency.[12] This growth reflects the late nineteenth century missionary expansion. Anglicans, Methodists, Presbyterians, Lutherans and Baptists all were active, with the Anglican and Methodists spreading their work into all parts of the country.

The proliferation of Protestant churches and programs led to increasing awareness of the practical difficulties (and later to a recognition of the theological indefensibility) of uncoordinated and often competitive denominational efforts. Consequently Protestant churches in India have been among the leaders in ecumenical activity. Most notable have been the formation of the Church of South India, having its beginnings in 1905 and official constitution in 1947, the struggles towards a United Church of North India, the National Missionary Council (1914) and its successor, the National Christian Council, formed in 1923.[13]

As Latourette points out, the development of Protestant indigenous leadership, so readily accepted in principle, has been very difficult to attain.[14] The problem is acute in all sections of the country and among all the denominations. For example, the Church of South India reported in 1963 that the average number of congregations served by each pastor in Tiruchchirappalli was 20, in Medak 16, in Krishna-Godavari

TABLE I

Protestant denominational families in India[15]

Denominational families	1954	1958	Percentage of change
Anglican and Episcopal	205,172	341,115	+ 66
Assemblies	32,923	33,478	+ 2
Baptist	1,251,330	1,276,957	+ 2
Church of South India	987,789	1,168,663	+ 18
Churches of Christ	4,206	3,999	− 5
Churches of God	15,551	19,051	+ 23
Lutheran	330,774	601,096	+ 82
Methodist	562,877	567,512	+ 1
Missionary Alliance	11,386	9,500	− 17
Presbyterian and other Reformed	135,745	161,067	+ 19
Salvation Army	158,978	209,585	+ 32
Seventh Day Adventists	19,133	19,133	..
Syrian Christians	789,000	846,410	+ 7
United Church of North India	422,776	487,771	+ 15
Other	97,618	108,889	+ 12
Total	5,025,258	5,854,226	+ 17

15.[16] Pay is abysmally poor (e.g. pastors in one C.S.I. diocese receive about $225 per year, or less than many cooks),[17] status is low, and most Christians come from economically and educationally depressed backgrounds. In the five major Protestant seminaries in India (Serampore, Leonard, Gurukul, United, and Bishop's College) there were a total of only 152 theological and 36 non-theological students in 1956. There are 15 lower-level theological schools offering a licentiate in theology, and requiring only a high school diploma for admission, with instruction in the vernacular. In 1956 these 15 theological schools had a total of 264 theological and 63 non-theological students.[18] In addition there were 12 schools, sponsored by more theological conservative groups, with 246 theological and 89 non-theological students. Further, Protestant seminary education is plagued not only by lower standard students, but by inadequate libraries, isolation from general educational trends in the country, language difficulties, and a variety of related problems.

Geographic distribution and growth

The dispersion of Christians throughout India reflects historical developments and mission patterns. Christians are

TABLE 2

Christian population in India (by state)[19]

State		Total population	Percentage of increase in population	Christian population	Christians as percentage of total	Percentage of increase in Christian population
Andhra Pradesh	1961	35,983,447	15·65	1,428,729	3·97	15·91
	1951	31,115,259		1,232,621		
Assam (excluding NEFA)	1961	11,872,772	34·45	764,553	6·44	56·89
	1951	8,830,732		487,331		
Bihar	1961	46,455,610	19·77	502,195	1·08	20·85
	1951	38,786,184		415,548		
Gujarat	1961	20,633,350	26·88	91,028	0·44	16·61
	1951	16,262,657		78,061	0·48	
Jammu and Kashmir	1961	3,560,976	9·44	2,848	0·08	··
	1951	3,253,852		NA		
Kerala	1961	16,903,715	24·76	3,587,365	21·22	26·95
	1951	13,549,118		2,825,720	20·85	
Madhya Pradesh	1961	32,372,408	24·17	188,314	0·58	
	1951	26,071,637		81,004	0·31	
Madras	1961	33,686,953	11·85	1,762,954	5·23	23·51
	1951	30,119,047		1,427,382	4·74	
Maharashtra	1961	39,553,718	23·60	560,594	1·42	29·39
	1951	32,002,564		433,255	1·35	
Mysore	1961	23,586,772	21·57	487,587	2·07	16·52
	1951	19,401,956		418,453	2·16	
Nagaland	1961	369,200	14·07	195,588	52·98	99·44
	1951	212,975		98,068	46·05	
Orissa	1961	17,548,846	10·82	201,017	1·15	41·63
	1951	14,645,946		141,934	0·97	

	Year	Total population	Decadal variation (%)	Christian population	Christians as % of total	Decadal variation of Christians (%)
Punjab and Haryana	1961	20,306,812	25·86	149,834	0·74	51·56
	1951	16,134,890		98,358	0·62	100·19
Rajasthan	1961	20,155,602	26·20	22,864	0·11	
	1951	15,970,774		11,421	0·07	−17·95
Uttar Pradesh	1961	73,746,401	16·66	101,041	0·14	
	1961	63,215,742		123,876	0·20	12·50
West Bengal	1961	34,926,279	32·80	204,530	12·52	
	1951	26,299,980		181,775	0·69	
Selected Union Territories						
Delhi	1961	2,658,612	52·44	29,269	1·10	56·64
	1951	1,744,072		18,685	1·09	
Goa, Daman and Diu	1960	626,667	5·14	227,202	36·25	− 2·66
	1950	596,059		233,403	39·16	
Manipur	1961	780,037	35·04	152,043	19·49	122·30
	1951	577,635		68,394	11·84	
Tripura	1961	1,142,005	78·71	10,039	0·88	90·78
	1951	639,029		5,262	0·82	
All India	1961	439,234,771	21·51	10,728,086	2·44	27·38
	1951	361,088,090		8,392,038	2·35	

a larger percentage of the population in the south (Kerala
21 per cent, Mysore 2 per cent, Madras 5 per cent, Andhra
4 per cent) than in the north, excluding Nagaland and Manipur (Jammu and Kashmir ·007 per cent, Madhya Pradesh
0·6 per cent, Uttar Pradesh 0·1 per cent, Rajasthan 0·1
per cent). Seventy per cent of India's Christians live in Mysore,
Madras, Kerala and Andhra. Syrian Orthodox Christianity
is a south-western phenomenon, although Christian leaders
from the south may be found all over India. Roman Catholics
are found all over India, but they predominate in the south
(78·4 per cent) ; the Chota Nagpur area in Bihar is a notable
exception, where since the 1920s Roman Catholics have
developed strong service programs and won many converts.[20]
Protestantism, largely consequent upon the British presence,
is also strongest in the south, but has a more even distribution
throughout the country, particularly around the former
British administrative centers and in the north-east tribal
areas.[21] Estborn puts the Protestant total in Tamil and
Telugu country, basically Madras and Andhra, at 1,557,332.[22]

A general perspective of the geographic distribution of
the total (undifferentiated) Christian community is shown in
Table 2, compiled from the 1961 census.

The growth of the Christian community is reflected in the
decade figures from 1881.[23]

TABLE 3

Growth of Christian population in India (1881–1961)

Year	No. of Christians	Percentage of population
1881	1,778,000	0·71
1891	2,164,000	0·77
1901	2,776,000	0·98
1911	3,666,000	1·21
1921	4,497,000	1·47
1931	5,966,000	1·77
1941	7,427,000	1·91
1951	8,392,038	2·35
1961*	10,728,086	2·44

* Not included by D'Souza.

These figures substantiate Baago's contention that 'the Christian Church in India is a growing Church, and contrary to the statements made in many church history books or histories of missions, the Christian population has increased at a greater rate in this century than in the last. About the year 1800, the number of Christians was about 0·7 per cent of the people. A hundred years later the percentage has increased to only 1 per cent, but in 1961 the Christians constituted 2·4 per cent of the population. The rate of progress during the last six decades has been almost three times that of the nineteenth century.'[24] It is not clear to what extent Professor Baago takes into consideration the partition of India, which must have made a significant increase in the overall percentage of Christians in India. Buddhism, although numerically small, is now the most rapidly expanding religion, by percentage, in India. Their numbers increased from about 180,000 to almost 3,250,000 between 1951 and 1961.[25] The relative position of Christianity in relation to the other major religions of India is clear from the following table.[26] Only 80,000 people were registered as atheists in the 1961 census.

TABLE 4

Major religions in India (1951 and 1961)

Religion	1951		1961		Percentage increase 1951–61
	Population	Percentage of total population	Population	Percentage of total population	
Buddhist	180,823	0·05	3,256,036	0·74	70·71
Christian	8,392,038	2·35	10,728,086	2·44	27·38
Hindu	303,575,474	84·98	366,526,866	83·50	20·29
Jain	1,618,406	0·45	2,027,281	0·46	25·17
Muslim	35,414,284	9·91	46,940,799	10·70	25·61
Sikh	6,219,134	1·74	7,845,915	1·79	25·13
Other	1,848,224	0·52	1,611,935	0·37	− 13·01
Total	361,088,090	100	439,934,771	100	21·51

Using the 1961 census figures, D'Souza has analyzed the urban-rural composition of the major religious groups.[27] Despite the fact that most Christians come from rural or tribal backgrounds and are generally referred to as a rural group, this table indicates that Christians are the third most urbanized of the the eight major religious groups in India. The population as a whole is 18 per cent urban, 82 per cent rural.

TABLE 5

Religion and urbanization in India (1961 census)[28]

Community	Total population	Urban population		Percentage urbanized of total population	No. of males per 100 females
Buddhists	3,250,227	M F	352,319 308,788	20·34	114
Christians	10,726,350	M F	1,299,538 1,239,615	23·67	105
Hindus	366,502,878	M F	32,854,503 27,481,384	16·46	120
Jains	2,027,267	M F	581,949 511,753	53·94	114
Muslims	49,939,357	M F	6,814,962 5,882,434	27·05	116
Sikhs	7,845,170	M F	801,776 639,594	18·37	126
Other	1,606,964	M F	84,059 83,929	10·45	100

The Parsis are probably the most urbanized religious group in India, but are not included in this table because of their size.

D'Souza suggests that one reason for the relatively higher incidence of Christian (and Muslim and Parsi) women in the city is their abandonment of the joint family system. There are certainly occupational and other reasons as well: commercial orientation of the Muslims and Parsis; heavy involvement of Christians in the civil service, especially in British times; establishment and running of medical and educational institutions by Christians, many of which are located in urban centers; relatively high literacy and education rate among Christians — to say nothing of the fact that many Christians probably migrate to cities to escape ostracism in a small rural community. A further breakdown shows that Christians are concentrated in cities in differing degrees in different parts of the country — West 69·63 per cent; Central 40·80 per cent; North 38·71 per cent; South 22·16 per cent; East 11·43 per cent.[29]

Growth of the Indian Christian community

We have noted that the Christian population is growing faster than the overall population. Latourette claims that ' most of the remarkable numerical growth of the Roman Catholic Church in India in the twentieth century was a result of the excess of births over deaths in its constituency '.[30] This may be true, given the higher education and health programs of Christians for their constituencies, and given the classical Catholic teachings on family life and family planning. But hard empirical supporting evidence is difficult to find. Indeed, some studies on relatively small samples suggest that, taking the urban Christian community as a whole, Christian families tended to have fewer children on the average than did their neighbor Hindus and Muslims, despite the fact that fewer of them had left their wives in the village. Two such studies are the Mysore Population Study, and a study of 1,018 wives in Kanpur and Lucknow, the two largest cities in Uttar Pradesh. The first was done under United Nations auspices, and the second by J. N. Sinha.[31] Perhaps conversions, as much as natural population increases, may have been largely responsible for the rising percentage of Christians in the total population. Conversions certainly have been an important element in the past.

In the 1930s Pickett analyzed four kinds of motives for joining the Christian community, and his findings on the percentage coming from each type of motive are as follows: (1) spiritual motives (religious and moral reasons) 34·8 per cent; (2) secular motives (economic or other material reasons) 8·1 per cent; (3) social motives (following the family, relatives or friends) 22·4 per cent; (4) natal influences (born of Christian parents, brought up in Christian environment) 34·7 per cent.[32]

Campbell asserts that people today are looking to government for their social emancipation, and it may even prove an economic and social liability to become a Christian today, whereas often in the past the danger was that the churches would attract too many 'rice' Christians.[33] Rural Christianity is in a difficult position ('sociologically speaking,' he reminds us) because of the following factors:[34]

(1) There is no place for the Christian in the village economy.
(2) Non-Christians are getting higher education now and Christians no longer enjoy their previous natural leadership role.
(3) Individuals and families now look to government and government service, rather than religion, for social and economic advancement.
(4) It is unlikely that mass religious movements can catch the imagination of the people today.
(5) Leadership of pastors is deplorably low, and
(6) It is extremely difficult to cultivate and sustain a Christian life in an isolated village, and Christianity tends to become just another set of rituals and beliefs, without vitality.

Despite the many obstacles which it has to face as a minority religion in an increasingly pro-Hindu environment, Christianity is making conversions in India — on a very modest scale. It would appear that between 1951 and 1961 there were approximately 530,921 converts, or 53,000 per year. Nevertheless, with the possible exception of eastern frontier areas, mass conversions are past. We no longer can imagine such increases as were experienced in the Punjab between 1881 and 1921, when the decade percentages of increase were 415, 94, 331 and 115, jumping the number of Christians from 3,823 in 1881 to 315,031 in 1921.[35] Yet there are still evidences of occasional fast growth even in India's heartland. For instance, Boal notes such growth in the Kond Hills of Orissa, and here also close traditional family patterns were a distinct advantage in bringing large numbers into the churches. 'Occasionally

Kond communities of considerable size and strength have joined an existing church or formed a new local church.'[36] This growth is seen in the rising number of churches, not including those still under construction.[37]

	No. of churches
1945	40
1950	49
1955/6	63
1958	73
1961	113

Therefore in the years:

 1945–50 there were 9 new churches in 5 years;

 1950–55/6 there were 14 new churches in 5 years;

 1955/6–61 there were 50 new churches in 5 years.

 Christianity in India is beset with difficulties, but growing sturdily, even remarkably, in some places.

Economic and occupational position

 Many in the Christian community are drawn from the poorer and tribal elements of society. There are, of course, Christians of middle- and upper-class background. Solid empirical evidence on Christians' financial position is hard to secure.[38] The socio-economic position of students in Christian colleges provides some data on the position of one segment of Christians in India. With a base sample from all over India of 1,800 respondents, we see the occupations of the fathers, given in percentages, in Table 6.

 Family income *per annum* is given in Table 7.

 This tends to confirm, but in a very tenuous way, the lower income characteristics of the Christian community. What is most striking in Table 6 is the relatively large number of Christian students from farming families. It is important to recall that these are the Christian families who sent their children to college, and may not be characteristic of the entire Christian community. Poorer Hindu and Muslim students *might* tend to enroll in government schools simply because

TABLE 6

Occupation of students' fathers (by students' religion, in percentages)

Occupation	RC	P	S	Hindu	Muslim	Other	Total
Farming	40	23	34	21	11	21	25
Professional	4	10	8	9	5	6	8
Skilled technician	4	6	3	5	6	4	5
Unskilled laborer	2	2	—	3	—	—	2
Clerical and Office	6	9	11	8	8	8	8
Government service and Military	7	13	8	17	21	14	14
Managerial	2	2	1	3	5	2	3
Business and Landlord	20	13	24	20	29	29	30
Education	8	12	10	6	2	4	7
Other	2	1	—	1	6	2	1
NA	5	9	1	7	7	8	7
Total	100	100	100	100	100	100	100

TABLE 7

Students' family income per annum (by religion, in percentages)

Annual income	RC 359	P 267	S 79	Hindu 948	Muslim 59	Other 40	Total 1,752
Up to Rs 1,000	26	19	19	23	31	—	23
Rs 1,001–2,000	24	29	28	19	17	25	22
Rs 2,001–3,000	13	12	11	10	7	10	11
Rs 3,001–5,000	11	14	24	12	8	16	12
Rs 5,001–7,500	6	9	4	7	10	9	7
Rs 7,501–10,000	5	4	4	6	3	3	5
Rs 10,001–15,000	2	4	3	5	12	6	4
Rs 15,001 +	2	3	1	5	3	—	3
NA	11	6	6	13	8	31	12
Total	100	100	100	100	100	100	100

tuition fees could be less. Even the poorer Christian students might enroll in Christian colleges.

Less solid empirical evidence is provided in Jai Singh and Alter's study of the church in Delhi, but in the absence of other materials, it is useful.[39] It is less solid because filled questionnaires were submitted by 16 of 22 Delhi pastors who gave impressionistic answers. Most Christians in Delhi were in some kind of government service (43 per cent), with other occupations as follows:

TABLE 8
Occupation of Delhi Christians

Domestic service	21%
Education	13%
Medicine	11%
Business	3%
Industrial labor	2%
Other	7%

Naturally Delhi is a special situation, not reflecting large numbers of Christians in such occupations as farming and tanning. On the whole, among Christians in India there are very few shopkeepers or independent businessmen. As for incomes, this Delhi survey concludes that 30 per cent of the families have incomes of below Rs 100 per month, 30 per cent have between Rs 100 and 200, 26 per cent receive between Rs 200 and 500 per month, and 14 per cent receive over Rs 500 per month. (At the time of that study Re 1 was worth 22 U.S. cents.) About one-third of the families received less than the amount officially considered the absolute minimum required for a family of five. Unemployment among Delhi Christians is a major problem, with one pastor reporting 20 per cent of the families in his congregation unemployed.[40]

Campbell's study of the churches in the Punjab also yields several insights into the socio-economic character of the Christian community. Again, however, synoptic empirical information is largely missing. In a transitional village adjacent to a city the occupation of Christians, largely converted from a very low caste group, was given as follows:[41]

TABLE 9
Occupation of village Christians in the Punjab

Work in the city	21
Bicycle repair man	1
Brick maker	4
Farm laborer	3
Tenant	3
Government road gang	6
Gate watchman	2
Hide and bone dealer	2
Landowning farmer	1
Shopkeeper	1
School teacher	1
Tailor	1
Village sweeper	3
Shoemaker	2

It would be very helpful to know how the 21 people in the city were employed! The author has mixed type of occupation with site of occupation. In any case, when this group of Christians is compared with the non-Christian caste group from which they originated, it is evident that Christians are socially and economically much better off.

Campbell also presented the composition of an urban church in the Punjab.[42]

TABLE 10
Income of urban Christians in the Punjab

Occupation	Rs 60 or less	Rs 60–100	Rs 100–150	Rs 150–300	Rs 300 +	Total
Laborers—part-time and apprentice	6	—	—	—	—	6
Industrial laborers	—	4	4	—	—	8
Sanitary workers	—	3	—	—	—	3
Clerks	—	—	4	—	—	4
Carpenters and masons	—	—	3	—	—	3
Teachers	—	—	2	1	1	4
Professors	—	—	—	—	2	2
Businessmen	—	—	—	4	—	4
Administrators	—	1	—	—	2	3
Total	6	8	13	5	5	37

While the evidence is not empirically sophisticated nor quantitatively sufficient, it gives an impressionistic view that Christians are predominantly rural and from the lower socio-economic level of Indian society. But their school systems and values make them one of the most literate and upward-mobile groups in the society, and Christian groups tend to be better off from a socio-economic point of view than are those from the same caste and tribal backgrounds who did not convert. This is true even though in some states Christians do not qualify for help under the government's program of economic assistance to underprivileged groups.

Organization

For a long time the effectiveness of the Christian Church in India was sapped by rivalries and lack of co-ordination. For the Catholics this was most noticeable in tensions between the Portuguese and indigenous Indian groups. Frictions were exacerbated by internal relationships in the Syrian churches and their differing rites. The Protestants, too, have long been plagued by denominational rivalries and tensions between the mission-sending bodies and local churches of India.

A complex of national organizations has been developed to help surmount these divisions. Most notable on the Roman Catholic side is the development of the Catholic Bishops' Conference of India, formed in 1944, but holding its first plenary meeting only in 1951. In addition there have developed organizations on a national scale to do specific types of work, such as the All-India Catholic University Federation, the Xavier Board of Christian Higher Education in India, the Xavier Association of Secondary Schools, and the All-India Catholic Medical Association. These and others are described in *The Catholic Directory of India* prepared for the visit of Pope Paul VI to Bombay in 1964.

Most notable on the Protestant side has been the evolution of the National Christian Council. Formed in 1914 as an agency of the mission boards, the Council became Indian in 1922, although its budget still comes largely from outside India. It began to assume a number of tasks on behalf of the churches for which it was not fully equipped — with staff, money, and sometimes authority. Baago notes the rise of many initiatives under the Council and reports the complaint, voiced by Manikam, that the National Council itself was like the former overseas mission boards; too few of the decisions devolved to the regional sections and the grass roots of the churches.[43] A major decision was taken in 1956 to divest the Council of all but its fundamental tasks, in the hopes that lower level regional councils would assume these responsibilities, but already by 1959 it was clear that local councils were too weak to do the job. The National Christian Council is, therefore, still in the process of defining its organization and functions toward its member churches. Some criticize it for being preoccupied with its own nature and organization and for not giving visionary and vital leadership in the mission and ecumenical life of the churches. One of its main functions continues to be as official representative of the churches to the Government. In 1967, the death of Korula Jacob brought additional leadership problems to the Council.

The Protestant churches in India have pioneered ecumenical activity by forming the Church of South India and the United Church of North India. The United Church of North India exists, but is still in the process of including all churches originally envisaged in 1924, and mooted at the first Round-Table Conference in 1929 at Lucknow — the chief abstainers being the Methodist Church in Southern Asia and the Church of India, Pakistan, Burma and Ceylon (Anglican).[44]

An encouraging phenomenon for the future is growing co-operation between the three major branches of Christianity in India. This collaboration follows the pattern of previous ecumenical initiatives within Protestantism itself — co-operation first in areas of service. One expression of this is the current collaboration of Protestants and Catholics in the action-research of the churches' participation in the development of the Chota Nagpur district. Another dramatic collaboration is through Action for Food Production (AFPRO), begun in 1965 and sponsored by the churches to increase food production — at first primarily through artesian wells and irrigation, but with a broad educational and development program to follow. Further, there are efforts now to foster joint socio-religious research related to development. Finally, in 1967, the National Board for Christian Higher Education in India was formed to strengthen the work of all colleges in the interests of improving education and accelerating development in the country. Other modes and areas of co-operation are likely to evolve in the near future.

II

UNIVERSITY EDUCATION IN INDIA

THIS chapter discusses only modern university education in India, having its roots in the western education of the late eighteenth century. There were, to be sure, important educational centers in ancient India, notably at Taxila and Nalanda, frequently with religious connections. But these centers were essentially different in character from modern university education. Furthermore, they had long ceased to exist when the present college and university system materialized.

The Portuguese, French and Dutch did not develop higher education institutions in India; it was the British who first established them. The East India Company first opposed introducing education into India because it feared its potentially disruptive effect upon the populace. This opposition persisted until the early nineteenth century, though the Company's policy was increasingly attacked in England by Wilberforce and others. By 1817, however, a first western-style college was founded in Calcutta, with Serampore College (1818) and Bishop's College (1820) following immediately thereafter[1] — the latter two being Christian colleges. Universities were not introduced until 1857.

During this formative period there was considerable controversy about the purpose and value of western education in India. Some opposed it because it would undermine Hindu culture and 'oriental' learning, while others thought this was precisely what it could and should do. These two approaches were symbolized by the attitudes of Lord Hastings and The Committee on Public Instruction ('orientalists') on the one hand, and Lord Macaulay, favoring Western and English education, on the other. A more practical question was how to stretch the meager sums allocated for education to cover the millions who needed it. The filtration strategy won the day; if the potentially powerful and influential elements could be educated, their influence would filter down to the rest of society. The famous Macaulay Minute on Education, in 1835, set its stamp on all education which was to follow in the country. Macaulay's arguments for western-style education, in English, were based primarily upon his disdain for 'oriental' learning and philosophy, the absence of tests, and upon practical considerations for governing the country. Acceptance of the Macaulay Minute as the standard for education in India deepened the entrenchment of western-oriented education.

If the Macaulay Minute set the general tone for education in India, Lord Hardinge's resolution of 1844 further crystallized its character as a tool of British hegemony. This resolution gave practical preference to English-speaking graduates of English-oriented schools, usually missionary schools, in civil service. Thus Christian schools were fortified, and it gave strong impetus to making education a narrow training instrument for lower level government service — a psychological handicap from which Indian education has not yet fully recuperated. It trained to execute decisions (and that at a fairly low level), but not to make them.

By 1854 ferment for freedom was finding political expression, giving rise to the Mutiny in 1857, after which the British government took control from the East India Company. The Wood Despatch on Education, in 1854, was primarily for elementary and secondary education, but it opened the door for the establishment of full-scale universities, and in 1857 a government university was established in each of the three administrative centers — Calcutta, Madras, Bombay. These were to be supported by public funds and styled after the newly-founded University of London, thus being primarily affiliating bodies rather than instructional ones.[2] Teaching was to be done in affiliated colleges, with the university setting syllabi, administering examinations and granting degrees. Only later, in 1902–4, was the principle of university instruction, the teaching university, adopted. This state involvement in education prompted Lamb to note that 'because of the policy of government inspection and grants to private educational institutions, India had a state-dominated system of education far earlier than countries in the West.'³

The centralization which resulted was resented by many missionary colleges. Indeed, the Hunter Commission of 1882 resulted largely from missionary agitation for a review of government policy. The Commission also reflected the concern that government was not adequately discharging its responsibilities for primary and secondary education, as had been stipulated in the Wood Despatch almost thirty years earlier. In the period between 1854 and 1882 no new universities had been founded, but many colleges had sprung up, with about seventeen of them being under Christian auspices. Not all of these have survived to the present.

The Hunter Commission was charged with reviewing the effects of the Wood Despatch. One consequence of the Hunter Commission's work was to reverse the strong preferential treatment accorded to government schools as distinguished from private institutions. The Commission recommended that government should actively encourage the transfer of control of government schools to local control, and that private colleges should be permitted to charge lower fees than government institutions. In addition, moral instruction should be included at all levels. At the higher secondary stages pupils would be channeled into streams commensurate with their abilities — collegiate and vocational. This report stimulated the rapid growth of private institutions; in ten years the number of pupils in secondary English schools jumped from 149,233 to 300,000 in 1892. 'In 1882 there were 7,429 candidates for Matriculation in the four [sic] universities; in 1885–6 there were 13,093; in 1889, 19,138; and in 1906, 24,963.'⁴ Bengal had the most dramatic rise in numbers at the Matriculation stage.

A significant movement to extend the scope of Indian education was highlighted, in 1890, with the Voelcker Conference. Delegates deplored that education was too narrowly conditioned by training for administration and that agricultural education was being ignored. There was also widespread feeling that, at least at the higher levels, quantity was submerging quality.

Notwithstanding the Hunter Commission's attack on centralized government control, the problem remained unresolved, and yet another Commission was formed — the Indian Universities Commission, under Lord Curzon (Viceroy, 1899–1905). Although this Commission focussed on Calcutta University, its recommendations had wider relevance. The report, published in 1904, claimed that universities paid too much attention to preparation for government service, that too much prominence was given to examinations, that courses were too literary, and that memory work beclouded the whole educational effort.[5] It urged a tightening of university administrative procedure and organization. Grants-in-aid would henceforth require more stringent inspections, even though such grants were to be more generous when merited. In addition, universities themselves were to become teaching units and set the standard for the colleges, and more Indians were to come into the administration of the universities. Siqueira notes, further, that a 1906 reform brought science into the Indian university curriculum for the first time — at Presidency College, Calcutta.[6]

Other efforts were being made during this period to indigenize education, and to relate it to the experiences and needs of the people. It is symbolic that Tagore's school, Santiniketan, was founded in 1904 as an effort to simplify education and make it more relevant to the Indian scene. The Wardha Scheme, publicized by Gandhi and his followers, was another attempt to bring education closer to the realities of Indian life, and to restore or preserve values which were, it was thought, being eroded by Western education in the country. The Wardha Scheme had political overtones as well, as an expression of the resistance movement. Not to mention the agitations of Tilak, endorsing education for girls, and Gokhale, would be remiss. Their efforts on behalf of universal and free education led to the 1913 Government Resolution calling for widespread improvements in primary education.

Siqueira notes that the demand for more university education places was met, between 1887 and 1917, primarily through the establishment of additional colleges, and not universities.[7] By 1917 there were only seven universities; in addition to the

three ' presidency ' ones already mentioned there were Allaha-
bad (1887); Banaras Hindu (1916); Mysore (1916); Patna
(1917). Numbers then increased rapidly: Osmania (1918);
Aligarh Muslim (1921); Lucknow (1921); Delhi (1922); Nagpur
(1923); but the pace slackened before the advent of World
War II, with only four additional universities being founded.
The major expansion in university numbers came, of course,
after World War II, with forty-two universities having been
founded between 1948 and 1966. Most new universities represented extensions of educational facilities more than new
approaches to education. Banaras Hindu University and
Aligarh Muslim University, both teaching universities, were
interesting additions to government universities, and paralleled
the Christian colleges.

Helping to account for the expansion of universities between
1917 and 1923 was the work of the Sadler Commission
(Calcutta Commission) in 1919, which reviewed university
structure once again. Noting that the Hunter Commission had
paid little attention to universities, and that the Curzon Resolution paid scant attention to secondary education, the Sadler
Commission examined the relationship between secondary and
higher education. In general, this Commission sought to
strengthen government control over the universities, and to
stimulate the development of universities as unitary and
teaching bodies. The Commission also wanted to minimize
intermediate work at the universities themselves, to increase
educational opportunities for girls, to expand facilities for
Muslims, and to improve vocational and professional education. Probably as important as any other recommendation
was a proposal for a number of junior colleges, many of which
would offer vocational training. Suggestions pertaining to the
junior colleges were not implemented.

To counteract the centralization of education, the 1921
Montagu-Chelmsford reform established the authority of the
states (not the central government) over the universities in
their own territories, but by 1924 it was increasingly felt that
some co-ordination of the work of the various universities was
essential; they could not be left to the vagaries of special

interests in each state. This co-ordination was advanced by the establishment of the Inter-University Board in 1926, a voluntary board of universities whose credentials are acceptable to the Board. This Board has had an uncertain history, but is active today. The Hartog Commission (1927), principally concerned with primary education, sounded a recurring theme: 'More attention to quality and less to quantity.'

Of special interest in the evolution of Christian higher education in India was the Lindsay Commission, established in 1930 to evaluate the work of the Christian (Protestant) colleges in India.[8] At this time there were approximately thirty-three Protestant and sixteen Roman Catholic colleges in India. The Commission grew out of a meeting in Agra in 1929, with representatives from a majority of Protestant higher education institutions in the country. The work of the Commission, and the Report itself, represents a landmark in Christian higher education in India. Among the major recommendations of the Report were the following.[9]

(1) Some colleges (many thought there should have been more on the list) should be closed, and others merged.

(2) Christian colleges should stress quality and not quantity.

(3) Christian colleges should maximize the advantages of being a residential community, and should limit their numbers to achieve this goal.

(4) Without creating a Christian ghetto, more attention should be paid to getting qualified Christian staff, and providing a Christian atmosphere.

(5) Classwork should relate, wherever possible, to the needs of the community, and expanded programs of social service should be stimulated.

(6) Research and emphasis on academic excellence should be actively encouraged.

(7) Colleges should cultivate relationships with the larger Christian community and church life.

(8) Colleges should express in a creative and imaginative manner (despite university restrictions) the special commitments for which Christian colleges stand.

(9) Means should be devised to co-ordinate the work of the various Christian colleges, and to include in decision-making more members of the Christian community in India.

This Report was received with widespread interest and enthusiasm, especially throughout the 1930s. Most of the recommendations were not implemented successfully, for a variety of reasons. One of the most profitable experiments was the establishment of a committee for higher education in the framework of the National Christian Council, which functioned with some success until the 1950s. The Lindsay Commission was the only survey and evaluation of Christian higher education work in India, on an inter-denominational basis, until the Consultation of Christian college principals and other responsibles, in 1966–7, at Tambaram.[10] There have been, in addition, denominational evaluations such as that by the Methodist Church, in the late 1940s, and by the Presbyterian Church of its North India educational institutions (not only colleges), in 1962.[11]

By 1937–8 the Abbott-Wood Report stressed the need to increase vocational training, and the Laubach group made major efforts to reduce adult illiteracy and to develop adult education. But these recommendations and efforts received scant attention with the fast pace of political and social developments both within India and outside. World War II had already come to India by 1940. Congress continued its agitation for freedom, even though a majority of Indians backed the British during the war, with the notable exception of S. C. Bose and the Indian National Army. Mohammed Ali Jinnah was increasingly militant for a solution of the Hindu-Muslim problem. In England itself there was heated controversy over the India policy, and the ' Quit India Movement ' was in full throttle by 1942.

With the dawn of Independence (15 August 1947) such vast changes had occurred in India that a new education commission was established, under the chairmanship of the distinguished philosopher and later President, Dr. S. Radhakrishnan (himself a graduate of Madras Christian College). The ensuing massive Report, issued in three volumes, became the guideline for university education. The challenge of the newly independent India set the tone of the deliberations and conclusions. The Report deplores the low educational standards in the country's universities, and urges a new education relevant to India's cultural heritage and to its promising future as an independent state. It calls for a deeply humanistic education, improvement of teaching, revision of the school system so that students would enter the university at a more mature age, development of tutorials and closer teacher-student relationships, reform of the examination system to make it more continuous and directly related to the ongoing work of the students, development of forms of student initiative and responsibility in the community life of the college, use of the mother tongue as the medium of instruction, provision for professional and vocational education, entrance to the universities on a much more stringently controlled basis, etc.

Among the more useful and promising recommendations was that to establish a University Grants Commission, similar to that in England. While the University Grants Commission would not have administrative authority over the universities, it would exercise considerable influence and power through its (limited) budget to foster certain kinds of programs and studies. Since its inception in 1956 the Commission has done invaluable service in gathering and publishing information about the colleges and universities, on the basis of which more sophisticated judgments can be made. It has also inaugurated many worthy and well thought-out programs for upgrading college and university life — such as the series of summer institutes it has supported, its ' centenary grants ' to institutions on their hundredth birthday, and its support for libraries and laboratories in deserving institutions. The Commission has contributed in many creative ways to the improvement of higher education.

An important controversy which has become sharpened since Independence pertains to the locus of authority of the university. Some argue that universities, perhaps unlike primary and secondary schools, are matters of national importance and national interest, and should come under the purview of the central government. Others vehemently insist that universities are state responsibilities. There have been efforts to put universities on a 'joint' list with central and state governments sharing responsibility, but all efforts to get universities even partially under central control have failed. The latest legal ruling to this effect was made in 1966, in response to a central government inquiry about the juridical status of universities. This ruling, for the most part, upholds the authority of state governments in higher education.[12]

In conjunction with the Second Five-Year Plan, a committee under the chairmanship of C. D. Deshmukh studied present conditions and projected needs in higher education. This committee, convened in the late 1950s, made several important proposals. Universities should adopt a three-year instead of a four-year course. The standard of education should be improved by increasing libraries, expanding laboratory facilities requiring inter-disciplinary work (as between arts and sciences in particular), reducing of college size to between 800 and 1,000 students by 1961, revising of syllabi and tutorials, etc. No new intermediate college should be recognized. The University Grants Commission was to help effect these changes, and by 1963 most of the universities had accepted the basic changes regarding the three-year course. Bombay retained the two-year intermediate and two-year degree courses.

Another significant landmark was the Sri Prakasa Committee Report on student discipline and values, in 1959.[13] In view of widespread student unrest and general malaise in colleges and universities, and in response to the increasingly vocational and scientific orientation of education in certain segments, the committee recommended a sustained effort to inculcate religious and moral values throughout the entire university curriculum. Starting with general ethical and moral instruction during the first year, students would then be introduced to the lives and thinking of great world religious leaders in their second year, and during the third year great religions of the world would be studied. This general plan has been supported in the most recent Education Commission Report. Christian leaders have generally, but not universally, criticized this approach as implicitly syncretistic and relativistic, arguing that it favours a Hindu *Weltanschauung*.

The most promising development in education in recent years has been the Education Commission, which met in various working groups from 1964 to 1966, under the direction of Dr. Kothari, Chairman of the University Grants Commission.[14] A striking feature of this Commission's work was its mandate for a comprehensive look at all Indian education in relation to national development needs. It was directed, therefore, to do what most other commissions could not do, to consider how all aspects of education in the country could be harmonized into a national educational plan. Mr. J. P. Naik, Secretary-Member of the Commission, to whom fell much of the actual formulation of the final report (presented in June 1966), argues that this is the first effort, at least since Independence, to develop a co-ordinated plan for all Indian education. There was, to be sure, the Sargeant Plan, developed in 1944, but this was in many ways irrelevant to the conditions which were to pertain after 1947. Naik argues that India has for many years needed such a long-term comprehensive plan so that reforms will have maximum effectiveness in a total scheme of development.[15]

The Education Commission Report is explicitly concerned with national development. Indeed, some feel that it puts too much emphasis on social rather than individual values. However, it is the first report which addresses itself so explicitly to calculated manpower needs, and Government of India Five-Year Plans. This frame of reference has provoked much discussion and not inconsiderable dissension, but it also brings a certain often-missing realism to discussions about educational reform because it considers priorities and budgets. Needless to say, more refinement and resolute action is necessary before many of the ideas and recommendations can be implemented — if they ever are — but the Report injects a note of healthy realism into educational planning.

One especially exciting and controversial feature of this realism is the Report's advocacy of six special universities and fifty autonomous colleges. Opposition to this proposal comes from those who feel that all institutions should be treated impartially, a hangover from the era of the struggle for Independence, when many colleges fought to be treated as equals with missionary and British colleges. They resented the perpetuation of their disadvantaged position. The Report strongly urges the establishment of six outstanding universities, comparable to the best universities anywhere in the world (two of which would be a technical university and an agricultural one). If there are already sixty-four universities, why should six more be necessary, or how can six of the existing institutions be elevated to special rank? The Commission argues that to upgrade all the universities is physically impossible, and impossible for other reasons as well. If there is to be first-class education in India it must evolve through a conscious strategy of investment in a few select places, even if this entails some partiality. This is a hard reality. Whether or not it is possible to create six such universities in the near future, or even one such university, comparable to the best universities anywhere in the world, it is a healthy sign that the principle of legitimate partiality has been mooted.

Similarly, the recommendation that perhaps fifty of the best colleges in the country should enjoy autonomous, or semi-autonomous, status is most encouraging. One disease of the Indian university system is that, in order to upgrade the poorer colleges, which are probably the vast majority, better colleges are confined and cramped by the same rules. All colleges, good and bad, are subject to the same university rules. Creativity is stifled; new initiatives are stymied. Pervading the whole life of the university and individual colleges is a common syllabus and examination which atrophies true education. The Commission argues that a number of the best colleges should be permitted to experiment, to set their own syllabi and examinations, to develop their own teaching staff and teaching patterns. Such autonomous status could be revocable, or even simply partial. The important thing would be to experiment with autonomy in a few colleges and gradually extend this advantage to other institutions, if and where warranted.

Again, this suggestion challenges the principle of impartial treatment for all colleges, but it is both sound and essential if higher education is to get untracked and on to new rails.

These suggestions for preferential status are particularly urgent in view of the general situation in Indian universities today, so aptly described by Robert Gaudino and Edward Shils, both of whom wrote before this semester of discontent, from September to February 1966-7.[16] Perhaps the tap-root of the problem is the explosion of secondary school graduates clamoring to capitalize on their political right—a seat at the university and a passport to a degree and a job (possibly) which it symbolizes. Twenty-three new universities have been created since 1960; every year the number of colleges increases by almost 10 per cent, totalling approximately 2,700 in 1966-7, and almost 3,000 in 1967-8. Can any country finance and find personnel for 250 to 300 new colleges per year? Many existing institutions expand as well. The number of students in higher education is now approximately 1,100,000 or about 2 per cent of the population in the relevant age-group. About 40 per cent of those in college or the university are under seventeen years old, either in the Pre-University Course or the Intermediate Course (different streams of advancement for different parts of the country). About 80 per cent of these students are in the colleges affiliated with the universities, as distinguished from the 20 per cent who are enrolled in constituent colleges of the university. Of these 2,700 university related colleges, approximately 85 per cent are private, although they come under university and state regulations. The Education Commission extrapolated that by 1985 there would be eight million students in higher education, and concluded that to meet even half this demand, assuming that the numbers could be curtailed, strenuous efforts would have to be made.

Beyond the provision for mere quantity, however, considerations of quality came to have paramount significance in the Report. To provide suitable teachers is all but impossible, even with an accelerated expansion of teacher-training and post-graduate instruction. Our own survey shows how young, inexperienced, and inadequately trained many teachers in Christian colleges are, and the picture for other institutions or groups of institutions can hardly be brighter.[17] It is a startling fact that many private colleges are operated for other than educational motives — for making money or securing status and political strength.[18] In such institutions physical plants are anaemic, teaching staffs are grossly inferior and often maltreated (hence teachers representing private colleges in Kerala have recently agitated for government take-over), libraries and other study materials are appallingly limited, courses which cost extra money (sciences), and services which support the student in his work (guidance services, orientation programs) are curtailed. Such conditions threaten all of Indian private education, even though it is unlikely that Government will expropriate private colleges.

To improve quality, the Commission also promulgated other recommendations of great potential significance. One is examination reform, with less stringent reliance on the end-of-studies external examination. These put a premium on rote memorization and the regurgitation of facts rather than on demonstrating an ability to solve problems. Likewise the Education Commission advocates the emancipation of the college syllabus from the tyrannical control of the university, especially in those colleges which have demonstrated maturity enough to use freedom intelligently. If these two reforms could be effected a fresh breeze could sweep through the classrooms of the better colleges, thus having a dramatic effect on collegiate education as a whole.

Another high priority recommendation relates to the kinds of courses offered in the colleges. The Commission notes the dearth of sociology, anthropology, and similar empirically oriented social science courses which are of critical importance in an emerging understanding of Indian traditions and India's future. The Commission urges universities to provide as quickly as possible broad scope for these studies, attaining as soon as feasible approximately 30 per cent of their total enrollment. It is also a matter of deep concern that about 53 per cent of students in arts and sciences colleges still pursue an arts degree, notwithstanding the fact that this degree is a glut on the employment market. Presumably many more students would choose the sciences were facilities available. The Commission also urged broadening the curriculum for maximum possible exposure to various fields of study. At present it is customary for students in, say, arts to pursue a course which offers no contact with physical and social sciences; the science course is likely to afford no familiarity with the arts. The Commission deplores this narrow and unimaginative approach, urging a vastly expanded inter-disciplinary experimentation.

Students come to the university at an impressionable and vulnerable age; this compounds the college and university's obligation to provide them with direction and special service. Yet most Indian colleges provide nothing of the sort, despite the fact that this may be the student's first major experience outside the authority patterns and morals of his own family. There are few other sources of help to which a confused student can turn. The Education Commission strongly urges concerted attempts to provide services for students, and that students should learn internalized norms through participation in responsible student organizations at their college.

Further, the Report observes that a major function of the university, especially in developing countries where human and material resources are scarce, is to actively promote the welfare of the community at large — through research, community outreach programs, social service projects. Several universities and colleges promote embryonic programs of this type, but only a handful (Ahmednagar College is an important exception) of institutions pay adequate attention to this aspect of a college's functions. Adult education programs, special courses for community leaders, involvement of students and staff in community-wide studies and relief programs, are but a few of the ways that a university may become more vitally connected with the life of the community in which it is set. On the larger scene, it is urged that colleges and universities develop enrollment patterns which reflect future manpower needs in particular areas of the country, and that present ratios of graduate to under-graduate students be accelerated from 11 per cent to 30 per cent in post-graduate work. Further, as a matter of practical policy, it is urged that post-graduate work should ordinarily be done in the universities rather than in the colleges.

Finally, to provide qualified teachers at an accelerated pace, several new patterns were suggested: teachers' salaries should be raised as an important first step (some people contend that while this is important in itself it is likely to have no appreciable effect on the overall situation without additional remedies); teacher-training should be put into the mainstream of higher education and taken out of isolated teacher-training institutions; grants-in-aid should be denied to schools which employ teachers who do not meet the minimum standards; teachers' organizations should be encouraged.

In addition to these major reforms, which are culled out of the text of the longer document, a number of lesser suggestions are important. For example, several changes in the pattern of advancement from one academic stage to another have been urged — e.g. the abolition of the Pre-University Course in the college. Such changes could have a profound effect on the whole educational structure. There are recommendations about language instruction, hostels, women students, library facilities, science facilities, extracurricular programs, and a wide variety of other subjects which cannot be reviewed here. In particular there are many suggestions about the language problem, one of the most difficult and pervasive of all problems, but we have not dealt with that directly in this study. It is a study in itself.

This list of advocated reforms points to two things — the areas of broadly recognized weakness and those areas where there is likely to be major effort for improvement in the years immediately ahead. Therefore, the Report is not simply a judgment and critique, but also a blueprint for action in the future. Administrators of colleges in India are in a position to evaluate trends and to develop their particular institutions in the most relevant and effective manner, consistent with these overall objectives. They have never before had such a clear framework with which to work and plan. It is important, however, that not only individual colleges reflect on their role in this new formulation of aspirations, but that groups of colleges should think and act in concert. Only then will the necessary reforms take root.

III

THE DEVELOPMENT SETTING

WE are interested here in three specific aspects of the development setting, as they are related to the theme of the volume: the planning process in India, the Churches as agents of development, and the educational setting. Throwing these into broad relief will prepare the necessary groundwork for the consideration of the specific role of Christian colleges in development, which is the subject of Chapter IV and onwards.

1. PLANNING IN INDIA

Since before World War II India has been committed to the concept of national planning for economic development. The purpose of planning was to begin ' a process of development which will raise living standards and open out to the people new opportunities for a richer and more varied life '. ' Economic planning has to be reviewed as an integral part of a wider process aiming not merely at the development of resources in a narrow technical sense, but at a development of human faculties, and the building up of an institutional framework adequate to the needs and aspirations of the people. '[1]

The first of four Five Year Plans was initiated in 1952, with heavy emphasis on the development of an infra-structure to support agricultural and industrial development, stressing power, transport, irrigation and agriculture. The First Plan fell short on several targets, partly because of the difficulty of initiating projects, rapid population growth, unfamiliarity with executing centralized plans, lack of factual data on which to base action. But it did not fail, and the Second Plan was written with optimism — with a stress upon industrialization (although agricultural programs still amounted to 20 per cent of the Second Plan, as compared with 31 per cent in the First).

The Second Plan espoused the goal of a ' socialist pattern of society ', and posited a large new injection of external assistance

(90 per cent of the First Plan and 76 per cent of the Second were scheduled to come from internal resources). It is judged that the first two plans were considerably successful, with national income having been increased in the ten years by 42 per cent, and *per capita* income having been increased by 16 per cent. Shortfalls in attaining the plans' objectives were attributed to the following points:[2]

(1) inadequate and sporadically successful agricultural growth;
(2) foreign exchange difficulties and consequent shortage of essential imports;
(3) stagnation in the export programs; and
(4) delays in the formation of certain industrial and agricultural programs.

Nevertheless these same authors conclude that ' the national income figure . . . does not adequately indicate the actual growth potential built up in the economy. Even the striking rise in the index of industrial production of about 95 per cent (average annual rate of about 9·5 per cent) does not reflect fully the extent of industrialization that has taken place . . . The decade witnessed the beginning of an industrial revolution. Particularly in the five years of the Second Plan, the growth and diversification of industry were remarkable.'[3] Agricultural and industrial production had increased by 41 per cent and 94 per cent respectively, which were indeed dramatic advances, even though they were somewhat blunted by a concurrent 22 per cent population growth.

The Third Five Year Plan aimed to attain and sustain a 4 per cent annual increment in national income; to achieve self-sufficiency in food; to expand basic industries — like steel, chemicals, fuel and power; to use more fully the manpower resources of the country; to bring about more equal distribution of wealth. Specifically, the Third Plan foresaw a 30 per cent increase in national income from Rs 14,500 crores in 1961 to Rs 19,000 crores in 1966 (1 crore equals 10 million). Unfortunately, these goals were unfilled, most noticeably in food production, partly because crucial sections of the country have been plagued with droughts. Also important was the fact that the community development programs have not taken root; fertilizer production has fallen far short and distribution has been a problem ; external and internal political problems have drained off desperately needed money and attention. The target for foodgrain production was 101 million tons, but only about 76 million tons were realized. Essential fertilizers should have been 1 million tons, but only 600,000 were actually produced. Money available for short and medium-term loans for co-operatives and similar economic efforts amounted to only about 55 per cent of the anticipated total; about 65 per cent of irrigation programs were achieved; 50 per cent of the hoped-for acreage under cultivation; 66 per cent of the anticipated production of steel; 90 per cent of hoped-for aluminum. However targets were far exceeded in training of doctors, in technical education, in general education in schools, in shipping tonnage, and were almost attained in road transport vehicles, power (installed capacity), cotton cloth in the decentralized sector, refined petroleum products.

In résumé, the Third Plan financial targets were basically realized, but the production was not, attributed largely to unfavorable weather conditions which seriously retarded agricultural production, failure to take preparatory action, delays in finalizing schemes, time taken in negotiating foreign assistance and obtaining equipment, hangover of certain shortfalls in the Second Plan, aggression over the borders and the long gestation period and phasing for most of the projects and programs.[4]

National income increased at about 4 per cent *per annum* instead of the hoped-for 5 per cent, and *per capita* income rose to Rs 317 (in 1964–5) rather than the Rs 385 postulated for 1965–6. The devaluation of the rupee in mid-1966, from 4·7 to 7·5 per U.S. dollar dramatized the decline in the purchasing power of the rupee, both externally and internally, thus eroding or cancelling the *per capita* income rise. Agricultural production was almost stagnant, due partly to adverse weather.

To overcome these handicaps revision of the community development and agricultural sections of the Plan led to an

increased allocation of about Rs 450 million. Industrial production was good in the first part of the Plan, but dwindled
toward the end, and power development was hampered by
lack of foreign exchange. Road transport was appreciably
improved, but many service programs atrophied because of
the troubles with China and Pakistan. Unemployment
remained a major problem.[5] To pay for the Plan, large new
taxations, especially from the states, were implemented, with
substantial foreign assistance increments (Rs 1,723 crores),
and sizeable deficit financing (Rs 686 crores). These two items
are about 30 per cent of the total Plan expenditure.

The Fourth Plan (1966–71) aims at an annual agricultural
production growth rate of 5 per cent; high priority to producing fertilizers, pesticides and agricultural tools (it is estimated
that rats in India eat more than the annual import of foods);
accelerated production of essential consumer goods; increased
production of cement and other building materials; greater
production of metals, chemicals and power; provision of a
broader network of social services; and decrease of unemployment.[6]

The comparative emphases evident in the provisions for
the Third and Fourth Plans, as reflected in the anticipated
expenditure in major areas (in crores of rupees, with a rupee
roughly equivalent to 14 U.S. cents) are given in Table 11.

In terms of concrete targets (rather than expenditures) the
Fourth Plan visualizes 120 million tons of foodgrains by 1970–1
as compared with a realization of about 76 million tons in
1965–6; steel production would double between 1966–7 and
1970–1; cotton production would increase by 33 per cent;
fertilizers would quadruple; railways would carry 50 per cent
more freight; five times as much newsprint would be produced;
cement production would double; commercial road vehicles
would be doubled. These are but examples of the kind of
ambitious thinking being done for the Fourth Plan. As for
employment problems: ' On the basis of an outlay of Rs 21,500
to 22,500 crores, the employment potential in the non-agricul-
tural sector is estimated at around 1·55 to 1·62 crores against
the requirement of about 3·5 crore employment opportunities,

TABLE II

Comparative provision in Third and Fourth Plans (in crores of rupees)[7]

Head of expenditure	Third Plan		Fourth Plan	
	Total	Percentage of Plan	Total	Percentage of Plan
Agriculture	1,090	13	2,372	16
Irrigation	648	8	924	7
Power	1,187	15	1,828	13
Small industry	233	3	395	3
Organized industry	1,662	20	2,866	19
Transport & communications	1,940	24	2,768	18
Education	557	7	1,260	9
Scientific research	72	1	148	1
Health	345	4	578	4
Housing & construction	112	1	297	3
Water supply	—	—	371	3
Backward Classes aid	104	1	188	1
Other social welfare schemes	250	3	426	3
Total	8,200	100	14,421	100

including a backlog of 1·2 crores at the beginning of the Plan and an additional 2·3 crores to the labour force during the five-year period of the Plan.'[8]

In view of the defence expenditures it appears unlikely that large amounts will be available for development programs over the next five years. Morarji Desai (Finance Minister till 1968) has officially announced that, without sacrifice to the military budget, the development allocation has been curtailed. Military expenditure accounts for about a third of the national budget — about Rs 9,700 million — or $ 1,100,000,000.[9] In rough terms, this means that military expenditures were about one-half as much as development expenditures during the Third Plan, and the situation is likely to be more disadvantageous for development during at least the initial stages of the Fourth Plan. Even with optimum conditions, Rs 3,200 crores of external assistance would be needed to fulfil the financial requirements of the Plan.

Educational planning can be understood properly only in the context of this larger planning effort. It, too, has been almost overcome by the enormous and complex nature of its task. Since Independence great strides have been made in the quantitative extension of education at all levels. Despite this, one of the wisest men in Indian education, Sri J. P. Naik, notes that even on the quantitative level much more needs to be done. At the same time he generally argues for greater attention to quality even at the probable sacrifice of quantitative expansion during the Fourth and successive Plans. Only 60 per cent in the age-group 6–14 years would be enrolled by 1966; only 17 per cent of young people 14–17 years old would be in a full-fledged secondary school by 1966; by 1966 only 2·4 per cent of the college age group would actually be enrolled.[10]

The following table shows enrollments at various stages over the past fifteen years. The growth of educational expenditure, shown in Table 13, is also revealing for its scope and the areas of changing interest suggested.

TABLE 12

Enrollment ratios at all levels of education
(1950–1 to 1965–6)[11]

Level of education	1950–1	1955–6	1960–1	1965–6
First level Primary stage (Standards I-V) (Age 6–10)	43·1	50·0	62·2	78·5
Middle stage (Standards VI-VIII) (Age 11–13)	12·9	15·9	22·5	32·2
Second level[1] (Age 14–16)	6·7	9·4	12·9	19·6
Third level[2] Colleges and University[3] (Age 17–22)	1·0	1·7	2·3	3·0
All levels (Age 6–22)	18·4	22·2	28·6	37·9

[1] Including general, vocational, technical, and special education.
[2] Including post-graduates and research.
[3] Including general education, professional and special education.
(The long term growth of education in the country as a whole is presented in the Education Commission Report, Table 12.)

TABLE 13

Growth of educational expenditure in India according to objects (1881–1960, in thousands of rupees)[12]

	1881-2	1891-2	1901-2	1911-2	1921-2	1936-7	1946-7	1960-1
Primary schools	7,087 (44·0)	9,614 (31·5)	11,876 (29·6)	20,726 (26·4)	50,908 (27·7)	81,260 (29·9)	184,853 (32·1)	734,461 (21·3)
Secondary schools	3,912 (24·3)	9,896 (32·4)	12,684 (31·6)	20,789 (26·5)	48,727 (26·5)	81,300 (29·9)	170,230 (29·5)	1,118,336 (32·5)
Vocational and special schools (including training)	453 (2·8)	1,711 (5·6)	2,280 (5·7)	5,374 (6·8)	13,701 (7·5)	18,595 (6·8)	34,657 (6·0)	146,088 (4·3)
Boards of Intermediate and Secondary Education	—	—	—	—	—	324 (0·1)	974 (0·2)	24,133 (0·7)
Total (Schools)	11,452 (71·1)	21,221 (69·5)	26,840 (66·9)	46,889 (59·7)	113,336 (61·7)	181,479 (66·7)	390,714 (67·8)	2,023,018
Universities	163 (1·0)	473 (1·6)	772 (1·9)	1,588 (2·0)	7,341 (4·0)	13,208 (4·9)	22,977 (4·0)	141,388 (4·1)
Arts and science colleges	1,332 (8·3)	2,044 (6·7)	2,601 (6·5)	4,799 (6·1)	11,042 (6·0)	16,662 (6·1)	43,915 (7·6)	236,139 (6·8)
Professional and special colleges	—	829 (2·7)	1,197 (3·0)	2,253 (2·9)	5,978 (3·2)	8,138 (3·0)	18,659 (3·2)	167,166 (4·9)
Total (Universities)	1,495 (9·3)	3,346 (11·0)	4,570 (11·4)	8,640 (11·0)	24,361 (13·2)	38,008 (14·0)	85,551 (14·8)	544,693 (15·9)

Direction & inspection	1,628 (10·1)	2,250 (7·4)	2,545 (6·3)	4,775 (6·1)	9,335 (5·1)	11,407 (4·2)	18,238 (3·2)	70,123 (2·0)
Buildings	838 (5·2)	2,182 (7·1)	2,573 (6·4)	9,730 (12·3)	19,761 (10·8)	18,197 (6·7)	28,453 (4·9)	428,158 (12·4)
Scholarships	399 (2·5)	727 (2·4)	912 (2·3)	1,340 (1·7)	3,170 (1·7)	(a)	(a)	200,222 (5·8)
Miscellaneous	298 (1·8)	794 (2·6)	2,681 (6·7)	7,219 (9·2)	13,784 (7·5)	22,766 (8·4)	53,657 (9·3)	171,711 (5·1)
Total (Indirect)	3,163 (19·6)	5,953 (19·5)	8,711 (21·7)	23,064 (29·3)	46,056 (25·1)	52,370 (19·3)	100,348 (17·4)	870,214 (25·3)
Grand Total	16,110 (100·0)	30,520 (100·0)	40,121 (100·0)	78,593 (100·0)	183,753 (100·0)	271,857 (100·0)	576,613 (100·0)	3,443,801 (b) (100·0)

(a) Included under Miscellaneous.

(b) Includes expenditure on pre-primary schools also.

NOTE: The figures in brackets indicate the percentage of total expenditure.

(From the Education Commission Report, p. 470.)

In preparation for the Fourth Plan formulation several task forces of educators were appointed to recommend 'irreducible minimum' amounts to be spent in various education sectors during the Plan period. The composite irreducible minimum turned out to be Rs 25,000 million or from two to three times the money likely to be available during the Plan period.[13]

As part of the emphasis on quality, Naik insists upon the need for new structures and departures, so well reflected in the Education Commission Report. Continuing education for teachers and administrators, intensified or deepened education (compressing and accelerating studies), adult education, increased vocational work (only 12 per cent of India's secondary school students are in vocational training, as compared with about 70 per cent in West Germany and 60 per cent in Japan), are but a few of the new emphases needed if education is to make the contribution to economic and national development which leading educators in India believe it can and must. This is the meaning of the Commission Report, *Education and National Development*.

2. THE CHURCHES AND DEVELOPMENT

Christian churches have been deeply involved in development activities in the now newer nations for the past two hundred years. Without doubt they have contributed immeasurably to the revolution of rising expectations and to the physical and social emancipation of individuals and groups. The scope and depth of this activity is suggested in the following statistics.

Christians comprise roughly one-third of the world's population, with two-fifths of these Roman-Catholic, two-fifths Protestant, and one-fifth Orthodox. There are upwards of 90,000 missionaries, including both evangelistic and social service efforts. Most Protestant missionaries (about 85 per cent) come from 'Anglo-Saxon' countries, including the U.S.A. Education, health, and rural development have been the most prominent types of church effort in the developing countries, although there are now modifications of these traditional approaches, both within these fields and in new types of ventures.

It has been estimated that between $ 200 million and $ 300 million are annually sent from churches in the more industrialized world to the developing world, for social service type activities alone. While this is a small amount in relation to inter-governmental programs and budgets, it is more than double the expenditures for this kind of work through all the United Nations agencies and special funds. It is estimated that 90 per cent of education in sub-Sahara Africa was under Christian auspices as late as 1960; that Protestant churches operate 14,000 hospitals and dispensaries in developing countries; that 13 million patients are served per year in Protestant institutions in Asia alone; that several million dollars are spent *per annum* for Palestine refugees; that 22 Protestant radio and television stations operate in Latin America; that $ 17 million were given for hunger relief by National Christian Council of Churches constituents in North America in 1965; that 3 Protestant medical colleges in Asia have an annual output of 150 trained doctors; that there are perhaps 20,000 Roman Catholic schools in Latin America; that 140 Christian colleges are run in India alone, with many others in South and South-east Asia. In addition to this there are hundreds of projects of rural development, community development, publishing, vocational training, co-operatives, family welfare, community centers. These figures suggest the deep involvement of the churches in development programs, even though there is current widespread questioning of the justification, efficiency, and methods of such involvement.

What is new for the churches is not participation in development projects, but a new environment both within the church and in the countries where work is to be done. This new environment poses fundamental questions for the churches' development activities; one truth some churchmen are beginning to learn slowly is that such involvement is not a one-way service from the churches to the recipients, but also a vital contribution to the continuing dynamism of the churches themselves. The Inter-Church Aid program of the World

Council of Churches is predicated on the 'renewal of the churches through practical help which the Christian may render one another, through the relief of human need, and through service to refugees'.[14] This help goes two ways. Such activities have opened new horizons of understanding and forced upon the churches a kind of pragmatic relevance which can continually purify the churches' thought and action.

The churches' environment is different. Where once the churches were practically the only overseas development agency, scores are now in the field — foundations, universities, governments, private agencies, businesses. Each has its own characteristics and problems. The situation in the developing countries has also changed; among other things there is frequent hostility to the religious character of Christian aid and institutions. In addition, governments in developing countries increasingly take responsibility for those spheres of public service traditionally espoused by the churches — schools, hospitals, community development. Further, a massive volume of study has been done on the means and problems of development, which cannot but affect any alert agents involved in the development process.

Within the churches, too, the environment has changed. Missionary theology is in a tangle. Over the past twenty years the energies of some of the best leaders of the churches have been turned to internal problems — reflected in the ecumenical movement (and the movement itself, while urging the churches to frontiers of social thinking, may have inadvertently, and perhaps temporarily, diminished support for mission work because it is difficult for some churches to shift from denominational to ecumenical thinking). Even before it was popularly recognized, the processes of secularization were raising questions about the role of the churches in society. At the same time, a resurgence of traditional world religions, the search for 'authenticity' in newly emerging countries, and the yearning for self-identity has led many developing peoples to insist on developing a home-grown ideology in the midst of rapid social change. This challenges the churches not to be easily content with mighty new efforts along old lines, but to probe into the adequacy of the old motivations for, and types of, service and involvement.

The churches are not discovering for the first time a responsibility for development, but they are confronting their old responsibilities in new forms, and with a new urgency. A fundamental question still to be answered is the relation between mission and service. For example, Christians in India ask whether a Christian college should explicitly propagate the tenets of Christianity and seek to win converts, or whether they should let their actions alone — the kind of ideals they stand for, the way the college is run, the way they relate to other faiths — be their sole witness.

But there are more than theological questions. How sort out and arrange priorities? How relate development efforts to the special ethos of the churches? How incorporate new insights, but conflicting theories, about development into the decisions taken by churches? How mobilize old resources and develop new ones? How create an effective ecumenical decision-making and administrative process? These are partly questions of effective strategy, but more deeply they are issues questioning the nature and function of churches in development. These larger questions affect the actual operations by posing more specific ones.

One immediate difficulty is how to bring the insights and experiences of the churches in the developing countries into the counsel of the mission boards and the potential donor churches, and vice versa — to make development a truly sharing and mutually growing effort. Representation in meetings costs a great deal, but it might prove even more costly to steal trained men and women from the local scene, where good leadership is always scarce, to become part of the international civil service of the churches, either part-time or full-time. Beyond these costs, however, there is the cost to the donor churches of their relative freedom in determining what projects shall receive support and which not. Here conflicts of vested interests become clearer, but it is most frequently not cynical self-interest which causes tension, but legitimate differences of judgment about the merits of divergent approaches, and temperaments of different groups and individuals. Can church leaders in 'donor' and 'recipient' countries divorce themselves sufficiently from their national psychological and intellectual syndromes to make honestly competent unpolitical judgments?

Another similar problem then appears. If one is committed to working with the church leadership of the developing countries, some of which is unimaginative and reactionary, directly or indirectly it frustrates and alienates those emerging young leaders who insist that churches should resolutely identify themselves with movements for social reform. These young church leaders often feel that at present churches are irrelevant or even detrimental to social justice. It is alleged that sometimes church social service programs simply buttress the authority and power of a reactionary government, thus delaying the changes ultimately required for justice. How can church leaders in the developing countries work effectively with both existing church leadership and young reformers in the developing countries?

Again, how can aid be tailored not to the preservation of the church, but to the church as servant of people in need? There is a fuzzy line of distinction between supporting the church in order that it may serve (perhaps as an independent center of power), and supporting it for its own perpetuation. Distinctions between these made for analytical or operational reasons cannot be hard and fast. Insistence that church aid to developing countries must pass through the churches in the recipient countries subtly nourishes the predisposition to think of the church as an end in itself. There is much talk of ' changing structures for mission' (which raises red flags for many existing leaders). What is needed is not changing structures in general, but articulation of specific organizational changes in line with the principle of shared and diverse responsibilities, to achieve specific objectives.

We have questioned to what extent aid programs should be channeled through the churches, and used explicitly for the advantage of the Christian community *per se*. One dimension of this question is how to evolve open and dynamic leadership in the churches, alive to currents in their own country. Churches in developing countries are perhaps even more pastor-centered than those in more developed areas, putting extra burdens on the pastor to comprehend and interpret social questions. Actually, however, this is frequently what he is least capable of doing. Often recruited from the lower economic and educational levels of society, which are traditionally unrelated to the questions of policy formulation and decision implementation; often receiving a theological education which has little or no place for social questions and social analysis; frequently pastoring a flock which lives at the margins of society; the pastor often tends to be insecure and defensive about getting involved in other than theological and biblical discussions. He feels threatened, because he senses that he is out of his depth, when laymen in the church, or outside, ask what the church should do about particular social issues. Pastoral leadership in general does not provide the forward-looking and critical vision necessary for the churches to become transforming agents in their own social setting. Among other remedies, theological education must find this a challenge vital to the health of the church itself; if the church is not socially relevant, it will die both numerically and spiritually.

Another question is to what extent the churches can shift their own thinking. Traditionally the churches have served development purposes either implicitly or explicitly through charity motives. In the long run, charity alone is inherently dangerous because it vitiates relationships between peoples. What is needed is a transformed and transforming conception of social justice, and this requires basic questioning of conceptions of property, natural resources, exchanges of value other than purely monetary ones (e.g. the 'brain drain'), a deeper understanding of the rights of the disinherited and the duties of the more favorably endowed, a practical realization of the inclusiveness of the community of responsibility, and related questions. The churches do not and cannot have blueprint answers to these fundamental questions — often they can learn much from those outside the church — but they can be powerful catalysts in raising these questions and pursuing adequate answers. This search and pursuit can be stimulated by churches being involved in practical operations in society. Stress upon charity as the grounding principle will have to be transformed into more profound conceptions of justice, justice constantly informed and renewed by true *caritas*.

Still further is how the churches can use development programs to create understanding — about the particular relationships between the donor and recipient, but also about the larger issues of the human community. Most development aid ignores this aspect. Yet a potentially significant element in aid programs is the enlarged vision and understanding which can come to all parties concerned. As important as the $ 25 given by a local churchman to support a particular mission work is how the local church, as a community, uses giving as a means for self-education and spiritual growth. More important to both sides than the giving and receiving of material gifts, important as they are, is the sense of solidarity which can be fostered through sensitive deepening of the process of aid. Generosity and gratitude are important feelings in the building of community, but true community and solidarity must be based on a wider network of feelings and understandings.

Increasingly it is questioned whether churches ought to continue in types of activities which have now been taken up by governments and other private agencies. Christians were pioneers, for example, in women's and harijan's education in India, but now governments are increasingly responsible for this work. Is there justification for simple quantitative extension of work, or must there be something qualitatively different? What is the line between these? Is good hospital administration in itself a justification for starting or maintaining Christian hospitals, even though government is committed to developing national health programs and facilities? Is the establishment of schools in unschooled parts of a country justified because the government either has not the resources, or refuses to begin schools in the knowledge that Christians and others will start them? These are down-to-earth but tormenting questions about missionary strategy today. Is it the churches' basic task to pioneer new interpretations of justice and to constantly work themselves out of jobs in particular areas in order to work in new ones? Is it the churches' task to open new vistas of justice for society, *hoping* that work thus initiated will be taken up by others? What criteria define a pioneering activity, and at what stage should Christians leave the field to others and pass on to new pioneering activities?

The perennial danger is that churches will become prisoners of their own institutions, perpetuating them for the wrong reasons. It is characteristic that when the original motivation for an institution becomes no longer tenable, the institution carries on with a changed formulation of its objectives (or even without a new formulation). While this may be justified, it may reflect in many cases that the organization has become an end in itself more than a means to social service. Admittedly in some ways churches have been city-dwellers rather than pioneers; they often have lagged behind sensitive social critics; there is an endemic tendency for the churches to preserve rather than create, to protect rather than to pioneer, to come late to the field of battle instead of supporting the advance guard. Churches have often become ' bogged-down ' in running traditional programs, without time or vision to see perhaps more significant opportunities.

Many Christians are increasingly unhappy with this state of affairs — about the churches' priorities in social service. They contend that there is too much emphasis upon relief work — victims of natural and human disasters — without enough attention to preventive work. Why are the churches so deeply committed to the treating of diseases and not to preventing them? Why is so much spent on refugee care, but so little on building the relationships of peace? Why is so much hunger relief given, and so little to the development of viable agriculture in the impoverished countries? What is the proper balance between preventive work and emergency relief? If churches think of themselves as special patrons of the disinherited, can they develop more imagination about where the trouble spots in society are coming, thus treating diseases as well as the symptoms? Some are uncharitable enough to opine that churches do not shift tactics because they find satisfaction in these dependency relationships. There is some embarrassing evidence to support this contention, but not much. Nevertheless, it is true that many Christians find it difficult to shift from emphasis on charity to a broadened and deepened conception of social justice. Further, treating symptoms demands so much attention that churches have little energy or resources left over to treat diseases in a fundamental way. This is particularly difficult when one's way of life in the Western churches and countries is likely to be changed, as could be the case if international economic justice were taken more seriously. One encounters the curious logic that we expect major shifts in the life of the developing countries without sacrificial change in the developed ones, on whom the former are so dependent.

This leads to the somewhat artificial, but frequently asked, question about institutions. Many former missionaries in China have forced upon the churches in an imperious way the question about the value of heavy institutional investments. Some regret the 'losses' of the 1949 revolution, and fear that the church stands to forfeit its investments in other troubled nations as well. But there are better bases for questioning how deeply the churches ought to commit themselves to institutions — buildings and facilities. It is a mixed business, both positive and negative. Running institutions forces the churches into choices, into studies, into establishing priorities for its limited resources and criteria for applying these priorities. It forces the churches to see spiritual-religious problems in the concrete context of human life, to see realities about the nature of the church and human society which preclude either utopianism or nihilism.

Running institutions can have a salutory effect on the whole life and thought of the churches. But they also have liabilities — bureaucratization, preoccupation with making a successful business, hardening of routines and a consequent inflexibility to abandon the old and take up new positions of service, the expenditure of human and material resources which might be more prudently invested elsewhere, with greater witness. These are only a few of the liabilities. There is no answer to this dilemma in the abstract, but there must be answers in the concrete. Some people talk about decreasing institutions and expanding programs, but essentially this is a false dichotomy; what is needed is maximum flexibility to envisage new opportunities and to implement these new visions. This will mean sitting loose to existing forms of service, but it does not mean choosing between programs and institutions.

Aside from the difficulties of raising money for work in the developing countries, many ask how money can be used without imperialistic overtones. Churchmen from developing countries should share in formulating and implementing churches' development activities, but a mature partnership of financial sharing has not yet emerged. Churches in the developing countries have not been brought fully into the system of sharing, even though spiritually and financially it is important that this be done. More sophisticated stewardship is needed to support programs of assistance in the developing countries. For example, churches in the West have usually taken the position that after a certain fixed period, projects should become self-supporting on the local level. Yet often local churches have not been fully consulted about the propriety and wisdom of initiating these programs in the first place, and they may resent being charged with programs and institutions which they cannot possibly support. Even National Councils of Churches and aid-channelling organizations are expensive institutions to run. Under pressure from the outside these have been started, but would die if overseas money were curtailed. Many other examples could be cited of how financial arrangements between the churches become sources of constant friction, and often bitterness and alienation. Church leaders of the 'North' (developed) and 'South' (developing) need to work toward a more realistic and sensitive conception of the potentially corrupting character of all development work, and of the financial aspects of this work in particular. Giving and receiving aid is fraught with enough psychological problems that the least Christians can do is to recognize the explosiveness of the relationship, and to defuse it wherever possible.

There are also strategic questions. On the very realistic level, the churches need to ask continually how they can elicit the interest of the potential donors. Some kinds of *projects* are popular, others are not; some *countries* are more inherently interesting for a variety of reasons. Other factors also enter in, such as whether the request comes from someone known to the donor, or whether it comes with all the personal elements strained out through the sieves of church bureaucracy. Many of these popular efforts are not germane for development; the popular may not be the most necessary.

On other levels, however, problems are more complex. Because churches have been involved in development work for years, they have reaped a vast harvest of experience which gives them an advantage in many situations. Yet the complexity of development theories has increased with the vast amount of new information available, and by the urge for jet-paced development in cultures and countries not equipped to handle this supersonic rate of change. Churches have tended to work in traditional fields of endeavor — education, health, rural development — and in microcosmic situations, despite the integrated approach of the traditional mission compound. The whole ethos of churches' development work is called into question in contemporary development schemes, and while there is obviously a significant place for their continued involvement, they must carve out a philosophy which is distinctively related to their own resources and character. Not the least important task they have is to share in the give-and-take with other development agents to discover a more strategic approach to development. Actually the churches have not used even their limited resources in a co-ordinated way, with competition between groups and denominations constantly afflicting planned involvement. Keeping and sharing records is deplorably weak, and it is difficult to conceive of a strategically oriented program without such empirical information. In this situation the churches need to build their own social science skills and resources, as well as to exploit the information available from others.

Churches are also beset with tactical questions, such as how to relate with other agencies and especially with governments. Efficient operation increasingly requires knowledge of what others are doing, and at times to structure efforts in a complementary way. Yet some contend that it is just in those areas where others are not working, or have no vision for work, that the churches should invest most; the task of the church is not to duplicate, but to pioneer. It is also urged that churches have a distinctive ethos and heritage which should determine what they can and should do; this should be more important than trying to fit into government plans which have evolved in a quite different framework. Also some fear that too close collaboration between the churches and other agencies will contaminate or compromise the work of the churches, introducing into the decision-making process too many extraneous or unwanted elements. Necessary as these reservations are, other agencies are now deeply involved in development activities, and the churches cannot ignore them.

In the whole development process it is of crucial importance for the churches, with others, to constantly ask about the human consequences of development and the fundamental question — 'development for what?' There is abroad a tendency to let development programs be dictated by specialized technicians. However indispensable these technicians are for development, their presuppositions must be constantly questioned and their decisions put under constant surveillance for potential human consequences. In our day of human engineering and large scale social planning, good decisions have far-reaching consequences — and bad ones too! All the more reason for continuous scrutiny. The churches have no monopoly of concern here, but they would be remiss if they never asked fundamental moral and educational questions.

Protestants and Orthodox have tended to transfer the ethics of the small face-to-face community to the big city and national and international levels; individual morality has preoccupied many social ethicists. Individual morality is fundamentally important to ordered social change, but it is inadequate for the churches to think in only those terms. The churches need to absorb and use the knowledge and insight about man and community gained through the behavioral and social sciences. In particular they need more sophistication about the structures of society and the forces playing upon individuals' decisions. Society is process, and to keep the process in manageable channels requires sensitivity to the interplay of social institutions and groups. Christians must move, therefore, from a static view of institutional relationship to a dynamic one, a view which is already implicit in the concept of the ' responsible society '. They must move from exclusive preoccupation with individual morality to a deeper perception of the institutional characteristics and realities of social change. Only in this context can the churches' involvement in development activities be most effective.

These are some of the internal uncertainties of Christians as they re-think the churches' roles in development — questions of philosophy, strategy and/or tactics and organization. Regardless of how these questions are answered, the churches have several major assets in their favor, aside from the spiritual resources and character of the church. Firstly, and probably most important, is the religious conviction and commitment of those working through the churches — a deep motivation and a sense of corporate involvement and support which sustains them in adversity. This kind of motivation is essential for the establishment of rapport with those with whom one works. In the final analysis this rapport, along with the personal changes it brings about and the aspirations it inspires, is an indispensable ingredient of long-term and truly indigenized development.

Willingness to sacrifice has characterized the church worker, even though at times narrowness, parochialism and purely religious interests have made the worker unwelcome. A weakness of many development efforts is that the workers have no sustaining commitment to keep them at their job over years of difficulty and frustration — a sustaining interest in people more than in the achievement of a pet theory or plan. Experts sent out are usually short-term, often live quite apart from the people both physically and psychologically, and are often frustrated in not being able to apply the level of technical competence which has made them 'expert'. This type of person may make a great contribution in certain kinds of technical consultation, but he is usually not able to work patiently for years with groups of people who are simple microcosms of the needs of the larger situation. This kind of technical competence may not be the most important ingredient in development, but the ability to work with and inspire people certainly is. The churches have much to offer in supporting workers with the right motivations in demanding human relations work.

Secondly, the scope and influence of the churches makes it potentially an important instrument for progress or reaction — as for example, in family-planning attitudes. As an international and inter-racial community, grounded in a common ethos and with administrative links and lines of communication, the churches are in a position (a position not fully utilized) to speak with breadth and depth on development questions, and to act ecumenically.

Thirdly, the past experiences of the churches in development, through which they have developed a broad network of contacts and relationships, and through which they have stored up a reservoir of knowledge — anthropological, tactical, organizational — can be drawn upon today. While there is suspicion of some Christian efforts, their reputation for service is generally good, and they are in a position, through long-term identification with the people, to do that sensitive development work which depends so much on local attitudes, relationships and resources.

Fourthly, much has been said elsewhere about the relative advantages and disadvantages of government-sponsored, as distinguished from private, development efforts. The role of the private sector in aid is increasingly appreciated, even though many governments in developing countries prefer direct government to government programs. The advantages of experimentation, avoiding political controversies, cutting needless red tape, flexibility to meet changing situations, are all advantages which, with other private agencies, the churches share.

Fifthly, churches also can mobilize considerable material and personnel resources. The fact that the churches are identified with the affluent portions of the world, along with their association with colonial and non-colonial patterns, is considered a liability of the churches.[15] But with intelligent and earnest effort, this liability could be overcome. Despite diminished enthusiasm among young people for working through the churches, these churches are nevertheless able to find a great deal of money and expertise to serve development goals.

The churches have been, and are, deeply involved in development. Despite their long traditions and experience they, like all other agencies, are novices because conditions in the world are in such rapid and fundamental transition. The church, *in* the world, is itself deeply affected by these seismic changes in the human landscape. What the churches can contribute as participants in the process ('*in*, but not *of*, the world') is not a blueprint, or even a systematic theory of society, but a responsible, sustained and critical involvement in service. This will help the churches as much as they help the world.

3. EDUCATION AND NATIONAL DEVELOPMENT

It is widely contended that education is a fundamental ingredient in development. Studies by Harbison and Myers, Schultz, Aukrust, and others purport to show a growth or development factor not accountable for except in terms of the input in educated manpower and citizenry.[16]

In his succinct, comprehensive and lucid introduction to a UNESCO volume on educational planning, Phillips reviews economists' efforts to measure and assess scientifically the 'residual' factor in economic development — that which is not explainable in terms of normal population growth, physical inputs, new natural resources and similar sources.[17] The 'X' element is attributed to human resource development — through education — and is more and more striking as economies and societies develop. Human and educational factors apparently become increasingly important in growth and development. Phillips refers to the 'extremely interesting research undertaken in recent years to show retroactively the proportionate contribution education has made to economic growth in particular countries. These studies indicate that the major part of the growth in production in developed countries over the last half century cannot be accounted for except by the inputs of physical capital, man hours and natural resources. The major part must be ascribed to technical progress and human factors among which education plays a prominent role. Professor Sulow estimated that only 10 per cent of the growth could be accounted for by population growth and physical resources, leaving the remaining 90 per cent due to residual factors falling under the general heading of technological progress. Dr. Massel has published an independent estimate for United States' manufacturing industry taken alone, which comes to the same conclusion. In Europe, Professor Aukrust made calculations for Norway . . . and his conclusions were similar. In the United Kingdom, Professors Reddaway and Smith have shown that capital and labour inputs accounted for only a quarter of the increased output per head in manufacturing industries between 1949 and 1954. . . . The criticisms of this approach are not directed at the importance of the role of education but at the measurement procedures involved and the assumptions made as to the basis on which the factors of production are actually distributed in the economies represented. . . . A difficulty with this type of analysis is that the importance of the residual factor varies at different stages of development, tending to be lower in the developing countries.'[18]

Phillips goes on to show that Schultz and others have attempted to use the same measurement procedures in the developing countries, and their conclusions are similar. Japan and Denmark were cited as interesting cases where natural resources were scarce, but where heavy investment in education yielded remarkable development returns. Israel is cited as another case where human factors are dramatically important, as also the post-war recovery in Germany, but in both instances large amounts of external capital were also available.

In short it is a natural assumption that education is an important ingredient in development and that it becomes increasingly important as social organizations and productive specialization become more complex and interdependent. Planned economies in particular require long-term prognostication of manpower needs and the evolution of institutions to meet these needs.

We accept the argument that there is a causal connection between education and development, but there is a danger of claiming too much from these studies. Correlations of variables do not prove a causal relationship. For example, in Harbison and Myer's study the correlation between rapid continuing development in the more advanced countries and high education investments and yields is not surprising because more technically developed nations have the resources, including leisure to make huge, and often unproductive, expenditures on education. They are less close to the subsistence margin and can afford schools. It may be that availability of money and leisure produce more education, and not vice versa.

What is less clear from these various studies, however, is how one moves from the general to the specific — from the observation that education is conducive to development to the specification of what types of education are instrumental to development in particular situations. What we need to know, for practical guidance, is what specific priorities (everyone has to work with financial and personnel limitations) are important in specific situations. This raises questions about the segments of the *population* receiving education, about the *kinds* of education, about *levels* of education, about the areas of *disciplines* to be stressed, etc. This kind of question can be answered only in relation to concrete realities and aspirations. Let us take some examples.

Certainly various types of traditional and classical education contribute very little in a direct way to the development of a country, especially if they stress memorization and irrelevant information. Such education may even be dysfunctional for development if it creates a reservoir of discontented graduates.

This is not to say, of course, that traditional education has no merits, but only to argue that in many instances it does little to mobilize human resources for development work. On the other hand, many are frightened by the prospect of too much emphasis on vocational and utilitarian education, to the detriment of the humanities. Foster, for one, argues that real job training and competence come not through the schools, but only on the job itself. He contends that education should instill values, broad commitments and knowledge, which are themselves conducive to development.[19] This argument has more relevance to some situations than to others, and in general the more pressing issue is to find a place for more vocational education. In the long run what is needed is to hold the two elements, broad cultural concerns and personal motivations and knowledge on the one hand, and particular skills and competences on the other, in some kind of dynamic interplay.

Levels of education are also an important consideration. One disturbing thing about prognoses in the Education Commission Report is that they tend to relate more to levels than to kinds of degrees obtained. Nevertheless, political and economic growth require attention to levels of education made available to the populace. Should primary education and literacy be maximized, or secondary education (as some argue for many sub-Sahara African states), or is higher education the particularly crucial need? These would not be relevant questions were abundant economic and personnel resources available. Plainly, there are stringent limits of resources, and education for development has to set priorities based upon levels or years of education deemed most suitable. We shall see below how India's priority needs have been defined.

There arises also the question of under-utilized segments of the populace, and underdeveloped areas of the country. In most countries, and more particularly the developing ones, large sections of the populace are traditionally marginal to the national economy and life. In India large tribal areas are quite unrelated to the national system. Women, too, often have been an educationally underdeveloped segment of the populace. Education for development must be strategically deployed to exploit untapped human resources which (as some argue is the case of women and mothers who will set attitudes about culture and education for the rising generations) are critical log-jams in opening up possibilities for change and rapid growth.

Undoubtedly there needs to be more balance in the growth of educational opportunities for various parts of the country. It is politically tempting to concentrate education and other development efforts in urban centers and influential areas of the country, but education for development needs to be related to what is economically useful and not only to what is politically expedient. They may, or may not, be coincidental.

Further, educational investments must be complemented by other inputs. To maximize this investment, educated persons must be put into situations where their abilities are used. This is a major shortcoming of many developing countries; opportunities are not matched up with skilled people. The brain drain is a dramatic and tragic example of what happens when educational investments have not been matched with inputs in other areas, as, for instance, providing pay, job satisfaction, and family living conditions enticing enough to get trained leadership into the rural areas. Deplorable as is the exodus of talent from developing to more affluent countries, probably more devastating to the economy and growth of the former are mis-employment, under-employment and unemployment among those who remain. Kurien argues in a compelling way that there has been in India a startling and wasteful amount of disguised unemployment; there is also an accelerating open unemployment and under-employment, especially among the educated.[20] 'The First Plan provided employment opportunities to about 4·5 million, but left a backlog of 5·3 million — 2·5 million in the urban areas and 2·8 million in rural areas. The Second Plan provided new employment for about 6·5 million, but left a bigger backlog of over 9 million. During the Third Plan it was expected that there would be an addition of nearly 17 million to the labour force, thus making it necessary for the Plan to create job opportunities for 26 million. . . . The Third Plan accepted a target of 17 million jobs, and achieved about 13 million. The Fourth Plan thus begins with a backlog of between 12 and 13 million, and will have also to cope with an addition of nearly 23 million to the labour force during

1966–71. It will, therefore, have to provide job opportunities for 35 million if open unemployment is to be wiped off by 1971.'

TABLE 14
Educated unemployment in India[21]

Year	Matriculates	Post-Matriculates but not Graduates	Graduates
1955	164,061	25,872	26,224
1956	186,978	40,640	26,774
1961	463,632	70,811	55,786
1964 (first half)	559,420	128,217	73,457

Large new physical and capital inputs are needed to complement educational investments. Furthermore, these inputs have to be integrated with an overall development strategy; it is not only the amount *per se* that counts, but how it is deployed. In some Latin American situations, for example, heavy foreign aid contributions, or sacrificial internal capital formation, may have adverse 'development' effects if it is concentrated in the hands of traditional decision-makers who line their own pockets or buttress their own privileged positions. These inputs are not always financial. Sometimes basic modification in the social structure or the structure of power in a community will be necessary before educated manpower can be properly used in development. In short, investment in education is not, in and of itself, a guarantee of development, but must be combined with physical inputs of other types.

Still another difficulty in relating education to development is establishing areas of priority. Recently technology and physical sciences have attracted the greatest attention, partly because they had been almost completely absent in many of the developing countries, and because of the charm of the technology 'myth' (the constellation of values, relationships, and artifacts which moves a society). Almost universally, however, there has been an inordinate attention to higher level scientists and technicians — engineers and theoreticians without corresponding attention to the need for persons on the lower levels to either run machines or intelligently supervise technical projects. That these questions are interlaced with political considerations is evident from the allegation, on the one side, that developed countries have trained these high-level engineers and scientists more in the hopes of advancing their own pool of trained people than of helping the development of technology in the poorer countries. On the other hand in the developing countries there is resentment at too much attention to middle-level technological training because it is feared that advanced nations are trying to keep the poorer ones in an inferior and dependent position. Despite Foster's relevant warnings that too much attention to vocational education is dangerous, for most countries this is still a highly academic danger — something to worry about in the future. Notwithstanding the recent concentration on technical and science training, most developing countries have insufficient numbers of graduates in these fields for the implementation of development plans already in process. The regional meetings under UNESCO (Addis Ababa, Karachi, Santiago, Lima and Beirut), unrealistic as many of their recommendations are, attest to this fact.

Moreover, there are less glamorous but equally clamant needs for educated people in other areas crucial to national development. One is for more and better teacher-training. Even in a country like India, highly educated as compared with most African countries, the number of practicing but ill-trained or untrained teachers is alarming. The content of teacher education is hardly related to development needs in the country; it is divorced from the mainstream of Indian higher education. Agricultural training, too, such as that offered in the traditional land-grant colleges in the United States, is woefully inadequate, attracting neither many nor, on the whole, outstanding students. Of the 130 Christian colleges in India, only one is an agricultural college, and practically none of its graduates actually work in rural or agricultural areas. Even where agricultural training is available, it tends to produce administrators and not practitioners. These are but two examples of the need to tailor educational investments to particular priority areas; otherwise education is largely for consumption and not an investment.

An urgent need is to evolve an education which breaks away from the traditional classroom experiences. This has two facets. One is to create an experimental and pragmatic problem-solving approach in the classroom itself, which in itself will require, and bring in its wake, radical changes in the teaching and administration of existing institutions. The *content* and *method* of teaching are clearly of critical importance in determining whether education will, in deed as well as in theory, be conducive to development. Perhaps no area is more important, and yet in many developing countries nothing has been done to effectively bring relevant problem-solving approaches into the teaching-learning situation. Huge amounts of money can be washed away meaninglessly unless this basic problem is tackled.

Another aspect of the same issue is to create a system of programs and institutions outside the traditional classroom, designed to meet the dizzying changes taking place in all societies. The traditional network of schools is no longer quantitatively nor qualitatively adequate. Continuing education, to use one example, is critically important everywhere, to keep educated persons from becoming obsolete. Health clinics, vocational schools for the middle-aged as well as the young, adult education and literacy programs of various kinds, rural training centers, co-operative associations — a whole complex of new, pragmatically defined, institutional responses to new needs and new conditions is required. The old conception of teaching young people information, attitudes and skills to equip them for a lifetime is no longer tenable; it is no longer an adequate conception of either society or education. Investment in education as an instrument in development must be related to the new realities where an individual experiences as many fundamental changes in his lifetime as it took generations of his forefathers to experience.

Planning in India has itself reflected this belief in the fundamental relationship between education and national development; provision for education has played a prominent role in the articulation of each of the four Five Year Plans. The Third Plan stated, for example, that 'education is the most important single factor in achieving rapid economic development and technological progress and in creating a social order founded on the values of freedom, social justice and equal opportunity. Programmes of education lie at the base of the effort to forge the bonds of common citizenship, to harness the energies of the people, and to develop the natural human resources of every part of the community.'[22]

Expenditure on education, as a percentage of the national income, went up from 0·79 in 1948–9 to 1·90 per cent at the end of the First Plan, to 2·65 per cent at the end of the Second Plan, and was close to 3·50 per cent at the end of the Third Plan.[23] Kurien observes that 'under normal conditions, therefore, we have been spending more on education than on defence', but he maintains that expenditure per student is still too low.[24] Further, education targets, unlike most others, have been often 'more than fulfilled'. Something of the scope of increase in educational facilities is suggested in Tables 12 and 13. Naturally growth in education cannot be simply equated with quantitative enrollment increases, and improvements in educational organization and practice have been constantly encouraged. For instance, science and technological education have been greatly expanded; greater attention has been paid to Scheduled and Backward groups; scholarship programs have been accelerated and enlarged.

The Education Commission Report, 1966, further reflects the conviction in India that education is the key to national development; indeed, the title of this excellent report highlights this emphasis: 'Education and National Development'. The first of 700 large and compact pages starts, 'The destiny of India is now being shaped in her classrooms. This, we believe, is no mere rhetoric. In a world based on science and technology, it is education that determines the level of prosperity, welfare and security of the people. On the quality and number of persons coming out of our schools and colleges will depend our success in the great enterprise of national reconstruction whose principal objective is to raise the standard of living of our people. . . . But education cannot be considered in a vacuum. It has to be used as a powerful instrument of social, economic and political change, and will, therefore, have to be related to the long-term national aspirations, the programmes of national development on which the country is engaged.'[25]

It is also clearly enunciated that a major function of education in India is to be the midwife of change, without violence and upheaval. But there should be no false optimism about education; the Report warns against 'the naïve belief that all education is necessarily good, both for the individual and for society, and that it will necessarily lead to progress.'[26] It also argues that the present system of education is ' largely unrelated to life and there is a wide gulf between its content and purposes and the concerns of national development.'[27] In general, the Report envisaged that education should be reformed to meet broad national development purposes, through the following influences: (1) as an instrument of peaceful change; (2) to solve national problems like food shortages and the need for higher productivity and distribution; (3) to contribute to a sense of the Indian national community and national integration; and (4) to strengthen the spiritual and moral fiber of the people in the midst of this rapid change, and to share this strength with peoples from other countries.

Indeed, the Report put so much emphasis on the utilitarian, social and development aspects of education that the Xavier Board of Higher Education, representing the 100 Roman Catholic institutions of higher education in India, while generally approving it as a 'truly monumental accomplishment', felt constrained to raise some objection. They called the Report a ' marvellously comprehensive document, ranging over almost every aspect of Indian education. . . . It has also borne courageous witness to today's even greater need of training in spiritual and moral values. . . . We are happy to place on record our agreement with most of the views expressed.'[28] Their major reservation was that it was too preoccupied with development and with the nation, and not enough with the individual. ' We find a disproportionate emphasis on the need for fashioning our youth into tools for society, for productivity, for national reconstruction. The recommendations that follow appear to focus almost exclusively on this one aspect of the training of our youth. ... We insist with all emphasis at our command that as educationists we have to defend our educational system from becoming a mere instrument of the state.'[29]

Thus the consensus today is that the human factor in development, as end and means, is a crucial element, and that education, whether formally defined or not, is the key to integrating individual efforts with the national development. We have intimated above some caveats that need mentioning when ascribing to education such a fundamentally important role in development. We have seen, further, that India's national and education planners, from 1951 until the present, accord to education a centrally important place in India's development. All the more important it is to guarantee that this education be as sound as the best brains and the most dedicated practitioners can make it. The Education Commission Report is a monumental accomplishment in that direction.

IV

PROFILE OF INDIAN CHRISTIAN COLLEGES

THE Christian college is an integral part of Indian higher education. Indeed, it was largely under Christian auspices that Western style collegiate education was introduced into India — first at Serampore College in 1818. For almost a hundred and forty years India has looked to the Christian colleges to produce some of its greatest leaders and broad leadership cadres. A significant by-product of Christian efforts to develop colleges was the stimulation it gave to other religious and governmental groups to develop similar institutions. Although Christian colleges continue to play a strong role in the total higher educational structure and patterns of the country, they do not dominate the educational field in the way that was true even at the time of Independence. However, they remain a significant and influential group of colleges and can have an impact far beyond what their number would suggest.

There were, in 1966, 130 university-level Christian colleges in India — 78 Roman Catholic, 45 Protestant, and 7 Syrian non-Catholic. This is less than 5 per cent of all of the colleges in India, 85 per cent of which are private colleges. On the other hand, about one-tenth of all of the students in higher education in India are in the Christian colleges; in 1966 there were 117,000 students in the Christian colleges. About 70,000 of these were in the Roman Catholic institutions, 40,000 in the Protestant ones, and 7,000 in the Syrian colleges.

Some preliminary generalizations

Several generalizations should help to focus the picture of Christian colleges in India today, and particularly more recent developments. Firstly, it is important to note that the Christian colleges in India are for the most part indigenous. While most of the early Christian colleges in India resulted from missionary

69

endeavors, the newer ones are Indian in inspiration, management, personnel, and finance. To be sure, several institutions receive some support from overseas, through religious orders and congregations, or through mission boards or local churches, but the dominant influence in almost all Christian colleges is the local and Indian. This has become increasingly true since Independence, but even before that time there was a strong movement toward the indigenization of Christian colleges in India. Leadership is also indigenized: almost 100 per cent of the teachers, 85 per cent of the principals, and almost all of the members of the Boards of Governors are Indian.

Christian colleges have been greatly influenced by the explosion of education at all levels in India. This explosion has been manifest in the establishment of new colleges and the expansion of old ones. Fifty-nine new colleges have been founded since Independence; existing institutions have been greatly expanded — often 50 per cent or more in the student body, and sometimes without adequate physical facilities and staff commensurate with this expanded student population. The Lindsay Commission, in 1931, advocated two basic Christian college sizes — 200 students and 800 students; the recent Education Commission judges that colleges of at least 1,000 students should become the norm. Of the Christian arts and science colleges in India, 41 per cent are already over 1,000 students, compared with the national percentage of 23 per cent.

While Christian colleges once set their own pace and almost independently evolved their own patterns of operation, they are now hardly masters of their own destiny. University control over affiliated colleges has greatly increased. Since all colleges must be related to a university if they are to be integrally connected with the total higher education structure in the country, and if the colleges are to receive the benefits of that connection, Christian colleges have been obliged to tie their future to a university — although two Christian colleges have refused a university connection. All colleges feel the impact of the universities' strenuous efforts to up-grade the poorer colleges, which often adversely affect the better institutions.

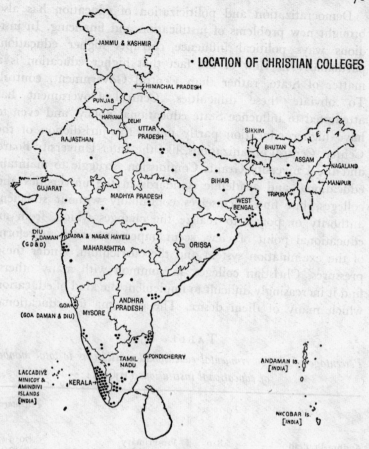

• LOCATION OF CHRISTIAN COLLEGES

Figure I. MAP OF INDIA SHOWING LOCATION OF CHRISTIAN COLLEGES

© Government of India Copyright 1967

Based upon Survey of India map with the permission of the Surveyor General of India. The demarcation of the Gujarat-West Pakistan boundary is in accordance with the Indo-Pakistan Western Boundary case. Tribunal Award is in progress (1969).

Tamil Nadu is referred to by its old name, 'Madras', throughout the book, as the text is up to date only till 1967.

Democratization and politicization of education has also brought new problems of justification and financing. In insidious ways political influence corrupts higher education, particularly in view of the fact that higher education is a matter of State, rather than Central Government, control. To obviate these difficulties, Central Government has attempted to influence State educational policy, and even to have higher education partly under the jurisdiction of the Center. Central organizations, like the Inter-University Board and the University Grants Commission, struggle to maintain educational and academic standards in the universities and colleges, but find themselves continually without sufficient authority or power to realize the changes which, from an educational point of view, seem imperative, such as reform of the examination system and the curriculum. Under these pressures, Christian colleges, in common with many others, find it increasingly difficult to implement the kind of education which many of them desire. The dilemma for educational

TABLE 15

Percentage of non-governmental educational institutions to total number of educational institutions (1960-1)

State	Percentage	Stage or sector	Percentage
Andhra Pradesh	8·0	Pre-Primary	70·9
Assam	19·1	Lower Primary	22·2
Bihar	74·0	Higher Primary	27·1
Gujarat	36·0	Secondary	69·2
Jammu & Kashmir	1·7	Vocational Schools	57·4
Kerala	61·6	Special Schools	79·0
Madhya Pradesh	4·6	Institutions for Higher	
Madras	33·0	(General) Education	78·8
Maharashtra	48·0	Colleges for Professional	
Mysore	34·3	Education	49·8
Orissa	65·3	Colleges for Special	
Punjab	7·4	Education	74·9
Rajasthan	3·5	(Local authority institu-	
Uttar Pradesh	14·5	tions are not included)	
West Bengal	36·3		
Total for India	33·2	Total for all sectors	33·2

(Source: Education Commission Report, p. 446.)

reformers is that, while most of the students in higher education are in the affiliated colleges, the educational decision-makers are in the State legislatures and universities. Naturally many college principals and professors serve on university bodies, and thus have potential influence. University relationship does tend to elevate inferior institutions which are too often run for status, political, or economic reasons. At the same time, however, these inflexibly applied regulations constantly thwart the creativity and ambition of many of the better colleges.

Another noteworthy feature in the evolution of the Christian colleges is that many older institutions, primarily under Protestant auspices, were located in the sparsely Christianized areas of the North. The basic purpose was to meet Hindu culture at its best and to initiate a dialogue with it. In more recent years there has been a heavy concentration of Christian colleges in the South — Madras, Kerala, Mysore and southern Andhra states (Table 16, and Figure 1).

This in itself suggests a different *raison d'être,* for new Christian colleges are placed most often where Christians are concentrated. Many Protestant institutions are to be found in areas where there are few Christians ; this may reflect a historically determined change more than an ideological difference between Protestants and Roman Catholics. In any case, the fact that there are now so many Christian colleges in a state like Kerala, many of them in close proximity with other Christian colleges (Tables 17 and 18), raises basic questions about the purposes of Christian colleges, along with practical considerations about how these colleges can be staffed and financed without depleting support for, and staff in, neighboring colleges. What is the saturation point, or optimal number, both from a philosophic and practical point of view ?

Since Independence, Roman Catholics have established many more colleges than have Protestants (see Figure 2). Seven Syrian colleges have been founded since Independence. The fact that 38 of the 50 Christian colleges founded since 1949 are Roman Catholic helps to explain why most have been in Kerala and southern states. There is no evidence that the pace of establishing new Roman Catholic colleges is slackening;

TABLE 16
Location of Christian colleges in 1966

State	Population	Christians as per cent of total Christian population of India	Christian population	Christians as per cent of state population	RC				P		S	Total			Total colleges
					W	M	D	S	U	S		W	M	C	
Andhra	35,983,447	13	1,428,729	4	6	1	–	–	–	–	–	6	2	1	137
Assam and NEFA	12,209,330	7	766,266	6	1	2	–	–	1	–	–	1	–	3	99
Bihar	46,455,610	5	502,195	1	1	1	–	–	1	–	–	1	–	2	189
Gujarat	20,633,350	0·8	91,028	0·4	1	1	–	–	–	–	–	1	–	–	133
Jammu & Kashmir	3,560,976	0·03	2,848	0·007	–	–	–	–	–	–	–	–	–	–	–
Kerala	16,903,715	34	3,587,365	21	6	5	14	1	3	–	7	9	5	22	123
Madhya Pradesh	32,372,408	2	188,314	0·6	–	5	–	–	–	–	–	1	–	2	234
Madras	33,686,953	16	1,762,954	5	8	5	–	1	13	–	–	12	8	6	137
Maharashtra & Goa	49,180,385	7	787,796	2	3	2	–	–	3	–	–	4	1	9	256
Mysore	23,586,772	4	487,587	2	4	2	3	–	3	–	–	4	–	4	134
Nagaland	369,200	2	195,588	53	–	–	–	–	–	–	–	–	–	–	71
Orissa	17,548,846	2	201,017	1	1	–	–	–	–	–	–	1	2	–	157
Punjab & Haryana	20,306,812	1	149,834	0·7	1	–	–	–	2	–	–	1	–	2	78
Rajasthan	20,155,602	0·2	22,864	0·1	–	–	–	–	–	–	–	–	–	–	–
Uttar Pradesh	73,746,401	1	101,641	0·1	1	–	–	4	3	–	–	2	–	5	293
West Bengal	34,926,279	2	204,530	0·6	2	2	–	2	4	–	–	3	3	4	246
Himachal Pradesh	1,351,144	0·005	592	0·04	–	–	–	–	–	–	–	–	–	–	–
Other Union Territories	2,434,740	2	214,856	9	1	–	–	–	1	–	–	–	1	5	–
Delhi	2,658,612	0·3	29,269	1	–	–	–	–	1	–	–	1	–	4	–
Total	439,070,582	100	10,725,273		35	21	20	13	32	7		44	23	61	2,360

TABLE 16 (continued)

State	Number of students in Christian colleges						Sex of students in Christian colleges			Total students in		Percentage of students in Christian colleges
	RC		P		S		W	%W	M	Christian colleges	Affiliated colleges	
	W	M	W	M	W	M						
Andhra	2,200	1,595	253	1,450			2,453	44	3,045	5,498	78,691	7
Assam & NEFA	461	3,008	46	114			507	13	3,122	3,629	48,197	8
Bihar	1,157	1,883	201	1,402			1,358	29	3,285	4,643	113,903	4
Gujarat	609	890					609	41	890	1,499	83,787	2
Jammu & Kashmir											13,023	—
Kerala	12,106	17,424	1,221	2,975	2,382	5,183	15,709	38	25,582	41,291	83,452	49
Madhya Pradesh	103	377	454	736			557	34	1,113	1,670	89,264	2
Madras	5,789	5,722	2,950	6,812			8,739	41	12,534	21,273	88,278	24
Maharashtra & Goa	2,734	2,649	2,138	4,536			4,872	41	7,185	12,057	166,334	7
Mysore	2,275	4,272					2,275	34	4,272	6,547	71,676	9
Nagaland												—
Orissa	108			1,392			396	31	1,392	1,392	27,202	5
Punjab & Haryana	168		288	904			168	100	904	1,300	79,830	2
Rajasthan										168	40,591	0·4
Uttar Pradesh	320		1,288	4,878			1,608	25	4,878	6,486	124,122	5
West Bengal	673	2,844	1,499	2,601			2,172	25	5,445	8,769	179,446	5
Himachal Pradesh	145						145	100		145		—
Other Union Territories												—
Delhi				703					703	703	30,431	2
Total	28,848	40,664	10,338	28,503	2,382	5,183	41,568		74,350	117,070	1,318,227	

TABLE 17

Other colleges within 25 miles

No. of other colleges	RCW	RCM	RCD	PS	PU	S	Total
0–3	6 (23)	1 (5)	4 (20)	3 (23)	7 (22)	4 (57)	25 (20)
4–7	11 (31)	5 (25)	3 (15)	1 (8)	4 (13)	2 (29)	26 (21)
8–12	2 (6)	7 (35)	2 (10)	1 (8)	6 (19)	—	18 (14)
13–20	1 (3)	1 (5)	3 (15)	2 (15)	4 (13)	—	11 (9)
21 +	1 (3)	1 (5)	1 (5)	—	2 (6)	—	5 (4)
Total	35 (100)	20 (100)	20 (100)	13 (100)	31 (100)	7 (100)	126 (100)

Numbers in brackets indicate percentages.

TABLE 18
Other Christian colleges within 25 miles

No. of other Christian colleges	RCW	RCM	RCD	PS	PU	S	Total
None	8 (23)	2 (10)	—	2 (15)	7 (23)	—	19 (15)
1 and 2	6 (17)	5 (25)	4 (20)	2 (15)	8 (26)	2 (29)	27 (21)
3 and 4	3 (9)	4 (20)	4 (20)	1 (8)	—	3 (43)	15 (12)
5–7	2 (6)	4 (20)	3 (15)	—	6 (19)	1 (14)	16 (13)
NA	16 (45)	5 (25)	9 (45)	8 (62)	10 (32)	1 (14)	49 (39)
Total	35 (100)	20 (100)	20 (100)	31 (100)	13 (100)	7 (100)	126 (100)

Numbers in brackets indicate percentages.

in 1967 nine new Catholic colleges have been sanctioned for degree work in Kerala alone. In 1968 a Roman Catholic women's college will be started in New Delhi, the first Roman Catholic college in the nation's capital. The total number of Protestant institutions has remained fairly stable since Independence, although there are recent signs of interest in establishing new Protestant colleges. Protestants are opening 3 new colleges in 1967–8. Much of the new effort in Roman Catholic circles comes from the Sisters' congregations, with 16 of the 38 post-Independence Catholic colleges being under Sisters' auspices; their rapid growth partially reflects the fact that education is one of the few areas of service open to women in India, and to the Sisters' congregations, minimizing staffing problems for these colleges. Most of the Roman Catholic women's colleges are in the South. Also, there has been a very sizeable increase in Roman Catholic colleges under diocesan auspices; three-quarters of the diocesan colleges have been founded since 1949.

Many new Christian colleges are explicitly vocational. Approximately one-third of the Christian colleges founded since 1949 are for teacher-training or are specifically vocational (Table 19). Indian higher education is still plagued with too many students in the arts and too few in the sciences and actual professional training; well over 50 per cent of the graduates of arts and science colleges are in the arts. And even much of the arts instruction is basically irrelevant to Indian situations. That Christian colleges have tended to be increasingly vocational is evident not only in the establishment of vocationally oriented colleges, but perhaps equally impressive is their much higher proportion of science than arts students, reversing the national trend and average. Christian colleges are also making heavy new expenditure to develop science training facilities and laboratories.

One reason for this emphasis upon teacher-training institutions is to provide personnel to teach in the great number of Christian primary and secondary schools spread throughout the country (Appendix II). Beyond this, however, there is growing concern to provide vocationally relevant education

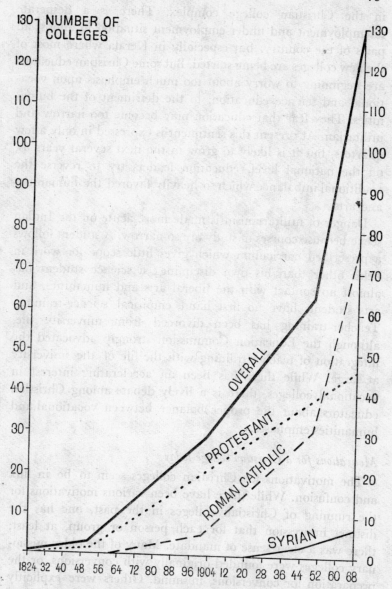

Figure 2. GROWTH OF CHRISTIAN COLLEGES

in the Christian college complex. There is a desperate unemployment and under-employment situation in almost all parts of the country, but especially in Kerala where most of the new colleges are being started. But some Christian educators are beginning to worry about too much emphasis upon vocational and science education, to the detriment of the humanities. They fear that education may become too narrow and utilitarian. At present this sentiment is expressed in only a few quarters, but it is likely to grow in the next several years as, on the national level, education leaders try to reverse the traditional imbalance which so heavily favored the humanities and arts.

Danger of utilitarianism is made more acute on the Indian scene because courses of study are so narrow. A student follows a prescribed curriculum which gives little scope for work in fields other than his own discipline; a science student has almost no contact with the liberal arts and humanities, and arts students have no first hand empirical science-training. Teacher-training has been divorced from university life, although the Education Commission strongly advocated the integration of teacher-training with the life of the university at large. While there has been an accelerating interest in vocational colleges, there is a lively debate among Christian educators about the proper balance between vocational and humanities emphases.

Motivations for a Christian college today

The motivations for Christian colleges seem to be in flux and confusion. While there have been various motivations for the running of Christian colleges in the past, one has the distinct impression that for each person or group, at least, there was a clear sense of mandate. Many of the older missionary colleges were founded originally with conversions, or the preparation for conversions, in mind. Others were explicitly designed to confront Hinduism with the ideas and faith of Christians.

Today there is a widespread and deep malaise about the *raison d'être* of a Christian college. Times have changed, and

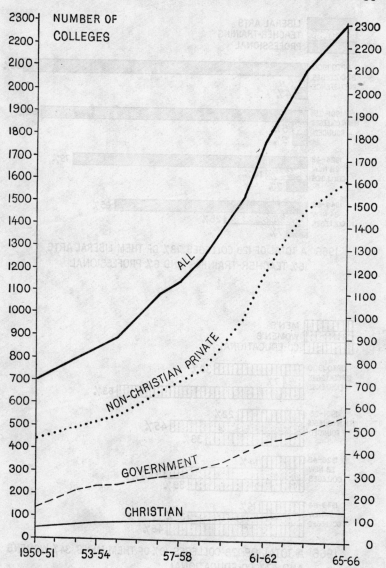

NUMBER OF COLLEGES

ALL

NON-CHRISTIAN PRIVATE

GOVERNMENT

CHRISTIAN

Figure 3. GROWTH OF AFFILIATED COLLEGES 1950-66

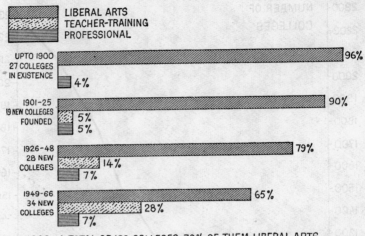

1966: A TOTAL OF 128 COLLEGES, 78% OF THEM LIBERAL ARTS,
16% TEACHER-TRAINING AND 6% PROFESSIONAL

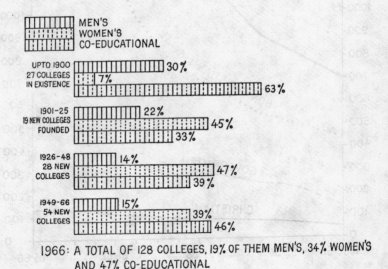

1966: A TOTAL OF 128 COLLEGES, 19% OF THEM MEN'S, 34% WOMEN'S
AND 47% CO-EDUCATIONAL

Figure 4. TYPES OF COLLEGE (BY PERIOD OF FOUNDING)

TABLE 19

Historical development of Christian colleges

Period	Religious sponsorship							Section of country			
	RCW	RCM	RCD	PS	PU	S	Total	North	South	Central	Total
Prior to 1850	1 (6)	2 (12)	—	4 (23)	10 (59)	—	17 (100)	8 (47)	8 (47)	1 (6)	17 (100)
1850–1900	4 (17)	7 (29)	1 (4)	3 (13)	9 (37)	—	24 (100)	9 (38)	13 (54)	2 (8)	24 (100)
1901–48	14 (37)	5 (13)	4 (11)	4 (11)	10 (26)	1 (2)	38 (100)	12 (31)	22 (58)	4 (11)	38 (100)
1949–60	10 (27)	6 (16)	13 (35)	1 (3)	2 (5)	5 (14)	37 (100)	5 (14)	28 (76)	4 (10)	37 (100)
1961–present	6 (46)	1 (8)	2 (15)	1 (8)	2 (15)	1 (8)	13 (100)	1 (8)	10 (77)	2 (15)	13 (100)
Total	35 (27)	21 (16)	20 (16)	13 (10)	33 (26)	7 (5)	129 (100)	35 (27)	81 (63)	13 (10)	129 (100)

TABLE 19 (continued)

Period	Type of education				Type of student body				Size of student body				
	LA	TT	Other	Total	Men	Women	Co-ed.	Total	1–300	301–1,000	1,001–2,000	2,001+	Total
Prior to 1850	16 (94)	1 (6)	—	17 (100)	3 (18)	1 (6)	13 (76)	17 (100)	1 (6)	3 (18)	11 (64)	2 (12)	17 (100)
1850–1900	22 (92)	1 (4)	1 (4)	24 (100)	10 (42)	6 (25)	8 (33)	24 (100)	2 (8)	12 (50)	7 (29)	3 (13)	24 (100)
1901–48	29 (76)	5 (13)	4 (11)	38 (100)	3 (8)	20 (54)	14 (38)	37(a) (100)	11 (29)	13 (34)	9 (24)	5 (13)	38 (100)
1949–60	26 (70)	10 (27)	1 (3)	37 (100)	5 (14)	12 (32)	20 (54)	37 (100)	13 (35)	8 (22)	13 (35)	3 (8)	37 (100)
1961–present	8 (62)	3 (23)	2 (15)	13 (100)	3 (23)	5·5 (38·5)	5·5 (38·5)	13 (100)	8 (62)	5 (38)	—	—	13 (100)
Total	101 (78)	20 (16)	8 (6)	129 (100)	24 (19)	44 (34)	60 (47)	128(a) (100)	35 (27)	41 (32)	40 (31)	13 (10)	129 (100)

Numbers in brackets indicate percentages.
(a) Information not available.

LA: Liberal Arts.
TT: Teacher-Training.

Christians feel under pressure to prove their identity with the Indian nation; many are deeply disturbed about how they can justify their efforts in a Christian way, with a sense of Christian vocation. How do they differ from others? While it is clear that proselytization and desire for conversions play an insignificant, almost non-existent, role in the functioning of the Christian college today, there is a basic ambiguity and confusion about the purposes of the Christian college in contemporary Indian society. This ambiguity results partly from the fact that Christian college educators find themselves caught between the pressures of the Church, and their commitment to the Church, on the one hand, and the secular State on the other. They are also under pressure from Hindu interests and agitations. An interesting concrete expression of this ambiguity was revealed when we asked principals how many conversions there had been at their college over the past three years (Table 20). In most instances, where we received any answers at all, the figure ranged between one and five, for all kinds of institutions.

TABLE 20
Converts by type of institution

Number of converts	College						Total
	RCW	RCM	RCD	PS	PU	S	
0	11 (31)	7 (35)	8 (40)	10 (32)	5 (48)	3 (43)	44 (35)
1–3	6 (17)	3 (15)	— —	4 (13)	— —	— —	13 (10)
4–10	— —	2 (10)	— —	2 (7)	1 (8)	— —	5 (4)
11–25	1 (3)	2 (10)	— —	— —	— —	— —	3 (2)
26 +	— —	— —	— —	— —	— —	— —	— —
NA	17 (49)	6 (30)	12 (60)	15 (48)	7 (54)	4 (57)	61 (49)
Total	35	20	20	31	13	7	126

Numbers in brackets indicate percentages.

Most principals did not answer the question. Often, of course, they did not know the answer. This suggests that the respondees may have felt torn in giving an answer which would be acceptable to both constituencies — to the churches and to the State. Perhaps a small figure sounded large enough to justify to the churches continuation of their effort, and small enough to the State to constitute no significant threat! However inaccurate may have been the figures which we received on this particular question, it is quite clear that evangelism and conversion are not significant factors in either the philosophy or practice of most Christian colleges. A few, but apparently not many, teachers and administrators in these colleges deplore this lack of emphasis upon conversion.

The trend seems to be in the direction of 'serving society as a whole', through good education, and through serving the Christian community as such.

TABLE 21

Principals' stated objectives
(Weighted scores on a base of 100 points)

Sponsors' aims	RCW	RCM	RCD	PS	PU	S	Total
Serve community of Christians	24	26	25	25	23	22	24·1
Social uplift of non-Christians	7	8	9	8	8	9	8·1
Social service to society as a whole	33	34	33	30	38	33	32·1
Evangelism or conversion	3	3	7	7	6	5	5·1
Lay foundation for the acceptance of the Gospel	17	9	11	18	16	10	14·1
Help needy individuals	8	8	8	7	9	16	9·1
Other	8	12	7	5	10	5	8·1
Total	100	100	100	100	100	100	100

Were we to take the principals' responses at face value, to serve society as a whole would be the dominant motive for the establishment and perpetuation of Christian colleges. But when we note the placement of colleges in particular parts of the country, and when we observe certain other aspects of the running of Christian colleges, such as preferential treatment for Christian students, it is clear that the Christian colleges may feel a special obligation to serve the Christian community first, and then to serve society as a whole. One hears the argument that there is so much discrimination against Christians in non-Christian institutions that something must be done to protect the Christian community. Also, there are many Christian institutions of other types — schools, hospitals, etc., for which personnel must be trained. It would be erroneous to neatly separate service to the Christian community and service to society as a whole, but the striking thing is that there has been a significant shift away from evangelization and conversion as the motivation for continuing Christian colleges, toward a more open-ended service to the broader community — either the broader Christian community, deprived groups, or to society as a whole.

Where are the Christian colleges?

While Christian colleges are sprinkled throughout India, the heaviest concentration is in the South, and the establishment of new colleges reinforces this concentration. A few new Christian colleges have sprung up in the Northeast area of Manipur and Assam. Figure 1 shows the distribution of the colleges throughout the country and in Kerala particularly. Table 16 (above) shows the location of colleges in relation to overall Christian population, numbers of colleges of all types, etc. The high proportion of Protestant institutions in the North helps to explain why Protestant colleges tend to have a smaller percentage of Christian students than do the Catholic institutions. It also helps to explain other differences between Catholic and Protestant institutions which might, at first glance, seem to reflect different denominational philosophies, policies or practices.

Christian colleges are often very close to one another, as well as close to other types of colleges under different sponsorship.

The fact that there are several Christian colleges, sometimes offering the same kind of courses, within a few miles of
one another, indicates inadequate planning and frequent
competition in starting new institutions. Competition seems to
be a major factor in Kerala, even within the same denomination.
Christian colleges are almost all in urban centers. Madras,
Bombay and Calcutta all have several Christian colleges, some
of them very prominent. Further, about 60 per cent of the
Christian colleges are in metropolitan centers of 100,000 or
more people, with about half of these being in cities of more
than one million. There are Christian colleges in 44 of the 113
(39 per cent) of the cities in India with 100,000 people or more.

Who sponsors the Christian colleges?

We have noted above that 45 of the 130 colleges are Protestant, 78 are Roman Catholic, and 7 are non-Roman Syrian
institutions. Table 22 breaks down denominational sponsorship
further. Among the Roman Catholic colleges, 35 are sponsored
by women's congregations, 20 by Roman Catholic men's
orders, and 21 by diocesan leaders. Most prominent among the
women's congregations are the Carmelites with 8 colleges
(men's Carmelite orders have 5 colleges). Franciscan Sisters
have 4, the Loreto nuns 3, the Daughters of the Heart of
Mary 3, while several other congregations have 2 or 1. The
Society of Jesus sponsors 18 colleges. Other congregations have
smaller efforts. Most of the diocesan colleges are in Kerala.

On the Protestant side, 13 of the colleges are run by single
denominations, while the remainder are under multiple
sponsorship. Most heavily involved, either in united or single
efforts, are Lutherans, Episcopalians, The Church of South
India, Methodists, United Church (congregational), Presbyterians, Baptists, and The United Church of North India. The
Church of South India and The United Church of North India
have been counted as united efforts, although it could be
argued that they are single denominations. Some institutions,
like Vellore and Ludhiana medical colleges, have broad Protestant support, with 60 different bodies contributing to the
operation of Vellore Medical College and Hospital.

TABLE 22

Profile of Christian colleges in India
(by sponsorship)

Colleges	RCW	RCM	RCD	RC Total	PS	PU	P Total	S	Grand Total
Number, by sponsor	35	21	20	76	13	33	46	7	129
Number of students	19,789	27,651	21,917	69,357	13,453	27,159	40,612	7,565	117,534
Men's colleges	0	12	2	14	4	6	10	—	24
Women's colleges	34	0	3	37	1	6	7	—	44
Co-educational colleges	1	9	15	25	7	21	28	7	60
INA	—	—	—	—	1	—	1	—	1
Liberal Arts colleges	28	17	15	60	12	26	38	4	102
Teacher-Training colleges	6	3	4	13	1	4	5	2	20
Other colleges	1	1	1	3	0	3	3	1	7
Colleges in North	8	6	—	14	8	12	20	—	34
Centre	3	2	3	8	3	4	7	—	15
South	24	13	17	54	2	17	19	7	80
Colleges founded before 1900	6	9	1	16	7	19	26	—	42
between 1921 and 1948	13	5	4	22	4	10	14	1	37
after 1948	16	7	15	38	2	4	6	6	50
Colleges with under 300 students	13	4	6	23	2	8	10	2	35
301–1000 students	15	2	4	21	4	15	19	1	41
1000 + students	7	15	10	32	7	10	17	4	53
Colleges with B.A. as highest degree	27	13	12	52	9	15	24	4	80
M.A. as highest degree	7	4	7	18	2	11	13	3	34
Ph.D. as highest degree	—	4	—	4	2	6	8	—	12
Other	1	—	1	2	—	1	1	—	3

How are the Christian colleges financed ?

This is the area for which it has been most difficult to get reliable and convincing information. Nevertheless, it is evident that fees and government support account for upwards of 90 per cent of the total annual budget, with church and mission boards contributing normally less than 5 per cent. Sometimes, particularly with the Roman Catholic institutions, a religious congregation subsidizes fairly heavily through special gifts or loans, and by providing teachers and administrators who serve at less than a normal salary.

Christian colleges receive almost no gifts from the community at large, and do not cultivate alumni giving. In fact, Christian colleges in India, as other colleges, have very little contact with their alumni. Most do not maintain up-to-date records of graduates, and only a few places, like Madras Christian College, attempt to relate alumni to ongoing programs. On the whole, neither Christian nor other colleges exploit the potential strength and values of closer continued contact with alumni.

On the other hand, Christian colleges have generally received a fair share of special grants from the University Grants Commission, a fact which reflects the traditional quality of the Christian institutions, as well as their age (since many colleges have been given centenary grants by the Commission for special projects). These special grants show not only the academic standing of the colleges, but also their physical potentialities, and Christian colleges generally have had superior physical facilities because they have been willing to invest heavily to develop them. As older institutions, they also were begun at a time when land was not so expensive. Several Protestant colleges, though few Roman Catholic ones, reported receiving some money from churches abroad. Almost half of the Protestant colleges received some money. Important as this is in the support of some colleges, it does not change the overall picture.

Because the vast majority of the money still comes from student fees and government, college students in India are obliged to pay a much higher proportion of their total educational cost than is true in either the United States or Britain.

Students in India pay 37 per cent of the total cost of their education, students in the United States 25 per cent, and students in England 12 per cent.[1] This is a very heavy burden upon the resources of the Indian student, particularly because many of them come from low-income families, as seen in Tables 23 and 24.

TABLE 23

Students' family income per annum

(by religion, in percentages)

Annual income	RC 359	P 267	S 79	Hindu 948	Muslim 59	Other 40	Total 1,752
Upto Rs 1,000	26	19	19	23	31	—	23
Rs 1,001–2,000	24	29	28	19	17	25	22
Rs 2,001–3,000	13	12	11	10	7	10	11
Rs 3,001–5,000	11	14	24	12	8	16	12
Rs 5,001–7,500	6	9	4	7	10	9	7
Rs 7,501–10,000	5	4	4	6	3	3	5
Rs 10,001–15,000	2	4	3	5	12	6	4
Rs 15,001 +	2	3	1	5	3	—	3
NA	11	6	6	13	8	31	12
Total	100	100	100	100	100	100	100

The overall financial position is both cloudy and quite gloomy, with the Catholic institutions seemingly somewhat better off than the Protestant ones. On the other hand, many Protestant institutions lack operating capital at present, but enjoy superior facilities inherited from the past. A major disadvantage of the fact that colleges are heavily dependent upon government, for economic as well as political reasons, is that they have been obliged to accept large numbers of pre-university degree students in order to have their fees. In some cases P.U.C. students number between 40 and 45 per cent of the total

TABLE 24

Students' family income per annum
(by institutional sponsorship)

Annual income	RCW	RCM	RCD	PS	PU	Total
Upto Rs 1,000	78 (17)	102 (24)	117 (29)	40 (19)	65 (21)	402 (22)
Rs 1,001–2,000	67 (15)	129 (30)	104 (26)	39 (19)	53 (17)	392 (22)
Rs 2,001–3,000	36 (8)	58 (14)	54 (13)	16 (8)	34 (11)	198 (11)
Rs 3,001–5,000	49 (11)	53 (12)	57 (14)	24 (12)	41 (13)	224 (12)
Rs 5,001–7,500	37 (8)	26 (6)	16 (4)	16 (8)	37 (12)	132 (7)
Rs 7,501–10,000	23 (5)	23 (5)	15 (4)	6 (3)	24 (8)	91 (5)
Rs 10,001–15,000	30 (7)	6 (1)	6 (2)	12 (6)	21 (7)	75 (4)
Rs 15,001–30,000	30 (7)	3 (1)	— (—)	6 (3)	10 (3)	49 (3)
Rs 30,001 +	7 (1)	5 (1)	1 (—)	2 (1)	2 (—)	17 (—)
NA	96 (21)	21 (5)	32 (8)	45 (21)	26 (8)	220 (12)
Total	453 (100)	426 (100)	402 (100)	206 (100)	313 (100)	1,800 (100)

Numbers in brackets indicate percentages.

student body, tending to give a secondary school quality to the college's work (Table 54). Considering such pressures, it is to the credit of Christian colleges, as a whole, that they have not opted for cheaper P.U.C. and arts education, as distinguished from science, technical and medical education. In 1963-4 it was calculated that it cost Rs 205 for law students, Rs 307 for commerce, Rs 431 for arts and science, Rs 845 for teacher-training. It costs four-fifths as much money per student for arts as for science instruction.

Inadequate financing has brought tremendous pressures on all colleges, and a few Christian colleges have been forced to relinquish their sponsorship to Government. Even where out-right government operations does not eventuate, governmental pressures are often keenly felt in most areas of policy and operation, causing many Christian college administrators to ask whether the fight is worth the candle.

Are physical facilities in the Christian colleges adequate ?

While there are glaring exceptions, most Christian colleges are reasonably well-endowed. By comparison many non-Christian colleges operate with wholly inadequate facilities. Many Christian institutions have enough acreage for further expansion ; most have adequate classroom space despite the fact that there have been large increments in the student population, (the use of existing facilities needs to be rationalized) ;[2] libraries are generally superior (Table 25) ; hostel facilities are usually quite good, although more hostels are needed (21 per cent of students in Christian colleges are resident, while the comparable national figure for all colleges is 13 per cent) ; and there is adequate provision for most other basic needs at the Christian colleges. One striking feature is their heavy investment in both hostels and new laboratories, which have been the major non-recurring expenditure over the last several years in Christian colleges taken as a whole. Many Christian colleges have large assembly halls, a chapel, good playing-fields, and good extra-curricular facilities. Student common rooms and lounges are often found ; canteens or messes are usually adequate, but not inspiring!

TABLE 25

Library volumes (by sponsorship)

Sponsorship	Liberal Arts		Teacher Training		Others	
	Total	Average	Total	Average	Total	Average
RCW	250,978	9,295	27,538	4,590	4,500	4,500
RCM	594,729	34,984	16,913	5,638	4,000	4,000
RCD	218,343	15,596	17,853	3,571	3,000	3,000
PS	243,595	20,300	1,650	1,650	—	—
PU	512,226	20,489	26,759	6,600	44,857	14,952
S	45,420	11,355	5,500	2,750	3,447	3,447
Total	1,865,291	18,841	96,213	4,582	59,804	8,548

The vast majority of these titles are in English. Subject areas in order of strength appear to be the following: English Literature (20 per cent), History (15 per cent), Languages (14 per cent), Physical and Natural Sciences (11 per cent), Social Sciences (11 per cent), and Philosophy and Religion (9 per cent).

There is room, however, for selected and significant improvement in facilities. For example, much more needs to be done to provide more space for administrative staff; they are frequently squeezed into quarters which preclude efficiency. Teaching staff desperately need office space where they can work and meet students. Other priority needs are residences for staff and students, and special facilities for day-students. There are, of course, great differences between colleges, and many of the newer institutions are much harder pressed for space and adequate facilities than older colleges. There are shortages, but these are not as acute as in many of the non-Christian institutions. Government colleges are likely to catch up to even the best-endowed Christian colleges in the near future; in physical facilities many are already superior to the weaker Christian colleges.

Who administers the Christian colleges?

Several generalizations can be made about the Boards of Governors or Trustees. First, they are a fairly homogeneous

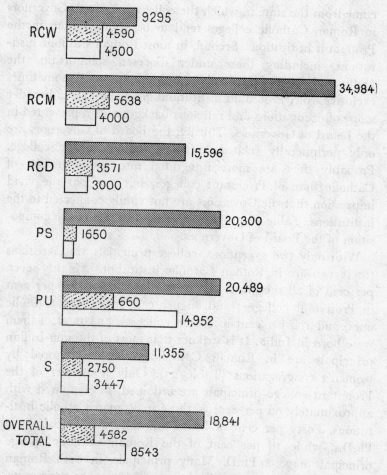

Figure 5. AVERAGE NUMBER OF
VOLUMES IN COLLEGE LIBRARIES (BY SPONSOR)

group, 90 per cent of them being church related and/or educators, with very few other professional, business or community groups represented. About 30 per cent of the principals are members of the Board of Governors in other Christian institutions and 44 per cent are on the Board of Governors of other colleges. Ninety per cent of them are Christian, most come from the state in which the college is located. Governors in Roman Catholic colleges tend to be younger than in the Protestant institutions. Second, in most Roman Catholic institutions, including those under diocesan sponsorship, the 'religious' or ordained play a dominant, and sometimes exclusive, role. Protestant institutions generally have a broader scope of occupations and religious backgrounds represented in the Board of Governors. Thirdly, the Board of Governors are only peripherally related to the operation of the college. Probably they are more integrated into the operation of Catholic than of Protestant colleges, but one gets the vivid impression that the Governors are not vitally connected to the institutions. Table 26 provides a general profile of the composition of the Board of Governors.

With only two exceptions, college principals are Christians (these two are in Roman Catholic institutions). Eighty-seven per cent of all the principals are Indian citizens (93 per cent in Protestant colleges; and 80 per cent in Roman Catholic ones, and 100 per cent in Syrian colleges), and most of them were born in India. It is striking that most of the non-Indian principals are in Roman Catholic colleges sponsored by women's congregations (Table 27). Only a quarter of the Protestant college principals are ordained, as compared with approximately 90 per cent of those in Roman Catholic institutions. Forty per cent of Protestant college principals have Ph.D.s, while 18 per cent of the Roman Catholic college principals have a Ph.D. Many principals, in both Roman Catholic and Protestant colleges, are fairly new to their posts. Principals in Protestant colleges tend to be older than those in Roman Catholic ones, with one-third of the Catholics and two-thirds of the Protestants being over fifty years old. Most principals teach in addition to their administrative assignments.

TABLE 26
Profile of trustees

Sponsorship	Religion							Profession					
	RC	P	S	Hindu	Muslim	Other	INA	Education	Business	Community	Church	Other	INA
RCW	154 (76)		2 (1)	37 (19)	2 (1)	5 (2)	5	101 (51)	5 (3)	8 (4)	70 (36)	13 (6)	11
RCM	92 (85)		2 (2)	12 (11)	1 (1)	1 (1)	5	40 (40)		6 (6)	44 (44)	10 (10)	13
RCD	105 (78)		22 (16)	8 (6)			3	64 (50)		2 (1)	50 (38)	14 (11)	8
RC total	351 (79)	3 (1)	26 (6)	57 (13)	3 (1)	6 (1)	13	205 (48)	5 (1)	16 (4)	164 (38)	37 (9)	32
PS	1 (1)	88 (72)	7 (6)	25 (20)	1 (1)		20	55 (45)	2 (1)	8 (7)	44 (36)	14 (11)	19
PU	2 (1)	328 (90)	20 (5)	15 (4)	1		231	167 (49)	12 (4)	6 (2)	89 (26)	65 (19)	258
P total	3 (1)	416 (85)	27 (6)	40 (7)	2 (1)		251	222 (48)	14 (3)	14 (3)	133 (29)	79 (17)	277
S total			118 (97)	3 (2)	1 (1)			22 (67)	1 (3)	2 (6)	4 (12)	4 (12)	89
Total	354 (34)	419 (40)	171 (16)	100 (9)	6 (1)	6 (1)	264	449 (49)	20 (2)	32 (3)	301 (33)	120 (13)	398

TABLE 26 (continued)

Sponsorship	Age					Sex			Home state			Total	Average age
	Upto 40	41-50	51-60	61+	INA	Male	Female	INA	Yes	No	INA		
RCW	29 (18)	62 (38)	48 (29)	25 (15)	44	54 (27)	144 (73)	10	89 (46)	105 (54)	14	208	8
RCM	15 (18)	31 (37)	29 (35)	8 (10)	30	106 (95)	5 (5)	2	60 (63)	36 (37)	17	113	7
RCD	17 (19)	28 (32)	24 (27)	19 (22)	50	120 (87)	18 (13)		94 (72)	36 (28)	8	138	9
RC total	61 (18)	121 (36)	101 (30)	52 (16)	124	280 (63)	167 (37)	12	243 (58)	177 (42)	39	459	8
PS	3 (4)	20 (29)	28 (42)	17 (25)	74	130 (95)	7 (5)	5	66 (62)	41 (38)	35	142	16
PU	21 (8)	87 (34)	100 (39)	47 (19)	342	460 (79)	123 (21)	14	199 (56)	159 (44)	239	597	23
P total	24 (7)	107 (33)	128 (40)	64 (20)	416	590 (82)	130 (18)	19	265 (57)	200 (43)	274	739	21
S total	4 (17)	9 (38)	6 (25)	5 (20)	98	122 (100)			116 (97)	3 (3)	3	122	18
Total	89 (13)	237 (35)	235 (34)	121 (18)	638 (77)	992 (23)	297	31 (62)	624 (38)	380	316	1,320	13

Numbers in brackets indicate percentages.

Percentages are based on the trustees for which there is the relevant information. One-hundred and fifty-six trustees belong to Vellore Medical College (PU), and almost no information was available about them, thus causing the large INA in the PU tabulation.

TABLE 27
Profile of principals

Sponsorship	Ordained		Christian		Indian citizen		Highest degree			
	Yes	No	Yes	No	Yes	No	Ph.D.	M.A.	B.A.	Other
RCW	33	2	33	2	23	11	4	25	5	1
RCW NA					1					
RCM	20	1	20		17	3	5	14	1	1
RCM NA			1			1				
RCD	16	4	20	2	20		4	14	1	1
RCD NA				1						
RC total	69	6	73		60	14	13	53	6	1
RC total NA		1				2				3
PS	4	9	13		13		4	9		
PU	7	24	31	1	28	3	14	16		1
PU NA		1				1				1
P total	11	33	44	1	41	3	18	25		1
P total NA		1				1				1
S	1	6	7		7		1	5		1
Grand Total	81	45	124	2	108	17	32	83	6	2
Grand Total NA		2		2		3				5

TABLE 27 (continued)

Sponsorship	No. of years in present post				Age				Now teaching		Years of teaching experience		
	1	2-3	4-10	11+	30s	40s	50s	60s	Yes	No	0	1-5	6+
RCW	2	11	13	8	5	18	7	2	31	4		2	32
NA				1				3					1
RCM	3	5	10	2		12	7	1	20				19
NA				1				1		1		1	1
RCD	3	2	12	2	3	6	6	3	18	1		1	19
NA			1					1		1			
RC total	8	18	35	12	8	36	20	6	69	5		4	70
NA			3					5		2			2
PS	5	2	3	3	1	4	5	3	12	1			13
NA													
PU	4	4	17	6	1	9	13	8	29				29
NA				1				1			1		2
P total	9	6	20	9	2	13	18	11	41	3			42
NA				1				1			1		2
S		4	1	1	1	1	3	1	6	1			6
NA				1				1		3			1
Grand total	17	28	56	22	11	50	41	18	116	6		4	118
NA				5				7		6	1		5

A major weakness of Christian colleges in India is their lack of properly-trained administrators. Many become principals without any prior interest in, or preparation for, administration. This is complicated by the fact that most principals are heavily overworked, with only tiny office staffs to assist them. Furthermore, there is a tendency for them, like principals all over India, to centralize administration, thus burdening themselves beyond their efficient capacity. More imaginative, experienced, and involved administrative leadership in the colleges could yield very significant advantages, both in changes on the local campus, and in educational reform in the university as a whole. Looking across Indian higher education, one is stunned by the inadequate preparation for educational administration. It is difficult to see how vigorous and imaginative reform can spring up in colleges and universities until much more adequate administrative training procedures and structures are devised.

It is interesting to note the attitudes of teachers toward the Christian colleges' administration, as shown in Table 28. For clarity and simplification we have made a general 'good'-'fair' dichotomy, including in the fair category all those who responded 'poor'. As anticipated, older teachers were generally less critical of the administration than younger ones. Teachers were most critical of administration for their lack of a sense of involvement in social and public issues, and for their lack of involvement in the life of the university as a whole. Forty-two per cent found administrators' 'rapport with teachers' only 'fair', and 40 per cent found only a 'fair' concern for academic excellence, with more critical attitudes expressed toward Protestant than Roman Catholic principals. Generally speaking, Roman Catholic principals were rated higher on both 'concern for the religious program of the college' and on 'dedication to student welfare'. The only significant difference between Christian and non-Christian respondees was that Christian teachers tended to be much more critical of the administration's lack of concern for the religious program of the college, most strongly felt by the Protestants (Table 29).

TABLE 28

Teachers' assessment of administration
(by sponsorship and age)

		Roman Catholic			Protestant			Totals		
		Under 40	Over 40	Total RC	Under 40	Over 40	Total P	Under 40	Over 40	Total
Rapport with teachers	Good	57	60	58	57	61	58	57	60	58
	Fair	43	40	42	43	39	42	43	40	42
Dedication to student welfare	Good	64	74	67	50	68	57	60	71	64
	Fair	36	26	33	50	32	43	40	29	36
Interest in religious program	Good	62	71	65	53	50	52	59	62	60
	Fair	38	29	35	47	50	48	41	38	40
Concern for academic excellence	Good	72	88	77	58	71	63	67	82	72
	Fair	28	12	23	42	29	37	33	18	28
Sense of involvement in social issues and problems	Good	19	21	20	13	30	19	17	25	20
	Fair	81	79	80	87	70	81	83	75	80
Involvement in the life of university	Good	29	39	32	29	36	32	29	38	32
	Fair	71	61	68	71	64	68	71	62	68
Concern for extracurricular affairs	Good	53	52	53	50	56	52	52	54	52
	Fair	47	48	47	50	44	48	48	46	48

TABLE 29

Teachers' assessment of administration

(by religion)

		RC	P	S	Other	Christian total	Grand total
Rapport with teachers	High	44	45	25	46	40	42
	Fair	52	43	75	48	52	51
	Poor	4	12		6	8	7
Dedication to student welfare	High	74	55	50	59	61	61
	Fair	26	33	48	34	33	33
	Poor		12	2	7	6	6
Interest in religious program	High	71	51	35	57	56	56
	Fair	24	35	53	41	34	36
	Poor	5	14	12	2	10	8
Concern for academic excellence	High	86	63	73	67	74	71
	Fair	12	33	27	31	24	26
	Poor	2	4		2	2	3
Sense of involvement in social issues and problems	High	14	20	16	14	17	16
	Fair	65	48	44	59	53	55
	Poor	21	32	40	27	30	29
Involvement in the life of university	High	26	26	20	19	25	23
	Fair	57	51	44	64	53	57
	Poor	17	23	36	17	22	20
Concern for extra-curricular affairs	High	50	51	54	42	51	48
	Fair	40	38	42	48	40	43
	Poor	10	11	4	10	9	9

Who are the teachers in Christian colleges?

Indian college teachers work under very difficult circumstances and are much maligned. Gaudino has contributed to a very good impressionistic account of the Indian college situation, and his description of both teachers and students is very rewarding.[3] Table 30 shows the teachers' fathers' occupational background, and Table 31 shows the teachers' religious affiliation. What is most striking is the high number of farm family backgrounds among teachers in colleges run under Roman Catholic men's congregations and diocesan auspices.

TABLE 30

Staff: Fathers' occupation

Occupation	RCW 171 respondents	RCM 138 respondents	RCD 60 respondents	PS 115 respondents	PU 157 respondents	Total 641 respondents
Farming	19 (11)	38 (27)	29 (48)	16 (14)	8 (5)	110 (17)
Professional (Medicine, Law, etc.)	21 (12)	11 (8)	3 (5)	18 (16)	43 (27)	96 (15)
Skilled technician	5 (3)	2 (1)	— —	3 (3)	5 (3)	15 (2)
Clerical and Office	16 (9)	7 (5)	4 (7)	6 (5)	14 (9)	47 (7)
Govt. servant & Military	30 (18)	16 (12)	6 (10)	27 (24)	26 (17)	105 (16)
Business/ Landlord	30 (18)	23 (17)	3 (5)	12 (10)	18 (11)	86 (14)
Educators	16 (9)	28 (20)	4 (7)	12 (10)	23 (15)	83 (13)
Other	2 (1)	1 (1)	— —	4 (3)	5 (3)	12 (2)
NA	32 (19)	12 (9)	11 (18)	17 (15)	15 (10)	87 (14)
Total	171 (100)	138 (100)	60 (100)	115 (100)	157 (100)	641 (100)

Numbers in brackets indicate percentages.

It is also surprising to note how few Protestant teachers are in Roman Catholic colleges, and vice versa. One would have

TABLE 31
Staff: Religious affiliation

Religion	RCW 171 respondents	RCM 138 respondents	RCD 60 respondents	PS 115 respondents	PU 157 respondents	Total 641 respondents
Roman Catholic	60 (35)	68 (49)	33 (55)	— —	3 (2)	164 (25)
Protestant	12 (7)	2 (1)	2 (3)	36 (31)	98 (62)	150 (23)
Syrian	5 (3)	1 (1)	6 (10)	2 (2)	11 (7)	25 (4)
Hindu	88 (51)	65 (47)	16 (27)	63 (55)	40 (26)	27 (42)
Other	6 (4)	2 (1)	3 (5)	14 (12)	5 (3)	30 (5)
Total	171 (100)	138 (100)	60 (100)	115 (100)	157 (100)	641 (100)

Numbers in brackets indicate percentages.

anticipated a greater degree of mixing. More refined information about the percentage of Christian teachers can be found in the listing of all the Christian colleges (Appendix I), as well as in Volume I of this study.

Table 32 gives a broader picture of the age distribution of teachers, reflecting on the whole a predominance of young people, which is probably attributable to the explosion of education during the post-Independence period. This probability is corroborated by the heavy proportion of teachers in their twenties and thirties in Catholic women's and diocesan institutions, which are themselves the younger colleges. If this younger leadership can be further trained, and kept in the teaching profession, the colleges will have a good reservoir of teachers for long-term development, but improving existing faculty members' competence must remain a high priority.

Christian colleges are parochial not only in administration and students, but also in teaching staff. About 75 per cent of the teachers in Christian colleges work in their home state, with a significantly higher number of home-state teachers in Roman Catholic institutions, which is probably explained by the location of many Protestant colleges in the sparsely

TABLE 32

Staff: Age composition

Age	RCW 171 respondents	RCM 138 respondents	RCD 60 respondents	PS 115 respondents	PU 157 respondents	Total 641 respondents
20s	104 (61)	57 (41)	34 (56)	57 (49)	65 (41)	317 (49)
30s	38 (22)	41 (30)	16 (27)	26 (23)	59 (38)	180 (28)
40s	16 (9)	15 (11)	6 (10)	20 (17)	16 (10)	73 (11)
50s	7 (4)	22 (16)	4 (7)	9 (8)	15 (10)	57 (9)
60s	4 (2)	3 (2)	— —	3 (3)	2 (1)	12 (2)
Totals	171 (100)	138 (100)	60 (100)	115 (100)	157 (100)	641 (100)

Numbers in brackets indicate percentages.

Christianized areas of the North. These import Christian teachers from the more densely Christian, less fully-employed, South. One finds expatriates from Kerala in colleges throughout the country.

A picture of the highest degrees earned by teachers in Christian colleges is shown in Table 33. Significant to note are the following points: there are comparatively few Ph.D.s (6 per cent overall); Protestant colleges tend to have many more Ph.D.s than do Roman Catholic colleges (10·4 per cent as compared with 2·2 per cent), and presumably considerably more than the national average in all types of colleges; there are more than twice as many teachers who have a Bachelor's degree as their highest degree as there are who have Ph.D.s. It is probable that the 'not known' category is predominantly a Bachelor's degree group. As a whole, the training of Christian college teachers compares quite favorably with the general situation for teachers in Indian colleges, although we do not have comparative statistics available.

We were surprised to find that about 14 per cent of the teachers in our sample had studied at some time outside of India, with about twice as many of these teachers (by percentage) coming from Protestant colleges under multiple denominational

TABLE 33
Staff : Highest degrees

Degree	RCW	RCM	RCD	RC Total	PS	PU	P Total	S	Grand total
Ph.D.	16 (1·5)	51 (3·1)	23 (2·1)	90 (2·2)	110 (15·2)	159 (9)	269 (10·4)	5 (1·3)	364 (6)
Master's	755 (69·6)	932 (70)	735 (69·3)	2,422 (69·4)	504 (68·9)	1,294 (74)	1,798 (72·6)	238 (71·6)	4,458 (71)
Bachelor's	233 (21·5)	272 (21)	166 (15·6)	661 (19·2)	60 (8·2)	169 (9)	229 (9·5)	58 (17·6)	948 (15)
Other	37 (3·4)	49 (3·8)	26 (2·4)	112 (3·8)	18 (2·3)	29 (1)	47 (1·3)	31 (9·5)	190 (4)
Not known	44 (4·0)	37 (2·1)	112 (10·6)	193 (5·4)	40 (5·4)	111 (7)	151 (6·2)	— —	344 (5)
Total	1,085 (100)	1,341 (100)	1,062 (100)	3,478 (100)	732 (100)	1,762 (100)	2,494 (100)	332 (100)	6,304 (100)

Numbers in brackets indicate percentages.

sponsorship. About 50 per cent of these who studied abroad did so in the U.S.A. and Canada, 25 per cent in England, 13 per cent in Western Europe, none in 'socialist' countries, and 12 per cent in other countries. Twenty-seven per cent of teachers in Christian colleges are teaching in the institution from which they graduated, and about a third of these have taught elsewhere in the interim.

Therefore, there is considerable in-grownness in college staffs, and considerably more in-breeding in the sciences than arts, partly reflecting the heavier emphasis on science in the Christian colleges. One-fifth of the teachers in arts and two-fifths of the teachers in science are graduates of the institution where they now teach. This in-grown character may be accelerating, judging from the fact that of teachers in their twenties, 52 per cent are graduates of the college where they now teach; 27 per cent of those in their thirties; 23 per cent of those in their forties; and 19 per cent of those in their fifties and sixties. Naturally, there is more in-grownness for Christians than for non-Christians. It is not clear how deeply this in-grownness affects attitudes about the college, but one series of generalizations may be indicative: teachers working in colleges from which they graduated tend to be more positive about the quality of staff-student relationship and good administration, as strengths of that particular college; they do not seem more enthusiastic about the religious atmosphere and program, nor about the sense of community, good discipline or physical plant as strengths of their college.

It is instructive to look more closely at a few attitudes which teachers have of the Christian college in which they work.[4] Most teachers seemed happy in their college, but 16 per cent of a sample of 232 teachers stated a preference for teaching in a non-Christian college, with dissatisfaction higher among teachers in Protestant colleges than in Catholic ones. It was surprising to find that, in both Protestant and Catholic colleges, teachers between the ages of twenty and forty were happier in a Christian college than were teachers above forty — about half as much dissatisfaction. While the sample is too small for comfortable generalizations, the pattern holds for both Protestant

STAFF: PERCENTAGE WITH BACHELOR'S AS HIGHEST DEGREE

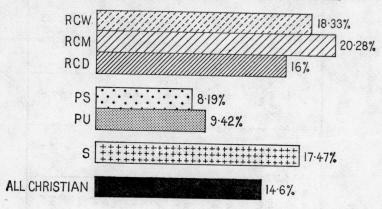

STAFF: PERCENTAGE OF Ph. D's

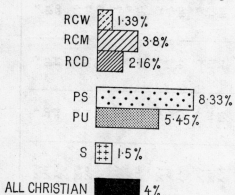

Figure 6. STAFF: HIGHEST DEGREES (BY SPONSOR)

TABLE 34

Teachers' assessment of their college
(by sponsorship)

		Roman Catholic			Protestant			Totals		Grand Total
		Under 40	Over 40	Total RC	Under 40	Over 40	Total P	Under 40	Over 40	
Attracts best students	Yes	82	77	80	76	62	71	80	71	77
	No	13	18	15	22	31	25	16	24	19
	NA	4	5	5	2	7	4	4	5	4
Higher moral and ethical values	Yes	89	91	89	89	83	87	80	88	88
	No	6	7	7	9	14	11	7	9	8
	NA	6	2	5	2	3	3	6	3	4
Better job of teaching	Yes	88	86	87	78	79	79	85	83	84
	No	4	9	9	13	17	15	7	13	9
	NA	8	5	7	9	3	7	8	4	7
Corporate life a special feature	Yes	71	56	66	74	83	77	72	67	70
	No	24	37	37	17	17	17	22	29	25
	NA	4	7	5	9	—	5	6	4	5
Overprotects Christians	Yes	23	14	20	22	3	15	23	10	18
	No	76	81	81	78	94	84	76	86	80
	NA	1	5	2	—	3	1	1	4	2

and Catholic institutions and this tends to confirm its validity. Teachers have a generally high assessment of their college. Table 34 shows their evaluation related to the kind of institution in which they teach, and Table 35 relates attitudes about the college based on religious background.

TABLE 35
Teachers' assessment of their college
(by religion)

	RC 59 resp. yes	P 64 resp. yes	S 26 resp. yes	Christian total 149 resp. yes	Others 83 resp. yes	Overall total 232 resp. yes
College attracts best students	83	77	69	78	85	80
Higher moral and ethical values	95	94	83	92	91	92
Better job of teaching	93	88	92	91	92	91
Corporate life a special feature	66	82	69	73	76	74
Overprotects Christians	17	17	19	17	23	19
Teach in non-Christian college?	10	17	15	15	19	16
No preference	—	9	3	5	9	6

A slightly higher percentage of non-Christian teachers would prefer to work in a non-Christian institution and feel that there is over-protection of Christians — 19 per cent as compared with 15 per cent, but these non-Christian teachers seem about as complimentary towards Christian colleges' work as their Christian colleagues do; they even feel *more* strongly that Christian colleges attract the best students. Protestant teachers seem to feel, and to lesser extent Roman Catholic ones, that their colleges stand out as superior in promoting a sense of community.

What do staff feel about their fellow teachers? Table 36 deserves study. For one thing, there is considerable criticalness of colleagues in general.[5] There was a feeling that colleagues were too little interested and involved in improving life in India, too little interested in the life of the college beyond the classroom, and too little concerned for participating in the community life around the college and in the college. They were, however, generally positive about colleagues' concern for academic standards. These suggest narrow conceptions of the function of a college and a college teacher, but it is interesting, too, that college teachers should themselves make these judgments.

Differences between Catholic and Protestant colleges were not of great importance. The major difference relating to the age of the respondee was that the over-forty group thought their colleagues' sense of community effort was stronger than the under-forty group felt. Non-Christian teachers were more critical than their Christian counterparts about teachers' dedication to student welfare, concern for academic and intellectual excellence, and staff's interest in self-improvement. Non-Christian teachers were less critical of their colleagues' involvement in non-academic life, both at the college and in the community at large.

What do teachers feel is the justification for Christian colleges?

Eighty per cent of the teachers felt that Christian sponsorship strengthened their college, and the older respondents were somewhat more positive on this point than younger teachers. Table 37 refers to the reasons for the continuation of Christian colleges, judged by different age groups. On a weighted scale, the imparting of personal values is the dominant motive expressed, while concern for promoting Christianity hardly finds a place; generalized personal and social values take precedence over specifically Christian ones. Younger teachers tended to emphasize general social values more than did the older teachers, whose perspectives were somewhat more particularistic.

TABLE 36

Teachers' assessment of other teachers

	Under 40		Over 40		Total	
	Good	Fair	Good	Fair	Good	Fair
	Roman Catholic					
Sense of community of effort among teachers	34	66	40	60	36	64
Dedication to student welfare	64	36	56	44	62	38
Concern for academic excellence	72	28	67	33	71	29
Interest in growth of college as first rate educational institution	66	34	65	35	66	34
Sense of involvement in improving life in India	21	79	33	67	25	75
Interest in self-improvement	55	45	47	53	52	48
Involvement in life of college beyond classroom	27	73	32	68	29	71
Working in the community in which college is located	26	74	29	71	27	73
Interest in religious program in college	38	62	49	51	41	59
	Protestant					
Sense of community of effort among teachers	24	76	44	56	32	68
Dedication to student welfare	48	52	50	50	49	51
Concern for academic excellence	48	52	61	39	53	47
Interest in growth of college as first rate educational institution	47	53	70	30	56	44
Sense of involvement in improving life in India	20	80	33	67	25	75
Interest in self-improvement	37	63	41	59	39	61
Involvement in life of college beyond classroom	35	65	32	68	34	66
Working in the community in which college is located	19	81	28	72	22	78
Interest in religious program in college	41	59	39	61	40	60

TABLE 36 (continued)

	Under 40		Over 40		Grand total	
	Good	Fair	Good	Fair	Good	Fair
			Totals			
Sense of community of effort among teachers	31	69	42	58	35	35
Dedication to student welfare	59	41	54	46	57	43
Concern for academic excellence	64	36	65	35	64	36
Interest in growth of college as first rate educational institution	60	40	67	33	62	38
Sense of involvement in improving life in India	21	79	33	67	25	75
Interest in self-improvement	49	51	44	56	47	53
Involvement in life of college beyond classroom	30	70	32	68	31	69
Working in the community in which college is located	24	76	28	72	25	75
Interest in religious program in college	39	61	45	55	41	59

There is one recurring difference between teachers in Catholic institutions and those in Protestant ones. Teachers in Catholic colleges tend to stress somewhat more the imparting of personal values, particularly 'discipline', while teachers in the Protestant institutions emphasized somewhat more the development of a sense of community and fellowship. These are interesting in view of the common stereotypes that Roman Catholic social thought is more communitarian and Protestant thought more individualistic.

In a prior study, based upon a small sample (208 respondees), teachers were asked to rank the reasons why, given the present

TABLE 37

Staff: Why continue Christian colleges?
(by age)

Reason	20's 320 respondents			30's 183 respondents			40's 73 respondents		
	w.f.	1st	%	w.f.	1st	%	w.f.	1st	%
Provide Christian environment	607	52	17	394	39	18	168	20	19
No rank		138			67			26	
Provide personnel for Christian institutions	248	6	7	103	3	5	61	0	7
No rank		213			134			47	
Impart personal values	981	117	27	572	55	26	227	24	26
No rank		72			34			17	
Provide educational facilities for Christians	536	27	15	318	13	14	127	8	15
No rank		122			66			30	
Provide fellowship and community	648	28	18	390	22	18	161	7	18
No rank		111			58			23	
Provide high quality education for evangelism	319	14	7	199	10	9	54	3	6
No rank		198			111			50	
Innovate and experiment	346	9	9	222	6	10	75	2	9
No rank		186			101			41	

w.f. = weighted frequency.

circumstances in secular India, Christian colleges should or should not be maintained. Only about 25 per cent of the respondees could be construed to have a distinctly or exclusively Christian concern, while the vast majority emphasized more general and secular values like academic excellence,

TABLE 37 *(continued)*

Reason	50's 57 respondents			60's 14 respondents			All ages 647 respondents		
	w.f.	1st	%	w.f.	1st	%	w.f.	1st	%
Provide Christian environment No rank	129	16 22	21	41	4 3	24	1,339	131 256	18
Provide personnel for Christian institutions No rank	46	1 37	8	17	0 7	10	475	10 438	6
Impart personal values No rank	173	18 14	29	48	5 2	28	2,001	219 139	26
Provide educational facilities for Christians No rank	86	3 28	14	21	— 5	12	1,088	51 251	14
Provide fellowship and community No rank	97	5 26	16	24	— 5	14	1,320	62 223	19
Provide high quality education for evangelism No rank	27	1 45	5	13	1 9	8	612	29 413	8
Innovate and experiment No rank	44	— 39	7	6	— 11	4	693	17 378	9

w.f. = weighted frequency.

maintaining discipline, moral and spiritual values. The most striking difference was, again, that the Catholic teachers (and non-Christian teachers) emphasized maintaining discipline, while Protestant teachers stressed the imparting of Christian point of view. Age differences were insignificant in this sample. The table is based on the weighted scale.

TABLE 38

Staff: Why maintain a Christian college?
*(by sponsorship and age, in percentages)**

Reason	Roman Catholic			Protestant			Total		Total (all ages)
	Ages 20-40	Ages 41+	Total	Ages 20-40	Ages 41+	Total	Ages 20-40	Ages 41+	
Impart a Christian point of view	20	24	22	31	29	30	23	25	24
Moral and ethical values	18	20	19	26	18	23	21	20	21
Inculcate social service	5	8	6	7	5	6	6	7	6
Academic excellence	28	22	26	28	31	29	28	26	26
Maintain discipline	19	14	18	3	7	5	14	12	13
Long tradition of good results	2	0	1	0	2	1	1	1	1
Provide for Christian minority	8	12	9	5	5	5	8	10	9
No justification	0	0	0	0	2	1	0	1	—

* 'Given the present circumstance : in the Church and in India (as a secular state), do you think there is justification for the continuation of Christian colleges? If so, what justification do you see?' (Based on 208 responses.)

Note : If the totals come to more than 100 it is due to the rounding off of the figures.

TABLE 39

Merits of respondents' colleges
(by sponsorship and age)

Merit	Roman Catholic				Protestant				Total
	20s & 30s	40s & 50s	60 +	Total	20s & 30s	40s & 50s	60 +	Total	
Good staff-student ratio; good lecturer-student relationship	17 (9)	9 (11)	—	26 (11)	18 (22)	8 (15)	2 (15)	28 (19)	54 (14)
Opportunity for student government	2 (1)	2 (2)	—	4 (2)	2 (2)	1 (1)	—	3 (2)	7 (2)
Religious atmosphere, training and program	21 (11)	7 (9)	1 (10)	29 (12)	12 (15)	7 (14)	2 (15)	21 (15)	50 (13)
Community feeling	6 (3)	2 (2)	1 (10)	9 (3)	5 (6)	3 (6)	1 (8)	9 (6)	18 (4)
Good discipline	42 (23)	17 (21)	1 (10)	60 (25)	8 (10)	4 (9)	2 (15)	14 (10)	74 (19)
Good administration or administrative methods	18 (10)	7 (9)	2 (20)	27 (11)	5 (6)	7 (11)	—	12 (8)	39 (10)
Good physical plant	11 (6)	4 (5)	1 (10)	16 (6)	8 (10)	8 (14)	1 (8)	17 (12)	33 (9)
Well trained staff	11 (6)	9 (11)	2 (20)	22 (9)	11 (14)	3 (6)	1 (8)	15 (10)	37 (9)
Variety of programs: undergraduate, post-graduate, research co-curriculum	8 (4)	3 (4)	—	11 (4)	3 (4)	4 (7)	1 (8)	8 (6)	19 (5)
Emphasis on education rather than results	3 (2)	6 (7)	—	9 (3)	4 (5)	5 (9)	1 (8)	10 (6)	19 (5)
Other	17 (9)	12 (15)	1 (10)	30 (13)	5 (6)	3 (6)	1 (8)	9 (6)	39 (10)

Numbers in brackets indicate percentages.

Finally, what does the Christian college teacher see as problems in Indian higher education as a whole? This is elaborated in Table 40. One generalization is unavoidable — that the three most significant problem areas mentioned are all practically beyond the individual teacher's scope of action ; all refer to basic educational reforms. Whether or not this is a realistic appraisal of the situation, it does reveal a widespread feeling of helplessness, which many, even most, Indian teachers experience. This sense of helplessness ('the government must do it, the university must change') is one of the most debilitating poisons which afflicts Indian higher education. All the more reason why, to exploit the human resources which are available, institutional rigidities must be eased to allow more scope to those who would improvise, invent, and inspire.

Briefly recapitulated, teachers in Christian colleges in India tend to be young and inexperienced ; about 55–60 per cent of them are Christian, although there are major differences from one part of the country to another ; a large number come from rural families, and many others originate from government servant and educator families ; a large number have graduated from Christian colleges, and many from the institution where they now serve ; most are teaching in their home area, although quite a number have studied abroad ; many have a Bachelor's as their highest degree and the number of Ph.D.s is higher in Protestant colleges ; many are critical of certain religious features of their college, but generally feel that Christian colleges have many strengths and should continue to be supported ; many are critical of the administrators of their college, especially about their minimal involvement in community and university affairs ; many are also quite critical of their teaching colleagues ; most are reasonably confident that the college is attracting students who are among the best in the area, and that Christian colleges are among the better institutions of the country, and most feel that their own institution in particular is doing a basically good job ; and most feel that the basic justifications for Christian colleges are more in terms of superior education and character-formation than in specifically religious or confessional objectives.

TABLE 40

Staff: Desirable changes in Indian higher education
(by sponsorship)

Desirable change	RCW	RCM	RCD	PS	PU	Total
Improve teaching	1		1	2	2	1
More central control of system	1		2	1	1	1
Less central control and more by teachers	14	12	11	9	11	12
Examination reform	22	19	22	21	22	21
Reduce number of students	3	6	4	5	3	4
Vocational guidance	2		1	3	2	2
Reform syllabus	18	18	20	17	16	17
Better staff remuneration	3	6	5	7	4	5
More selectivity of admissions	6	6	5	5	3	5
Vernacular medium of instruction			2	1		1
Smaller teaching load	1		2	3	3	2
Liaison schools and colleges	2			1	2	1
No student politicking	1	2	2		2	1
Improve staff facilities	1	1	1	2	2	2
Teacher refresher courses	1	1	1	2	1	1
Teacher exchange program						1
Promotion on merit	1	2	1	2	2	2
Improve overall facilities	2	4	5	3	5	4
More text books			2	2	1	1
Other	11	12	11	9	12	11
NA	10	5	2	5	4	5

Weighted on a scale of 100.

TABLE 41

Religious affiliation of students
(by sponsorship)

Religion	RCW	RCM	RCD	PS	PU	Overall
Roman Catholic	83 (18)	116 (27)	152 (38)	1 (—)	7 (2)	359 (20)
Protestant	43 (10)	47 (11)	51 (13)	52 (25)	74 (24)	267 (15)
Syrian non-RC	13 (3)	6 (1)	54 (13)	1 (—)	5 (1)	79 (4)
Hindu	279 (62)	227 (53)	128 (32)	116 (56)	198 (63)	948 (53)
Muslim	11 (3)	11 (3)	9 (2)	12 (6)	16 (5)	59 (3)
Other	16 (4)	4 (1)	— (—)	12 (6)	8 (3)	40 (2)
NA	8 (2)	15 (4)	8 (2)	12 (6)	5 (2)	48 (3)
Total	453 (100)	426 (100)	402 (100)	206 (100)	313 (100)	1,800 (100)

Numbers in brackets indicate percentages.

Who are the Christian college students?

It is frequently assumed that Christian colleges are operated almost exclusively for Christians. While there are wide variations in the percentage of Christian students and staff in Christian colleges, partly reflecting North-South differences, Christian students comprise less than 40 per cent of the total enrollment, as indicated in the Table 41.

A significant number of Protestants are enrolled in Catholic colleges, but almost no Catholics study in Protestant institutions. The high percentage of Roman Catholic students in diocesan colleges reflects their concentration in Kerala. While not a major difference, there is a higher percentage of Muslim students in Protestant colleges, which is also probably related more to the large number of Protestant colleges in the North than to possible ideological differences.

Twenty-five per cent of the students come from farm families, with 45 per cent of the students in diocesan colleges coming from farm families. Overall, 40 per cent of the Roman Catholic students come from farming families, as compared with 23 per cent of the Protestants, and 21 per cent of the Hindus. Business and landlord fathers are the second most prominent, but the major source of non-Christian students. Table 6 details this information.

PERCENTAGE OF CHRISTIAN STUDENTS/PERCENTAGE OF COLLEGES

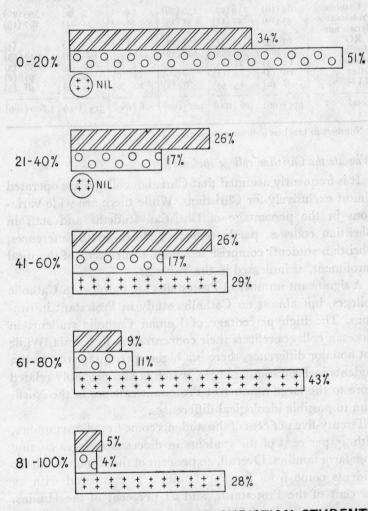

Figure 7. PERCENTAGES OF CHRISTIAN STUDENTS
(BY SPONSOR)

Related to fathers' occupation is family income (Table 7). Forty-five per cent of the students come from families earning less than Rs 167 per month ($ 24 after the currency devaluation of 1966). While there is a slight tendency for Hindu students to come from higher economic levels, this is not a major difference between Christian and non-Christian students. Deeper study would undoubtedly reveal important differences between individual Christian colleges, or perhaps even between categories of colleges. It is alleged that some Christian colleges are run for upper-class students, but we have not explored the situation in particular institutions. In general, however, it does not appear that this allegation is often warranted.

Indian college students are younger than their counterparts in other countries; this leads to special needs and problems. Table 42 shows the age distribution of students in all parts of the country and all types of Christian colleges. Six per cent of

TABLE   42

Students' age

(by sponsorship)

Age	RCW	RCM	RCD	PS	PU	Overall
14 and 15	37 (8)	21 (5)	35 (9)	4 (2)	2 (1)	99 (6)
16 and 17	203 (45)	128 (30)	133 (33)	69 (33)	89 (28)	622 (35)
18 and 19	148 (33)	151 (35)	135 (34)	86 (42)	109 (35)	629 (35)
20 and 21	51 (11)	103 (24)	84 (21)	43 (21)	90 (29)	371 (20)
23 +	10 (2)	20 (5)	14 (3)	4 (2)	21 (7)	69 (4)
NA	4 (1)	3 (1)	1 (—)	— (—)	2 (—)	10 (—)
Total	453(100)	426(100)	402(100)	206(100)	313(100)	1.800(100)

Numbers in brackets indicate percentages.

those enrolled are under sixteen years old (almost 10 per cent in Roman Catholic diocesan colleges), and slightly over 40 per cent are seventeen years old or younger, with 53 per cent of the students in Roman Catholic women's colleges in this age group. Generally speaking, students in Catholic colleges are younger than those in Protestant ones, which may be because so many of the former are in Kerala, which has a two-year pre-degree course prior to the three-year degree course. Most parts of the country have a one-year pre-university course, plus a three-year degree course; a few areas retain the old two-year intermediate, two-year degree system.

What subjects are being studied? This question takes an added significance because courses of study are narrow, offering little scope for broadening personal interests. Economics and

TABLE 43

Students: Subjects being studied
(by sponsorship)

Subject	RCW	RCM	RCD	PS	PU	Total
English	14	13	6	6	7	46
Language & Literature	2	—	4	1	2	9
History	4	2	5	1	4	16
Economics & Politics	100	93	68	33	55	349
Sociology	11	2	5	3	—	21
Philosophy & Religion	—	—	—	3	3	6
Art/Music	1	—	—	—	—	1
Home Science	1	—	6	—	—	7
Mathematics & Statistics	68	66	83	8	38	263
Education/ Teaching	9	—	7	13	9	38
Medicine	7	4	—	2	27	40
Chemistry	18	18	25	11	16	88
Physics	11	54	47	14	26	152
Zoology	17	6	13	1	16	53
Biology & Botany	107	45	52	7	36	247
Psychology	—	—	—	—	6	6
Social work	5	1	—	—	—	6
Commerce	1	46	32	1	22	102
Other	2	—	—	—	6	8
NA	75	76	49	102	40	342
Total	453	426	402	206	313	1,800

politics, traditionally joined together in this way, is the most popular current major subject, but the natural and physical sciences are also very popular. Many more would take science courses were seats available. It is a common and probably well-grounded belief that the best students opt for science and engineering. Mathematics and statistics are also popular. This table corroborates the widely deplored dearth of sociology and psychology students, as also the relatively low esteem of teaching. Art and music, religion and philosophy, language and literature are distinct also-rans.

A corollary question relates to the kinds of jobs sought by students. These are classified below by college sponsorship and religion of respondee (Tables 44 and 45 respectively). Both are based upon a weighted frequency, relating to respondee's ranking. Professional life is the most sought after, with college teaching, government service and research following in that order. Scrutiny of the tables reveals several interesting differences between types of college sponsorship, on the one hand, and between respondees of different religions on the other. But the basic pattern of preferences remains.

Students in Christian colleges generally come from the state and community in which the college is located — 39 per cent live within 5 miles of the college, and only 12 per cent live more than 100 miles away. Admittedly this is difficult to understand in view of the fact that so many students are from farming families, while 75 per cent of the Christian colleges are in cities of 100,000 or more people. Forty-eight per cent of the students reported coming from areas with a population under 100,000. Drawing students from such a narrow geographic base tends to make the institutions parochial; but the proximity of a college to students' homes enables many more economically under-privileged students to attend. In all, 55 per cent of the students came from within 15 miles of the college, and the only noticeable difference between Catholic and Protestant colleges was a slightly higher percentage of distant students in the Protestant colleges — which relates, no doubt, to the fewer number of such colleges, and to their dispersion throughout sparsely Christian areas of the North. There may also be a somewhat stronger emphasis in Protestant colleges on a heterogeneous student body with a few students coming from overseas. About 78 per cent of the students in Protestant colleges come

TABLE 44

Students : Type of job sought
(by sponsorship)

Job	RCW Total w.f.	RCW First place 453 respondents	RCW %	RCM Total w.f.	RCM First place 426 respondents	RCM %	RCD Total w.f.	RCD First place 402 respondents	RCD %
Govt. administration	249	17	6	352	32	9	316	36	9
No rank		338			282			278	
Govt. service	520	58	13	471	31	12	665	69	18
No rank		255			228			151	
College teaching	714	69	17	525	53	13	686	68	18
No rank		194			224			156	
School teaching	437	40	11	172	9	4	327	21	9
No rank		279			348			268	
Professional	809	153	20	682	111	18	649	115	17
No rank		218			213			194	
Research	373	34	9	477	58	12	274	21	7
No rank		307			252			287	
Business executive	56	2	1	170	18	4	117	11	3
No rank		423			358			351	
Private business	105	5	3	255	26	7	107	5	3
No rank		402			324			347	
Church work	97	7	2	130	15	3	126	12	3
No rank		410			378			351	
Social welfare	513	42	13	258	19	7	245	17	7
No rank		241			305			289	
Agriculture	83	5	2	147	5	2	78	2	2
No rank		407			353			354	
Industry	46	1	1	132	6	1	61	3	2
No rank		429			360			370	
Other, e.g. Military	91	9	2	146	18	4	64	8	2
No rank		416			367			378	

TABLE 44 (continued)

Job	PS			PU			Overall		
	Total w.f.	First place 206 respondents	%	Total w.f.	First place 313 respondents	%	Total w.f.	First place 1800 respondents	%
Govt. administration	148	18	8	258	32	9	1,323	135	8
No rank		146			213			1,257	
Govt. service	211	23	2	327	29	12	2,198	210	13
No rank		111			181			936	
College teaching	243	27	13	334	31	12	2,502	248	15
No rank		117			182			873	
School teaching	172	12	9	166	14	6	1,274	96	8
No rank		140			247			1,282	
Professional	308	52	16	463	85	16	2,911	516	18
No rank		111			174			910	
Research	258	26	14	370	33	13	1,752	172	11
No rank		115			178			1,139	
Business executive	47	—	2	140	13	5	530	44	3
No rank		182			260			1,574	
Private business	111	10	6	176	15	6	754	61	5
No rank		159			237			1,469	
Church work	77	10	4	90	8	3	520	52	3
No rank		175			277			1,591	
Social welfare	149	9	8	152	7	5	1,317	94	8
No rank		133			242			1,210	
Agriculture	68	3	4	121	10	4	497	25	3
No rank		172			255			1,541	
Industry	49	1	3	132	6	5	420	17	2
No rank		183			250			1,592	
Other, e.g. Military	65	8	3	101	11	4	467	54	3
No rank		183			275			1,619	

w.f. = weighted frequency.

TABLE 45
Students : Type of job sought
(by religion)

Job	Roman Catholic			Protestant			Syrian		
	w.f.	1st	%	w.f.	1st	%	w.f.	1st	%
Govt. administration	262	29	8	184	18	8	45	2	6
No rank		249			193			60	
Govt. service	409	36	13	301	32	12	106	9	14
No rank		188			153			36	
College teaching	508	48	16	359	43	15	118	11	16
No rank		167			135			34	
School teaching	274	26	8	198	17	8	61	2	8
No rank		246			183			52	
Professional	540	91	17	338	60	14	165	33	22
No rank		182			159			30	
Research	246	24	8	245	20	10	49	3	7
No rank		257			170			58	
Business executive	117	9	4	63	6	3	16	2	2
No rank		305			239			72	
Private business	155	12	5	100	11	4	29	65	4
No rank		284			224			5	
Church work	189	23	6	232	21	10	39	5	5
No rank		283			167			65	
Social welfare	276	21	8	185	11	8	62	3	8
No rank		236			174			49	
Agriculture	70	5	2	70	2	3	23	1	3
No rank		319			228			67	
Industry	83	4	3	48	3	2	13	1	2
No rank		313			241			74	
Other, e.g. Military	61	7	2	76	10	3	19	3	3
No rank		330			236			73	

TABLE 45 (continued)

Job	Hindu w.f.	Hindu 1st	Hindu %	Muslim w.f.	Muslim 1st	Muslim %	Other w.f.	Other 1st	Other %	Totals w.f.	Totals 1st	Totals %
Govt. administration	711	71	9	43	4	8	18	2	5	1,268	1,126	9
No rank		628			41			34			1,205	
Govt. service	1,182	112	16	74	6	13	44	6	13	2,116	201	14
No rank		469			29			26			901	
College teaching	290	118	4	85	10	15	52	8	15	1,412	238	10
No rank		450			28			24			838	
School teaching	621	44	8	43	2	8	28	1	8	1,225	92	8
No rank		683			40			30			1,234	
Professional	1,595	290	21	108	19	19	65	11	19	2,815	504	19
No rank		459			25			21			876	
Research	1,051	108	14	75	9	14	20	1	6	1,686	165	11
No rank		547			32			33			1,064	
Business executive	287	25	4	24	1	4	15	—	4	522	43	4
No rank		813			48			30			1,510	
Private business	393	30	5	26	2	5	26	5	7	729	58	5
No rank		764			44			41			1,411	
Church work	11	2	—	2	—	1	1	1	—	474	51	3
No rank		918			57			28			1,531	
Social welfare	667	46	9	40	4	7	40	—	11	1,270	90	9
No rank		635			40			35			1,162	
Agriculture	289	14	4	13	—	2	15	4	4	480	17	3
No rank		781			50			39			1,480	
Industry	227	9	3	12	1	2	9	—	3	382	53	2
No rank		819			50			38			1,536	
Other, e.g. Military	269	28	3	10	1	2	16	—	5	451	—	3
No rank		830			53			—			1,560	

w.f. = weighted frequency.

from the state in which the college is located, as compared with 91 per cent of students in Roman Catholic colleges. About 9 per cent of the students in Protestant institutions and about 5 per cent of those in Roman Catholic ones, are from different regions of the country than that in which the college is located.

We have noted above that 26 per cent of the students in Christian colleges are in college hostels, with Roman Catholic men's college and Protestant multiple-denomination colleges having the highest overall percentage. Table 46 shows where students (by religion) live during the school year, and the higher overall percentage in hostels (33 per cent) may reflect the fact that in some places there are hostels off campus not run by the college. Preference is given to Christian students in

TABLE 46

Students' residence during college
(by religion, in percentages)

Residence	RC	P	S	Hindu	Muslim	Other	Total
Hostel	36	46	33	30	29	27	33
Friends & other boarding	4	4	3	6	5	I	5
Home	54	48	62	62	63	72	58
Other	4	I	I	I	—	—	2
NA	2	I	I	I	3	—	2
Total	100	100	100	100	100	100	100

these hostels, with more partiality in Protestant institutions. Again, the different character of colleges in North and South is probably an important variable on this point. It is almost surprising that the disproportion of Christian students is not greater, and it is also something of a surprise that more than 90 per cent of the students are accommodated either in hostels or at home, with few apparently having to make other housing arrangements.

TABLE 47

Students' religion and school leaving position

Class	RC 359 respondents	P 267 respondents	Syrian 79 respondents	Hindu 948 respondents	Muslim 59 respondents	Other 40 respondents	Total 1,752 respondents
No class	186 (52)	134 (50)	46 (58)	366 (39)	23 (39)	11 (27)	766 (44)
First class	80 (22)	46 (17)	15 (19)	261 (28)	15 (25)	7 (18)	424 (24)
Second class	58 (16)	47 (18)	13 (16)	192 (20)	18 (31)	13 (33)	341 (19)
NA	35 (10)	40 (15)	5 (6)	129 (14)	3 (5)	9 (22)	221 (13)
Total	359 (100)	267 (100)	79 (100)	948 (100)	59 (100)	40 (100)	1,752 (100)

Numbers in brackets indicate percentages.

Do Christian colleges attract the best students, and do they give preferential treatment to Christian applicants despite low secondary school leaving examination results? Table 47 makes it clear that concessions are made for Christian students who have not attained the highest examination results. Preferences for Christians in admissions policy seem strongest in Protestant colleges, judging by the lower number of 'first-class' secondary school graduates in that group. It is important, however, not to conclude too readily that only the first and second class groups deserve admission to college. Table 48 is also instructive, as it suggests that the Protestant United and Roman Catholic Men's colleges have the highest percentage of first and second class (secondary school examinations) students. The difference is noticeable when one looks only at the percentages of first-class passes in these colleges, but supported even further when second classes are also considered. 'No class' would reflect several kinds of situations, but most often would be roughly similar to 'pass' without any kind of distinction. In some places there is no distinction between classes, but this is not regional or frequent enough to distort the conclusions above.

TABLE 48
Students' school leaving position
(by sponsorship)

Class	RCW	RCM	RCD	PS	PU	Overall
No class	257 (57)	135 (32)	239 (59)	45 (22)	107 (34)	783 (44)
First class	78 (17)	134 (32)	73 (18)	48 (23)	97 (31)	430 (24)
Second class	56 (12)	100 (23)	56 (14)	73 (35)	66 (21)	351 (19)
NA	62 (14)	57 (13)	34 (9)	40 (20)	43 (14)	236 (13)
Total	453 (100)	426 (100)	402 (100)	206 (100)	313 (100)	1,800 (100)

Numbers in brackets indicate percentages.

While 14 per cent of the students in Christian colleges as a whole are from the 'Backward Communities' (usually tribal groups, underdeveloped economically and educationally), there is again a strong showing by the Protestant United and Roman Catholic Men's colleges. Eleven per cent in Protestant Single Denomination colleges, and 9 per cent in Catholic Diocesan colleges are from Backward Communities. These percentages no doubt reflect, in part, policies of the various kinds of colleges, with the Protestants putting rather more emphasis on education in remote and tribal areas, where also they have other kinds of projects, and where some have strong evangelizing programs. A word of caution is necessary at this point. We fear that some students have confused 'Scheduled Caste' and 'Backward Community', and some may have used this term about themselves without actually being officially so classified. In general, however, we feel that the percentages are approximately correct. It is clear that Christian colleges are making strenuous efforts to provide for the Scheduled and Backward groups, even though the government is rightly urging a higher percentage in many colleges.

TABLE 49

Students of Backward Communities
(by sponsorship)

Community	RCW	RCM	RCD	PS	PU	Total
Backward	44 (10)	84 (20)	36 (9)	22 (11)	72 (23)	258 (14)
Not Backward	303 (67)	290 (68)	303 (75)	138 (67)	198 (63)	1,232 (68)
NA	106 (23)	52 (12)	63 (16)	46 (22)	43 (14)	310 (18)
Total	453 (100)	426 (100)	402 (100)	206 (100)	313 (100)	1,800 (100)

Numbers in brackets indicate percentages.

'Scheduled Caste' students are those who do not formally belong to any one of the major caste groups. There are about 75 million in this category in India. As with the Backward Communities, the Government of India is making strenuous efforts to correct the disadvantage of these groups, to make them more able to compete for higher posts in society, and to give their own communities greater prosperity and participation in the nation. Eleven per cent of the students in Indian Christian colleges represent this segment of the population. Again, the Roman Catholic Men's colleges were better than average in enrolling Scheduled Caste students, the Diocesan colleges were considerably below the average of other Christian colleges in this respect.

TABLE 50

Students from Scheduled Castes
(by sponsorship)

	RCW	RCM	RCD	PS	PU	Overall
Yes	63 (14)	55 (13)	23 (6)	33 (16)	28 (9)	203 (11)
No	326 (72)	322 (75)	311 (77)	137 (67)	237 (76)	1,333 (74)
NA	64 (14)	49 (12)	68 (17)	36 (17)	48 (15)	265 (15)
Total	457 (100)	426 (100)	402 (100)	206 (100)	313 (100)	1,800 (100)

About 28 per cent of the students receive some kind of financial assistance for their college work. Of these, 74 per cent reported receiving money from Government, 16 per cent from the colleges, 6 per cent from religious institutions, and 4 per cent from other sources.[6] Non-Christians received more government support than did Christian students — 80 per cent as compared with about 68 per cent. College aid was given about equally to Christians and non-Christians. Although it has been estimated that 90 per cent of the Christians in India are from the depressed classes, in some states Christians are not eligible for state aid to Scheduled and Backward groups. Men students receive financial help more often than do women students, but there did not seem to be a significant difference between men and women in the actual *amount* of help to each individual. (The Education Commission Report argues that women should receive preferential treatment in scholarships.)

TABLE 51

Education among Backward Communities (1961)

State	Population of Scheduled Tribes as percentage of population of state	Percentage of enrollment of Scheduled Tribes in total enrollment					
		Lower primary	Higher primary	Secondary	Higher	Vocational & professional	Total
Andhra Pradesh	3·7	2·3	0·7	0·6	0·4	1·8	1·9
Assam	17·4	24·0	16·2	9·3	9·8	32·9	20·9
Bihar	9·1	8·7	7·4	3·7	2·4	7·1	7·6
Gujarat	13·3	12·4	7·5	1·9	0·2	12·0	8·1
Jammu and Kashmir	—	—	—	—	—	—	—
Kerala	1·2	0·5	0·4	0·2	—	0·1	0
Madhya Pradesh	20·6	12·3	6·5	2·2	2·2	5·0	9
Madras	0·7	0·5	0·1	0·2	0·8	0·3	0·4
Maharashtra	6·1	6·6	0·1	1·0	0·6	2·6	3·4
Mysore	0·1	0·7	0·2	0·2	0·1	0·4	0·6
Orissa	—	—	—	—	—	—	—
Punjab	0·1	0·1	0·1	0·1	—	0·3	0·1
Rajasthan	11·5	2·3	0·9	0·6	0·2	4·5	1·9
Uttar Pradesh	—	—	—	—	0·5	—	—
West Bengal	5·9	3·5	3·2	1·4	0·3	8·5	3·4

SOURCE: Education Commission Report, p. 140. Data for Orissa were not available. Population of Scheduled Tribes in Jammu and Kashmir and Uttar Pradesh was negligible.

TABLE 52

Students: Why attending college?
(by religion)

Reason	Roman Catholic			Protestant		
	w.f.	1st	%	w.f.	1st	%
Best reputation	610	53	18	458	61	18
No rank		130			98	
Only one available	88	10	3	90	13	4
No rank		318			236	
Near home	320	27	10	164	14	7
No rank		233			202	
Inexpensive	150	9	4	114	5	5
No rank		283			212	
Family's wish	421	25	13	376	22	15
No rank		175			107	
Friends were going	94	2	3	71	1	3
No rank		302			222	
Good college education	986	159	29	694	110	28
No rank		49			45	
Good for getting a job	170	—	5	159	1	6
No rank		266			185	
Offers course wanted	464	41	14	310	18	12
No rank		162			123	
Other reasons	38	8	1	44	6	2
No rank		344			250	
Total	3,341			2,480		

TABLE 52 (continued)

Reason	Syrian			Hindu & Muslim			Overall		
	w.f.	1st	%	w.f.	1st	%	w.f.	1st	%
Best reputation	146	18	19	1,883	205	20	3,097	347	19
No rank		25			321			547	
Only one available	23	2	3	230	24	3	431	49	3
No rank		67			907			1,528	
Near home	24	5	11	725	61	9	1,294	107	8
No rank		42			556			1,133	
Inexpensive	24	3	3	277	3	3	565	21	4
No rank		66			849			1,410	
Family's wish	69	1	9	1,224	73	13	2,090	121	13
No rank		45			480			807	
Friends were going	26	—	3	316	8	3	507	11	3
No rank		65			823			1,322	
Good college education	215	33	28	2,844	495	30	4,739	797	30
No rank		11			141			246	
Good for getting a job	45	58	6	564	14	6	938	15	6
No rank		15			714			1,223	
Offers course wanted	134	27	17	1,236	82	13	2,144	156	13
No rank		1			465			777	
Other reasons	7	77	1	50	4	1	139	19	1
No rank					980			1,651	
Total	773			9,350			15,944		

w.f. = weighted frequency.

TABLE 53

Students : Merits of respondents' colleges
(by religion)

Merit	Roman Catholic			Protestant		
	w.f.	1st	%	w.f.	1st	%
Good academic standard	1,213	173	25	870	120	23
No rank		58			49	14
Fellowship	459	15	9	516	28	
No rank		184			106	8
Good job training	198	1	4	282	15	
No rank		283			171	7
Values it stands for	365	14	7	270	9	
No rank		229			164	6
Living conditions	217	2	4	219	8	
No rank		272			186	14
Quality of teachers and students	734	25	15	509	21	
No rank		113			97	4
Extracurricular program	262	4	6	168	2	
No rank		246			194	2
Active involvement with national issues	160	1	3	89		
No rank		286			227	6
Concern for individual student	324	14	7	236	7	
No rank		235			174	12
Character-training	837	80	17	468	35	
No rank		114			112	3
Moderate fees	125	2	3	128	4	
No rank		298			210	1
Other	11	2	—	23	2	
No rank		356			258	
Total	4,935			3,778		

TABLE 53 (continued)

Merit	Syrian w.f.	Syrian 1st	Syrian %	Other w.f.	Other 1st	Other %	Overall w.f.	Overall 1st	Overall %
Good academic standard	301	45	26	3,309	454	23	5,723	792	24
No rank		8			184			299	
Fellowship	142	5	12	1,625	64	12	2,742	112	11
No rank		30			430			750	
Good job training	45	2	4	609	33	4	1,134	51	5
No rank		61			795			1,310	
Values it stands for	85	2	7	925	34	7	1,645	59	7
No rank		48			694			1,090	
Living conditions	51	2	5	774	19	5	1,261	31	5
No rank		59			715			1,232	
Quality of teachers and students	188	6	16	2,143	110	15	3,565	162	15
No rank		20			343			573	
Extracurricular program	68		6	738	15	5	1,236	21	5
No rank		54			685			1,179	
Active involvement with national issues	16		1	376	13	3	641	14	3
No rank		71			847			1,431	
Concern for individual student	68		6	1,085	33	8	1,713	54	7
No rank		49			590			1,048	
Character-training	158	14	14	2,169	177	15	3,632	306	15
No rank		28			340			594	
Moderate fees	26	1	2	365	8	3	644	15	3
No rank		62			850			1,420	
Other	9	1	1	35	4	—	78	9	—
No rank		77			993			1,684	
Total	1,157			14,153			24,014		

w.f. = weighted frequency. % = weighted percentage. 1st = highest ranking.

For about 50 per cent of the students who receive help, the assistance amounted to more than half of their total school costs, while for 21 per cent of those who received help, assistance amounted to more than 75 per cent of their total expenses. Protestants received more support from non-Governmental sources than did any of the other religious groups — probably concessions or scholarships from the college itself, or from the churches.

We have referred to the teachers' belief that close staff-student relationships are a major asset of Christian colleges. Students do feel that teachers are interested in them, with 83 per cent strongly affirmative, and only 11 per cent ambiguous or negative. There was a slightly stronger positive feeling among Protestant students than among Roman Catholic ones (86 per cent to 79 per cent) and there seemed to be no appreciable difference between Christian and non-Christian students.

Asked why they attended this particular college, most students stated that it was the quality of education, or the reputation of the college, which attracted them — almost half the points on a weighted frequency scale. 'Family's wish' and 'offers course wanted' both received 13 points, while 'availability' (i.e. near home) received only 11 points. Obviously this could have been a more important reason than claimed, as so many students attend college near home. Other stated reasons were minor. The religious background of the respondee did not seem to make an important difference in the way he answered this question (Table 52).

What are the best things about your college? 'Good academic standard' was considered most important, with 'quality of staff and fellow students' and 'character training' somewhat less appreciated. 'Fellowship' too was considered valuable. Table 53 shows the scaling in more detail.

In another breakdown of the same material, by age of the student (in general, therefore, reflecting the number of years he had been in a Christian college), there were no severe shifts, but some noticeable trends. Students' appreciation increased on sense of fellowship, values the college stands for, and staff concern for India's development. It decreased perceptibly on character training, moderate fees, and quality of staff as

TABLE 54

Christian college enrollment levels and type of course, 1966

Sponsorship	PUC & Intermediate	Bachelors'						Masters'		
		Arts	Science	Comm.	Educ.	Other	Total	Arts	Science	Comm.
RCW	9,203	4,923	4,682	—	534	—	10,139	221	75	—
RCM	10,016	4,966	7,260	2,930	400	—	15,556	295	340	97
RCD	9,899	2,868	6,687	1,051	457	—	11,063	229	259	42
PS	2,989	2,988	3,450	210	251	—	6,899	617	139	44
PU	8,840	6,781	6,367	589	496	40	14,323	588	361	16
S	3,777	946	1,942	33	240	—	3,161	25	35	—
Total	44,724	23,441	30,388	4,813	2,398	149	61,189	2,065	1,177	155
Percentage of total	38	20	26	4	2	—	52	2	1	—

TABLE 54 (continued)

Sponsorship	Masters' (continued)			Ph.D.				Other	INA	Total	%
	Educ.	Other	Total	Arts	Science	Other	Total				
RCW	—	—	296	—	—	—	—	151	—	19,789	17
RCM	38	55	825	26	6	1	33	171	1,050	26,601 27,651	24
RCD	—	—	637	—	—	—	2	223	93	21,824 21,917	19
PS	6	—	806	—	48	—	48	414	2,297	11,156 13,453	11
PU	19	4	978	4	16	—	41	1,331	822	26,337 27,159	23
S	—	—	60	—	—	—	—	567	—	7,565	6
Total	63	59	3,626	51	70	1	124	2,903	4,262	1,13,272 1,17,543	100
Percentage of total			3				—	3	4	100	

Of the total number of students, excluding undifferentiated PUC, 38 per cent are in the arts and 49 per cent in science. Two per cent are in education, with 58 per cent of the education students in Roman Catholic colleges, 10 per cent in the Syrian ones, and 32 per cent in Protestant institutions. 'Other' refers to courses of study not mentioned, or a degree not cited.

strengths of the college. Student opinion remained fairly un-
changed through the age-span of five years on academic
standard, job training, quality of facilities, extracurricular
program, and involvement of the college in the life of the
community.

What courses are offered?

About 80 per cent of Christian colleges are arts and science
institutions, with two of these combined with teacher-training.
Table 54 above shows enrollments at different levels and in
different types of courses. The following points are worth
special attention: 38 per cent overall are enrolled in pre-
university degree courses; at the Bachelor's level there are
more science than arts students, with higher rates of science to
arts in Roman Catholic colleges, and especially in the men's
and diocesan institutions; about 3 per cent of the total enrollment are in Master's programs of some sort; there are a
very few Ph.D. students, with a significantly higher number
and percentage in Protestant institutions. Most of the Protestant
college Ph.D.s are in sciences, while Roman Catholic college
Ph.D. candidates are in arts, thus reversing the pattern of the
Bachelor's and Master's levels.

Table 55 is self-explanatory; it shows the number of institutions offering various degrees. There are a few additional
degrees which do not fit into these categories and are thus
excluded, such as the Medical Doctors, 'Intermediates'
(a vestige of the two-year plus two-year system in some states
in the North) and 'PDC' (two years prior to degree work, in
Kerala) are included under PUC.

What are the departmental (or faculty) strengths, as shown
by number of teachers in each of the departments? Table 56
gives an overall perspective on areas of concentration. What the
table does not reveal, unfortunately, is strengths and weaknesses within these broad categories. For example, the fact that
there are almost no sociology and psychology teachers is
hidden by the comparatively large number of history and
economics teachers. Heavy emphasis on physical and natural
sciences is also evident, being more than one-third the total

TABLE 55

Number of Christian colleges offering various degrees

Sponsorship	PUC	B.A.	B.Sc.	B.Com.	B.Ed.	M.A.	M.Sc.	M.Com.	M.Ed.	Ph.D.
RCW	18	23	19	11	10	6	3	—	1	—
RCM	13	17	17	11	3	5	6	3	1	4
RCD	5	16	13	7	4	7	6	3	—	—
RC total	36	54	49	18	17	18	15	6	2	4
PS	6	35	11	12	2	3	3	1	1	2
PU	16	24	24	2	6	8	10	1	2	6
P total	22	35	35	4	8	11	13	2	3	8
S	—	5	5	1	2	2	3	—	—	—
Total	58	93	89	23	27	31	31	8	5	12

number of teachers in the arts and science colleges. Religion and philosophy are startlingly low, considering the fact that these are Christian colleges. This particular weakness is more apparent in the Roman Catholic than in Protestant colleges, although there are many more religious or ordained in Catholic colleges.

Some broad observations can be made about courses of study. Firstly, in all colleges across the country the empirical social sciences are very weakly represented. Secondly, there is little breadth in the curriculum. Main subjects of study are compartmentalized; the traditional conception of a broad liberal arts foundation has had little influence in practice. Thirdly, because the syllabus and examination for courses are set by the university, there is little or no scope for an individual college, to say nothing of an individual instructor, to innovate and to move ahead in his field. While central control of the syllabus could have an emancipating effect, it has not worked that way in practice. The syllabus for most courses is antiquated, routine and traditionalist. It is buttressed by an external examination system which cuts the heart out of dynamic educational endeavor. Individual professors, and local colleges, are thus at a tremendous disadvantage in trying to arouse in the student, and in the college community as a whole, a spirit of active inquiry. The better colleges in the country, among them many Christian ones, find this a heavy burden.

Are there distinctive religious characteristics of Indian Christian colleges?

Already we have made many comments relating to this question. Most Christian colleges, patricularly Roman Catholic ones, have a considerable Christian presence in faculty and staff, who receive preferential treatment in hiring, residence, and promotions. Special consideration also is given to Christian students in admissions, scholarships (to some extent), and hostel space. These have been referred to above. About 60 per cent of the colleges have a chaplain, and religious programs generally include regular chapel services, some sort of religious

TABLE 56

Department strengths by number of teachers
(arts and science colleges only)

Subject	RCW	RCM	RCD	RC total	PS	PU	P total	S	Total
English	168 (17)	195 (15)	155 (16)	518 (16)	85 (13)	203 (15)	288 (14)	54 (17)	860 (15)
Languages	145 (14)	172 (13)	105 (12)	422 (12)	74 (11)	171 (13)	245 (12)	40 (13)	707 (12)
Mathematics	52 (5)	113 (9)	81 (8)	246 (7)	67 (10)	104 (8)	171 (9)	35 (11)	452 (8)
Physical Sciences	157 (15)	343 (27)	232 (24)	732 (24)	158 (25)	345 (24)	503 (25)	74 (26)	1,309 (24)
Natural Sciences	160 (16)	155 (11)	146 (16)	461 (14)	72 (11)	170 (12)	242 (11)	38 (12)	741 (14)
Social Sciences	214 (21)	232 (19)	129 (13)	575 (18)	100 (16)	243 (18)	343 (16)	31 (10)	949 (17)
Philosophy & Religion	4 (—)	3 (—)	3 (—)	10 (—)	26 (4)	22 (2)	48 (3)	—	58 (1)
Education	—	—	—	—	—	13 (1)	13 (1)	—	13

TABLE 56 (continued)
Department strengths by number of teachers
(arts and science colleges only)

Subject	RCW	RCM	RCD	RC total	PS	PU	P total	S	Total
Commerce	—	18 (1)	29 (3)	47 (1)	17 (3)	9 (1)	26 (2)	1 (—)	74 (1)
Professional	—	—	—	—	5 (1)	—	5	29 (9)	34 (1)
Other	31 (3)	12 (1)	22 (2)	65 (1)	—	—	—	2 (1)	67 (1)
INA	86 (9)	63 (4)	66 (7)	215 (7)	40 (6)	115 (8)	155 (7)	2 (1)	372 (1)
Total	1,017 (100)	1,306 (100)	968 (100)	3,291 (100)	644 (100)	1,395 (100)	2,039 (100)	306 (100)	5,636 (100)

Numbers in brackets indicate percentages.

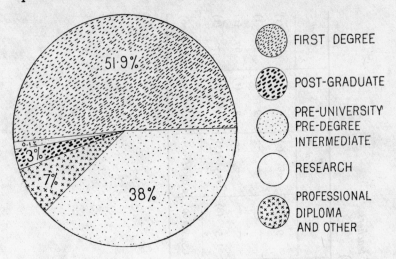

Figure 8. STUDENTS IN CHRISTIAN COLLEGES (BY LEVELS)

instructions for Christians, and moral instruction for non-Christians.

On the other hand, in many Christian colleges there is little evidence of a specifically Christian or sectarian emphasis. In 17 per cent of the colleges there are under 25 per cent Christian staff, and in 20 per cent Christians total 10 per cent or less of the student body. Corporate community life does not usually center around any religious traditions or experiences. Chapel programs are often minimal. Out of 67 colleges responding to this question, 4 reported no required chapel; 14 reported requirement once a week; 46 reported six or more times per week. Our visitors to the campuses felt that these figures were often unreliable, and reported that even when chapel was theoretically required, it was often sparsely attended and not treated very seriously by the students and staff. One researcher who received quite full and glowing information about the nature of the chapel program stayed adjacent to the chapel for three days and did not see it unlocked or used on any occasion. Through the windows it looked quite

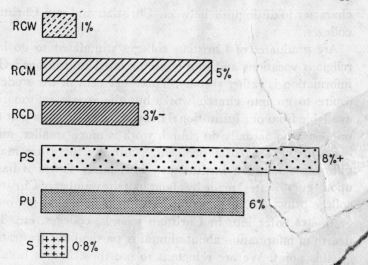

Figure 9. STUDENTS TAKING ADVANCED DEGREES (BY SPONSOR)

dusty and unused! The description sounded suspiciously like fiction!

It hardly needs to be said that the picture here does not apply to all situations; in some colleges there are good chapel programs, but the general picture is rather dismal. Fourteen per cent of the colleges responded that non-Christians were permitted to have worship and religious programs on campus (in 86 per cent they were clearly forbidden), but it was obvious that even where such programs would be tolerated, there was little opportunity (or inclination?) to practice this theoretical freedom.

In addition, religion and philosophy departments are notoriously weak. Religious instruction is outside of the regular academic curriculum, and colleges receiving state aid are unable to require involvement in religious programs. Many programs called 'chapel' have a scarcely distinguishable religious context. Examining these overall religious characteristics, one gets the general impression that except in a very broad and nebulous way, there is little of a sectarian character to distinguish between Christian and non-Christian colleges.

Are graduates of Christian colleges stimulated to go into religious vocations and into church-related institutions? Our information is rather sketchy. Three per cent of the students aspire to go into church work, but the sparse information available from our institutional questionnaire suggests that the number who actually do church work is much smaller, more likely in the area of 1 per cent. Naturally there are major differences between institutions. This latter figure is based upon 'guestimates' made by about half the number of Christian college principals. It is very difficult to believe that not more graduates enter jobs in Christian schools, colleges, etc. The dearth of information about alumni is particularly frustrating on this point. We are reluctant to use these figures because they are so tenuous, but do so in the hope of stimulating deeper and more adequate study of the real situation.

Summary: Some generalizations about Christian colleges today

We have reviewed in some detail selected major characteristics of Indian Christian colleges. To again catch a broad perspective the following points are highlighted.

1. Christian colleges were pioneers in the field of higher education in modern India, several of them having been established in the first half of the last century at a time when there were no other colleges of a similar nature. Christian colleges were also pioneers in bringing Western ideas of education to India, thus helping to pave the way for many cultural and political events and attitudes which were to follow. The majority of early colleges were Protestant.

2. Since Independence the rate of growth has accelerated, especially for the Roman Catholics, now numbering 76 colleges. All of the Syrian non-Roman colleges were founded after Independence. Since Independence the number of Protestant institutions has remained almost constant at 45. Some new Protestant institutions have emerged and some of the older ones have been abandoned. Of the Roman Catholic colleges, 36 are run by women's congregations, 21 are under the auspices

of men's orders, and 20 are sponsored by a diocese. Of the 45 Protestant colleges, 13 are run by single denominations and 32 are under united sponsorship.

3. Enrollment in the Christian colleges in India is about 117,000 or approximately one-tenth of the total number of students in affiliated colleges in the country, and about 7 per cent of all college students. This number includes only the Christian colleges with full degree instruction status (all but two are related to universities). The total staff in Christian colleges is approximately 6,300.

4. Several of the oldest Christian colleges are in the North, while most of the new colleges have been established in the South, especially in Kerala, Mysore, Madras and Andhra. Some new colleges have sprung up in Assam in the Northeast, while a Roman Catholic Women's college will be started in New Delhi in 1967. There are relatively more Protestant than Roman Catholic colleges in the North, and all 7 Syrian colleges are in Kerala.

5. Most Christian colleges are in large cities, with about 60 per cent of the colleges located in cities with a population of more than 100,000. Madras, Calcutta and Bombay have 19 Christian colleges. There are Christian colleges in 40 per cent of those Indian cities with over 100,000 population.

6. Roman Catholic colleges under the sponsorship of women's congregations have shown the most remarkable increase. There were no Christian colleges under women's auspices until after the turn of the century. Most of these are in Kerala.

7. About 39 per cent of the students in Christian colleges are Christian, with a much higher percentage of Christian students in the South (except in Assam) and in the Catholic colleges. Staff reflects the same North-South difference, and about 50 per cent are Christian. There are many Protestant students in Catholic institutions, but almost no Catholic students in Protestant ones. Many Protestant colleges, particularly in the North, have less than 10 per cent Christians in their student body and less than 25 per cent Christians among their staff.

8. Some Christian colleges have upwards of 80 to 90 per cent of the total enrollment from Backward Community and Scheduled Caste groups.

9. One hundred and one Christian colleges are for liberal arts, 21 are teacher-training colleges, and 8 are professional colleges. Of 54 new colleges founded since Independence, 35 per cent are either teacher-training or professional institutions, which marks a significant acceleration of the growth of Christian professional colleges. Eight of the teacher-training and professional colleges are under Protestant sponsorship, 1 is Syrian and 17 are Roman Catholic.

10. In addition to the 130 degree colleges under Christian sponsorship, there is a broad network of junior and intermediate colleges throughout the country. About a dozen of these junior colleges have already been sanctioned for instruction towards the Bachelor's degree, 10 of them being in Kerala. More new Protestant institutions are located in Madras than in Kerala while new Roman Catholic institutions are not concentrated in any particular state.

11. Because they need the additional fees which low-cost P.U.C. education represents, and because they are under certain pressures from the state, Christian colleges have a generally high percentage of P.U.C. students — about 38 per cent of their total enrollment. The burden of P.U.C. students affects the whole style and temperament of Christian colleges. Most principals wish this influence could be diminished.

12. Most of the colleges are plagued by financial difficulties, especially since overseas support plays a less significant role now than in the past. For various reasons the financial position of Roman Catholic colleges seems sounder than that of the Protestant ones, although some, but not all, of the old line colleges are in reasonably sound financial position. All institutions, however, receive support from government, and overall between 80 and 95 per cent of the support for recurring expenditures comes from fees and government.

13. Christian colleges are now indigenous operations, integrated thoroughly into the total Indian cultural picture and the Indian educational system. While this is basically a healthy

situation, they are, as a result, caught up in the problems which afflict all higher education in India, and enjoy only marginal freedom. They generally enjoy a good reputation based upon a tradition of excellence and continuing good performance, and this reputation gives them prominence and possibilities out of proportion to their numbers.

14. There is abundant evidence that the Christian colleges still live at the growing edge of higher education in such areas as science education, vocational training, the provision of facilities and services for students, examination results, etc. They are still growing in numbers too. This is a response to the explosion of students pressing for admission. Most colleges have admitted many more students than they did prior to Independence.

15. Administration of Christian colleges is notably weak because most principals are not properly trained for their tasks, and many have no fundamental interest in administration. This weakness is magnified by the fact that most principals tend to centralize power, taking upon themselves too many administrative tasks. Furthermore, most colleges are plagued with wholly inadequate administrative staff to keep records, write necessary letters and forms, and to do the thousand and one administrative details which characterize every college.

16. There is a basic confusion and ambiguity about the aims of a Christian college. While there is an obvious movement away from evangelization and conversion as a primary justification, there are still a few who think in these terms. On the other hand, service to society as a whole is often stated as the primary purpose of the Christian college, but closer analysis of how colleges actually are founded and operated suggests special help to the Christian community is considered very important. This is not a normative judgment, but a description.

For example, Protestants have made major efforts in the retarded and tribal areas of Assam and Manipur. What philosophy of involvement does this suggest? Roman Catholics have tended to develop colleges where there are already many Christians, and indeed where there are already several other Christian colleges. What is the implicit philosophy behind this

policy ? If for both Roman Catholics and Protestants service to
society as a whole is the major goal of the Christian colleges,
there are specific and different interpretations within each
group of how society as a whole should be served. It is these
considerations which are in a very fluid state, and the clarification of goals should be one of the major tasks of those who
sponsor Christian colleges in the next decade.

V

ASPECTS OF CHRISTIAN COLLEGES'
INVOLVEMENT IN DEVELOPMENT

I. THE COLLEGE AS A GENERAL
LEAVENING INFLUENCE

OF the many ways a college may contribute to development, perhaps the most important and the most elusive to measure is its leavening influence upon the educated populace as a whole — the values, motivations and general knowledge of its graduates. These graduates may be quiet agents of both change and stability, bringing to their work, their communities and their families a perspective and a style of life which deeply influences the lives of many.

Philip Jacob's study has shown how difficult it is to assess this aspect of a college's performance,[1] and this same difficulty is reflected in a more recent evaluation of church-sponsored colleges in the United States.[2] Even if a college has done superior work in preparing individuals to accept new values, the graduate is usually thrown back into a milieu which quickly neutralizes these perspectives; changes are short-lived. Much of the Patillo and MacKenzie study is based upon the status of college graduates in other educational endeavors, in scholarships, etc., and not necessarily in terms of their contribution to society. Not the least difficult obstacles to overcome in educational evaluations are: (1) the danger of ascribing to institutional influence what was really a factor in the selection of certain students in the first place; (2) the danger of confusing reputation and past performance with current excellence; (3) the difficulty of giving scientific sociological articulation to the characteristics which are 'progressive' or 'developmental', particularly when action indices, as well as verbalized attitudes, are called for.

Recognizing these difficulties, is there evidence that Christian colleges in India contribute significantly to national development through the general knowledge level and commitments of its graduates? One possible source of insight into this question is current policies and practices at the college which militate against, or contribute to, the development of sensitive and mature graduates aware of, and concerned to alleviate, social ills. A second source is evidence from alumni of the colleges; what they are doing, and what their attitudes are. This study has turned up a scattered kind of evidence on these two points, and while it does not present a clear and conclusive argument, the evidence does suggest important areas in which Christian colleges have succeeded and where they fail. We will refer to three main areas as examples: national integration, comprehension of national problems and goals, and training for democratic leadership.

National integration

A major obstacle to India's development is strife and tension between diverse linguistic, religious, regional, economic and caste groups. In the midst of these how can India develop political coherence and national integration? Destruction of property is but one manifestation of the economic and social disabilities brought on by this kind of tension, but even on this level the costs have been enormous. A more devastating and costly consequence is the constant need to balance opposing interests, often dictating that economic decisions cannot be made on sound economic judgments (where will a steel mill or dam be placed?); sound educational policy is subjected to political pressures which often render the educational program ineffectual (witness the struggle over the language formulae). Caste, religious, linguistic and other differences constantly frustrate the mobilization of resources for rational and effective solutions to economic, political and social problems. Are the colleges, and Christian colleges in particular, conscious of a role to play in promoting national integration in a more than propagandistic way? How do they envisage that role, and are they playing it?

Christian colleges show little alertness to their opportunities in this area. The peculiar ethos of Christian colleges suggests that they should have a special interest in promoting national development; their geographic and sociological position reinforces their prospects for success in these efforts, but the colleges have not implemented down-to-earth programs to this end. Even between Christian groups there are deep frictions. For example, there has been almost no contact between Roman Catholic, Protestant and Syrian Orthodox sponsors of Christian schools and colleges, even though they frequently face many of the same problems. Further, there is little cross-fertilization across state and regional boundaries, reflecting language areas, in many cases. Administrators of Christian colleges in the North have almost no contact with their counterparts in the South, and vice versa. This perpetuates a narrowness of perspective which inhibits the development of a deep national consciousness. The regional character of the staff and student bodies in Christian colleges has already been alluded to.

Clearly, Christian colleges would seem to be in a unique and enviable position to accelerate national integration: (1) given a sense of co-operation, they could develop the machinery for exchanges of staff and students on a fairly broad basis; (2) Christian colleges generally use English as the medium of instruction, and it would be comparatively easy for students in one part of the country to study in another, or for staff from one section to serve in another; (3) the reputation of Christian colleges in all parts of the country (although not all individual colleges) would make it easier to propagate the exchange idea to staff and students. These are offered merely as examples.

In addition to an intensified and extended exchange program within India, programs at the college itself could be greatly improved. The high percentage of resident hostel students means that Christian colleges are in a position to develop community life in ways which are not open to colleges without such hostels. But there is sparse evidence that colleges are alert to this advantage. Hostel and college life are seldom fully exploited to create a sense of solidarity among staff and students from diverse backgrounds. Christians were once segregated from non-Christians in hostels and dining halls, and happily this era is largely past, but there remain vestiges of the ghetto mentality. One occasionally hears the remark that the problems of the college would be solved if all or most of the staff members were Christian! There is no evidence to support this contention. Even where residential and dining policies have been modified, Christian colleges have not evolved institutional patterns designed to break down traditional barriers in Indian society. For example, less than 50 per cent of the colleges report a conscious policy of mixing people from different religions, caste and other backgrounds in their rooming assignments; there is still a tendency to put people of similar backgrounds together.

A difficult practical question relates to non-Christian worship on campus; most colleges take the position that non-Christian worship is neither necessary nor permissible. They fear that social pluralism in a secular state will become confused with religious pluralism, or into tolerant Hinduism itself. Elsewhere we have alluded to the poverty of much of the Christian worship at Christian colleges; here we are concerned only with non-Christian devotional life at the Christian colleges, especially public group worship.

Father Mathias has summarized the situation lucidly.[3] He says that there has been a definite evolution of Christian thought and practice on this point. The position generally adopted by all Christian colleges twenty or thirty years ago was a categorical refusal of permission to any religious group, other than the denomination running the college, to conduct public and organized worship. This refusal even included Christians of other churches. In many cases non-Christian students staying in hostels were not even permitted to display statues or pictures of their deities in their rooms or to burn joss sticks in front of them; still less to gather two or three companions and worship together in a hostel room on the occasion of important festivals.

But during the last ten years it has been recognized generally among all Christians that every student has the right to display images and pictures in his hostel room and to worship privately in it. Further, if a small group of students gather in a private room to worship, no action is taken against them. Most Christian colleges have more recently come to the position of allowing other Christian groups to have public worship on the premises, sometimes even facilitating this. But public worship for non-Christian groups is still not known, although several principals have admitted it in theory.

Among many Christians a deepening view of the natural and inalienable right of a freedom of conscience in religious matters has evolved, and is supported by Christian leaders throughout the world. For Christian colleges the pressing question is whether non-Christians should be permitted their own public worship on Christian college campuses. The most common arguments for such permission are that it is a natural right of students, that it will again demonstrate that Christianity is not narrow and bigoted, and that it might help to counteract the spread of atheism and *anomie* among students. On the other side it is contended that this will lead to all sorts of objectionable practices, that it is not practical nor administratively feasible (e.g. what of the contention that a piece of ground used for worship becomes the property of that deity?), that it will encourage the belief that Christians think of all religions as the same, that it might create dissensions and frictions on campus, and that the colleges have a juridical right to insist on exclusively Christian practices. These are still open questions which are subject to increasingly lively debate.

Carman properly notes that despite the reputation India has as a country of deep religious and spiritual concerns, university and college education does not make an adequate provision for religious instruction. He goes on to ask two difficult but pertinent questions of Christian colleges in particular. 'Is it reasonable or right from a Christian standpoint to expect the non-Christian student to grow to ethical maturity without seriously considering the religious basis for moral behavior given in his own religious tradition?' And 'Is it reasonable or right for Christian students to be guided in their growth to ethical maturity in a segregated course of study, separated from non-Christian students, and without any study of the religious principles and moral norms that have shaped traditional Indian society and to some extent still inform the behavior of Indian young people in the present — including Christian young people?'[4]

Another dimension of the same problem is the policy regarding Christian staff and administrators. There is a tendency in some Christian institutions to over-indulge Christian members of the faculty, even though this is accepted as normal by the non-Christian staff. A corollary of this general situation is that, particularly in Roman Catholic institutions, members of the sponsors' religious order tend to retain the dominant positions in the college. Boards of Governors, principals, and senior teachers are predominantly members of the particular religious order. An unsettling aspect of this partiality relates to faculty promotions, where it is sometimes alleged that 'religious' receive preferential treatment warranted by neither their training nor academic qualifications. Some outsiders allege that promotion policy is dictated more by religious and financial considerations than by educational and academic ones. While we do not have adequate data on the relative rank of 'religious' in Christian colleges, our statistics corroborate the contention that Christians are given some preferential treatment in promotions. Ten per cent of the Hindu teachers and 16 per cent of the Christian teachers were Professors or Heads of Departments. However, we did not find this to be a major problem in Christian colleges in general. Perhaps the situation was more keenly felt in Kerala than elsewhere.

It should be clear that partiality is probably not the only reason for the larger percentage of Christians in top positions of the college. Indeed, there is some justification for guaranteeing that a certain number of posts, especially certain key posts, should be retained by Christians. Christians may tend to come into the top positions because promotions are influenced by seniority more than by any other single factor. It is natural that Christian teachers should feel more at home and stay longer in a Christian college than elsewhere, where promotion opportunities may be more limited. Further, Christian teachers are more likely to be involved in the entire range of activities at the college — religious, extracurricular, etc. — and this participation enhances their identification with, and value to, the college. Christian teachers also usually feel deeply dedicated to the perpetuation of the principles upon which the college is founded. Therefore some partiality toward Christian teachers and staff is natural, and it is accepted as natural and right by most non-Christian staff. But haunting feelings remain that the true and full nature of the academic community may be quietly corroded by a constant tacit assumption of first- and second-class citizens, whether first-class is defined by being a Christian, or by belonging to a particular religious congregation.

Little is done in the extracurricular program to develop consciousness of the cultures and problems of all segments of the community and population. It is rare that a Christian college consciously programs exhibits, dances, plays, literature, etc. of life in other sections of the country. Lack of funds probably precludes travelling groups from one part of the country to another, but even in the absence of such groups, cultural exhibits could be planned; pictures, books and artifacts could be displayed; speakers could give sensitive insights and interpretation to life and customs in other parts of the nation. Libraries could serve as centers for continuing displays; perhaps groups of colleges could develop a series of displays which could be sent from one college to another, for perhaps two weeks at each institution. Some very expressive and attractive contemporary art, music, drama and dance are springing forth in various centers, to complement India's rich artistic heritage. Students and staff need a deeper sense of this vigorous cultural expression of the Indian people; it would increase their sense of identity and involvement, and help to lift their thinking above regional and parochial horizons.

It is appalling to find so much of the extracurricular cultural life of the college, where it is developed to any extent, is oriented to the West. More contact with non-Indian worlds is desirable, but much of the current contact is with a Western world that no longer exists, and there is little contact at all with other Eastern countries. In any case, this contact must not be to the detriment of a deeper appreciation of Indian life and culture.

11

As in extracurricular affairs, so also in the classroom itself, unconcern with Indian life as a whole is evident. Many things do militate against a fuller content of Indian-oriented studies; to name a few, the traditional syllabus; the paucity of text books, particularly books printed in India and about Indian circumstances; the inexperience and inadequate training of many teachers; the short and fragmented college program. Despite all obstacles, some outstanding teachers do, in fact, draw upon the corpus of Indian life and culture for illustrations, interpretation and analysis. But the picture as a whole is bleak; both Christian and non-Christian colleges are pitifully deficient in imparting a positive sense of identification with India's life and culture.

What evidence is there that Christian colleges reduce caste consciousness? Have they developed effective anti-caste programs? Our survey of 3,200 alumni suggests that caste consciousness among Hindu graduates of Christian colleges is as strong as that among Hindu graduates of non-Christian institutions. Naturally the overall picture shows less caste-consciousness among graduates of Christian colleges because a large proportion of these graduates are Christians and do not consider themselves members of any caste. However even 32 per cent of the Christians, graduates of both Christian and non-Christian colleges, regarded themselves as members of a caste; it made no difference whether they attended a Christian or non-Christian college. Sixty-six per cent of the Hindus consi-dered themselves to be caste members. Christian and non-Christian colleges had the same percentages of Brahmin and non-Brahmin Hindus (23 and 72 per cent respectively). We assume that these features have not changed fundamentally in recent years, and among more recent alumni.

Many Christian colleges have taken the lead in providing education for 'harijans' and the lower castes — not to confuse caste and class, although they possess many of the same socio-economic and psychological characteristics. Because of the government's scholarship support to the Scheduled and Back-ward students, it is doubtful whether today Christian colleges are playing the pioneering and unique role which typified their work in the past. Indeed, some allege that Christian colleges have become institutions for the economically privileged more than servants to the disinherited.

If there is any truth to the allegation, colleges are prompted to become class colleges not by ideological considerations *per se,* but by financial pressures of running first-class private colleges, where fees constitute up to 50 per cent of the overall operating budget. In addition, students from higher economic and social classes often have better secondary school preparations and higher matriculate test scores. Only occasionally a Christian college administrator argues that educating the upper classes is justified on strategic grounds, that because these graduates will be the leaders of society and in a position to make desirable changes, it is best to invest heavily in them. Whether this is realistic in the new India, and whether it is the right strategy, both morally and practically, deserve profound questioning.

Further, when disinherited groups are present on campus, the college has a major responsibility to see that they are properly integrated into the total campus community, particularly in view of language difficulties, inferior cultural preparation and inadequate formal education which many of them have had. Many are ostracized by fellow students. There is a tendency for them to be pariahs in the academic community, and thus they require additional personal attention and assistance to ensure their full integration into the college community.

Still another way of promoting a sense of identification with the poor, and thus building a sense of national integration, is the Social Service League, a voluntary extracurricular program of work projects and discussions related to special community needs. Roman Catholic colleges have enjoyed the very dedicated and imaginative leadership of Fr. Ceyrac, Fr. Colasco and Fr. Keough in this work. But with less dedicated and bold leadership Social Service Leagues easily become an excuse, or even a substitute for, significant involvement. The danger is that participants will play at social work rather than developing a mature understanding of the true conditions of the disinherited, and how their problems can be solved in a fundamental sense. A three-day work camp to build a stretch of road or dig latrines may help to give first-hand awareness of conditions which the average student has never even seen or felt before ; it may open his eyes to see people he never saw before. But there is a concomitant danger that this sporadic and piecemeal approach may anesthetize the conscience by allowing students to feel that they have paid their moral debt to the underprivileged through this one act of sharing.

There is danger, too, that this piecemeal approach may blind students in the Social Service Leagues to the realities of social powers and social justice, implicitly fostering a charity approach to the solution of social problems. The casual participant may always be able to see only the symptoms and never to identify the real diseases. It requires wise and sustained leadership to guarantee that the highly-touted Social Service Leagues actually engender among students a sense of identification with the less fortunate elements of the community, giving them practical and intelligent ways of helping the poor. To date, such leadership has materialized only in rare cases.

Comprehension of national problems and goals

So far we have been concerned with what the colleges are doing to develop a sense of the broader Indian community, across the traditional cleavages of the society. This is one way that colleges may contribute to national development by building up a general knowledge and concern among its graduates.

A second area is in stimulating students' awareness of, and sensitivity to, national issues and problems. Do Christian colleges make significant efforts to arouse in their students a sense of the Indian's titanic struggle to develop ? Do they help students to acquire an articulate understanding of social forces and pressures ? Do they stimulate their students to personally contribute to the solution of these problems ? Do they set before their students a vision of what Indian society might become and how that dream is frustrated ? The questions are enormous, of course, but straws in the wind may give some suggestions of an answer.

Table 57 shows where alumni of Indian colleges think the bottlenecks to development are. Government inefficiency tops the list, with reliance on foreign aid (this was much in the newspapers at the time when the questionnaires were mailed out), lack of moral values, and illiteracy all ranking very high. Lack of industry and too little free enterprise were cited as strong hindrances as well. What is most interesting to note is the basic homogeneity of the responses, whether respondees were graduates of Christian or non-Christian institutions. It is also interesting that 'senior citizen' graduates of both Christian and non-Christian institutions gave more importance to moral and ethical values than did the younger generations, who, in their turn, emphasized the institutional forms and structures of society.

As for 'action' involvement in national and community life, one indication is alumni voting behavior. Graduates of Christian institutions have been somewhat more active, and successful, in standing for elections than graduates of non-Christian colleges. Seven per cent of the graduates of Christian colleges have stood for some type of public election (municipal, district, state or central bodies), with 71 per cent of them having been successful. Five per cent of graduates from non-Christian colleges have stood for election, and 59 per cent of these have been successful. Approximately half of those who stood for election of any kind had done so for the municipal level.

There was little difference between the Christian and non-Christian colleges in the percentage of graduates voting in the 1961-2 elections, while in the 1964-5 elections the difference became more significant. In the earlier election 18 per cent of the graduates of Christian colleges did not vote, while 20 per cent of the graduates of non-Christian institutions did not vote. In the 1964-5 elections, the percentages were 18 for Christian college graduates and 23 for graduates of non-Christian institutions. The voting percentage is high in comparison with voting patterns in other countries, but it must be remembered that the sample group was already a select one, being those who had registered for voting in university affairs.

TABLE 57

Alumni: What are the keys to India's development?

	Christian colleges					Non-Christian colleges					Grand total
	20s & 30s	40s & 50s	60+	NA	Total	20s & 30s	40s & 50s	60+	NA	Total	
Literacy	387 (17)	210 (16)	86 (14)	13 (21)	696 (16)	666 (18)	420 (17)	109 (14)	15 (16)	1,210 (17)	1,906 (17)
Moral values	430 (18)	264 (20)	132 (22)	10 (16)	836 (19)	582 (15)	487 (19)	162 (22)	13 (14)	1,244 (17)	2,080 (18)
Efficient government	457 (20)	258 (19)	100 (17)	12 (20)	827 (19)	761 (20)	511 (20)	147 (20)	19 (20)	1,438 (20)	2,265 (20)
Free enterprise	242 (10)	170 (13)	90 (15)	5 (8)	507 (12)	368 (10)	263 (10)	76 (10)	11 (12)	720 (10)	1,227 (11)
Big industry	304 (13)	166 (12)	62 (10)	9 (15)	541 (12)	501 (13)	250 (10)	71 (9)	14 (15)	836 (12)	1,377 (12)
Less foreign aid	419 (18)	230 (17)	108 (18)	11 (18)	768 (18)	749 (20)	497 (20)	148 (20)	19 (20)	1,413 (20)	2,181 (19)
Communalism	5	1	—	—	6	2	3	1	—	6	12
Problems too vast	35 (2)	17 (1)	9 (2)	—	61 (1)	80 (2)	42 (2)	15 (2)	2 (2)	139 (2)	200 (2)
Don't think about it	10	9 (1)	1	—	20	21 (1)	11	3	1 (1)	36 (1)	56 (1)
Other	42 (2)	24 (2)	6 (1)	1 (2)	73 (2)	68 (2)	52 (2)	15 (2)	—	135 (2)	208 (2)
NA	1	3	7 (1)	—	11	5	6	4 (1)	—	15	26
Total	2,332	1,352	601	61	4,346	3,803	2,542	753	94	7,192	11,538

Numbers in brackets indicate percentages.

It is also interesting to note that graduates of Christian colleges were more likely to change the party for whom they voted, with 20 per cent of the respondees having changed their vote from one party to another in the two elections under study, while 16 per cent of the graduates of non-Christian institutions changed their party choice. All of these percentages are calculated only on the 85–90 per cent of those who answered these particular questions. Generally speaking, graduates of Christian colleges were more active in the election processes, and were perhaps less traditionalist.

Table 58 indicates major parties and the support they received from respondees to this questionnaire.

As for service and professional clubs, 44 per cent of the graduates of Christian colleges belong to some kind of social service club in the community (41 per cent of the Hindus and 45 per cent of the Christians); about the same percentage of non-Christian college graduates belong to service clubs (44). Among graduates of Christian and non-Christian colleges, 29 per cent of the respondees have held, or hold, office in these service clubs, with Christians tending to hold office more often than Hindus (32 as compared with 26 per cent). These statistics suggest that perhaps more of the social service clubs are under Christian auspices, and may even be in conjunction with churches. This is supported by the fact that a higher percentage of Hindus than Christians are members of professional associations. However, for both service and professional clubs, graduates of Christian colleges appear more active than graduates of non-Christian colleges.

What are the channels of communication to the educated *élite*? (Only 1 per cent of the respondees were employed in the field of mass communications, while 44 per cent were educators!) Newspaper and magazine reading habits afford some insight, even though more refined information would have been desirable. About one-third of all the alumni regularly read vernacular newspapers, with a somewhat higher percentage among graduates of Christian institutions than of non-Christian ones. The *Indian Express* was the most popular English paper (70 per cent); the *Hindu* was also widely read (16 per

TABLE 58

Alumni voting in National Elections, 1961 and 1965
(by type of college, in percentages)

Party	Christian		Other private		Government		All non-Christian		Total	
	1961-2 (1,039)	1964-5 (1,016)	1961-2 (768)	1964-5 (736)	1961-2 (835)	1964-5 (805)	1961-2 (1,665)	1964-5 (1,602)	1961-2 (2,705)	1964-5 (2,618)
DMK	2	2	2	2	1	2	2	2	2	2
Congress	74	62	58	56	55	59	61	57	66	59
Swatantra	2	4	2	3	2	3	2	3	2	3
Communist	2	2	9	7	4	3	6	3	4	4
Praja Socialist	2	2	3	3	4	3	4	3	3	3
Other	2	9	7	8	3	5	5	6	3	8
Did not vote	18	18	19	21	21	24	21	24	20	21

This shift from Congress indicates the disenchantment with Congress which many have reported. Graduates of Christian colleges less frequently support the Communists, and are stronger than average supporters of Congress. We have included DMK, but unfortunately not Jan Sangh. This was due to a simple clerical error. Where the figures do not add up to exactly 100 per cent, it is due to rounding-off of percentages.

cent); *Blitz* was named by 9 per cent and the *Times of India* by 7 per cent. Readership patterns for graduates of Christian and non-Christian institutions were not different. The *Reader's Digest* received top-ranking for magazines (14 per cent), with the *Illustrated Weekly* being second (13 per cent). *Life* scored 6 per cent; *Time* was read regularly by 4 per cent. *Desh* was reportedly read by 2 per cent of the graduates, and other Indian magazines were 1 per cent or under. Books about India, however, were most popular, with travel books second.

Does the Christian college academic program foster a more profound understanding of, and concern to alleviate, national problems? We have noted the dearth of empirical social sciences in all Indian colleges, although the Loyola Institute of Sociology in Trivandrum is a promising venture at providing high-level sociological training and experience. While statistics pertaining to non-Christian colleges are not available, there is no reason to believe that Christian colleges are any more advanced than non-Christian institutions in fostering empirical social sciences. While science training has been accentuated, awareness of the need for sociological training is only dawning. What is needed is not only specialized centers for sociological study, but the infusion of at least an elementary sociological perspective into the curriculum for every student. It is evident that this is not yet happening. Neither is it clear that Christian college leaders are working to achieve a broader and more integrated curriculum, or that they are sufficiently conscious of the need for interdisciplinary study. If students are not introduced to at least the rudiments of social analysis and interpretation, it is difficult to believe that they will become intelligently critical citizens who can act as a leaven in the lump.

Fifty-three per cent of the Christian colleges (66 per cent Protestant, and 48 per cent Roman Catholic) have inaugurated Planning Forum discussions, many of them at the request of government. These are designed to familiarize students with the issues and problems of planning, as well as with the specific goals of particular Five Year Plans. Generally speaking it is a sound idea badly executed. It is generally conceded that

Plan Forum discussions tend to become ephemeral and sporadic; they seldom are backed up by the discipline of continued work. Most are not integrally connected with the curriculum of any department.

Also Christian colleges do make serious efforts, on the whole, to keep abreast of the most significant Government of India publications, such as the *Census*, the *Yearbook*, the Education Commission Report and other major educational studies. Most colleges do have copies of the Third Five Year Plan in the library, and a high percentage also have copies of the First and Second Plans; the survey was made just as the Fourth Plan was being distributed, and several colleges already had copies. The Five Year Plans themselves are reportedly used in classes in about 75 per cent of the colleges. Yet while Plans may be used in the classroom, students are not immersed in national questions, especially in their extracurricular life. Student newspapers and magazines reflect almost no national or community issues, except with occasional references to something very close to home, like the language issue. Further, there is a hiatus between the college and the local community, despite the many ways this chasm might be partially bridged, and notwithstanding how deeply each needs the other.

Training for democratic citizenship

India's political framework is rooted in democratic principles; its success will largely depend upon how well her people, individually and through their institutions and groups, internalize the values and mores which support the persistence of these democratic principles. Yet the average Indian, even the educated Indian, has little experience in democratic traditions; they tend to remain for him a veneer which does not organically relate to most of his social experience. Family patterns are still paternalistic and in some cases authoritarian; caste patterns persist, adapting themselves to new social situations and entrenching themselves in old.[5] Roles tend to be ascriptive rather than achieved; age and tradition dominate the centers of power and decision-making. There are few opportunities for individuals to learn the nature of democratic process through experience. For one thing, there is no plethora of voluntary associations, each of which evolves its own leadership and routines for throwing up that leadership.

Therefore a college, with its variety of voluntary associations, is potentially an important laboratory of social relationships in which students can learn the character and art of democratic leadership and community. For many people, college is their first experience away from home, away from the womb of relationships which are defined for him. For many, it is the last such experience as well. While many students come to a Christian college for only one year, many others attend for three or four years. The college, therefore, has the possibility of playing a very significant role for the individual, and for the nation as a whole, by thrusting students into a variety of situations which require democratic decision-making, responsible leadership formation, and group responsibility for implementing decisions taken. It is a potential laboratory for the inculcation of values and attitudes absolutely essential for the formation of responsible citizens.

But are the Christian colleges alive to this opportunity? While some institutions seem to be, there is strong evidence that most are not. There is a pervasive fear that the student cannot be trusted and should not be given too much leash. Perhaps Roman Catholic institutions are more unyielding on this point than Protestant ones, but for both the picture is one of very limited expression for students. One aspect of this is the legalism which characterizes the life and rules of many colleges, sometimes even closely governing the conduct of students as they pass from one classroom to the next, minute rules about life in the hostels, codes of etiquette expected in relation to teachers, visitors, etc.

Many Christian college educators in India, mindful that almost 40 per cent of their charges are fifteen or sixteen years old, pride themselves in the discipline and strength of character which the college is reputed to impart, and indeed many alumni, as well as the community at large, respect the colleges for their success in developing discipline. We have had occasion to refer to this before. Notwithstanding the urgent need for developing self-discipline, many Christian colleges so cramp their students that the internalization of values, and the formulation of personal values in the midst of fundamental changes in their lives, is short-circuited.

It is all the more important, then, that in the midst of this discipline and character-formation, a broader intellectual framework, related as far as possible to concrete and corporate experience, should be explored. Yet religious and moral instruction has tended to become a deadening legalism, despite valiant efforts of many teachers to impart solid philosophical and religious content. Those developing the program for religious and moral instruction are continually plagued by the desire to make the teachings broad enough to be meaningful to all kinds of students, and the end product usually has not the scope of conception necessary for an intellectually satisfying commitment. The whole situation militates against a comprehensive and compelling faith, intellectually and morally satisfying. It tends to root ethics more in terms of laws than as a response to grace, and to separate ethics from a well-articulated philosophical system.

Christian colleges also need to become more alert to stimulating local democracy through activities on the college campus. In many Christian colleges there are student governments or student unions (66 per cent overall, with 57 per cent of Roman Catholic colleges and 81 per cent of the Protestant institutions), but deeper questioning showed that often students have a very narrowly defined sphere of responsibility; sometimes staff members possess absolute veto power. Only about 2 per cent of the Christian colleges had developed a code of student conduct and a student judiciary or court. All the student courts reported were in Protestant institutions. Often hostels do have their own internal government, and sometimes a miniature court for offenders, and these are positive signs. In other campus organizations too (e.g. Science Clubs, Economics Clubs), there are elective procedures, but one gets a very strong impression that neither the clubs, which in some institutions meet only once a year, nor the leadership developed through them, are very effective for training democratic leadership. Athletic organizations at the college are likely to do better.

Twenty-nine per cent of the Protestant colleges, and 32 per cent of the Roman Catholic colleges reported student-run newspapers, but frequently students did not readily run them. Shortage of newsprint, and prohibitive printing costs, are among the reasons why more colleges do not have student newspapers. When they do, it is usually with a publication frequency of between four and six issues per year. The main point here is that student organizations in Christian colleges do not make sufficient use of their opportunity for invaluable training in responsible citizenship and democratic leadership. Christian colleges are in an enviable position because of their high percentage of resident staff and student body, but most often they have fumbled their opportunities in this work.

In addition to this kind of experience in extracurricular affairs, it is of crucial importance to cultivate the problem-solving approach in the classroom itself. Indian higher education is traditionalistic, oriented toward the passing of information examinations. The entire educational endeavor is deadened by the weight of the examination and the cramming of facts. The paucity of library facilities and laboratories are sometimes used as an excuse for the traditional approach, but there is undoubtedly much that can be done to stimulate a pragmatic approach to the solution of problems, to promoting an inductive and empirical approach. This is completely out of character with most teaching in Christian colleges of India. Yet it is difficult to believe that graduates can become effective citizens amidst the swirling and startling changes of contemporary India unless they have developed the capacity to move with the times, and to see contemporary issues in the light of more comprehensive realities. To foster such a capacity in students requires a fundamentally different orientation than the now-familiar mocking-up of information to pass examinations. There are limits, naturally, to what can be changed as long as the system itself remains so perverse, but Christian colleges may pioneer in agitating and experimenting toward the realization of a more relevant type of classroom and academic work.

Christian colleges are doing a great deal to develop responsible citizens, of course. They have an excellent record in academic preparation, far surpassing that of the average college in India. Many have comparatively good facilities and broad extracurricular programs. A large percentage of Christian college graduates enter education careers, which may reflect the fact that there is comparatively larger number of women graduates from Christian institutions, and education is reputable work for women in India. Our random sample of alumni showed 67 per cent of the graduates of Christian colleges now 'educators', and only 37 per cent of the graduates of non-Christian colleges. And it cannot be insignificant that Hindu graduates of Christian colleges speak with deep appreciation of the moral and spiritual values they have encountered. This appreciation is expressed 50 per cent more often among graduates of Christian than non-Christian institutions, and it is expressed almost equally by Hindus, Muslims and Christians alike. These facts suggest that Christian colleges are still pioneering in many ways, and that they do often provide solid foundation for responsible citizenship. Yet there is much room for improvement.

We have not tried to prove here that Christian colleges contribute to national development through the general leavening influence of their graduates. Rather we have tried to suggest that such leavening influence is important to development, that there is some evidence that Christian colleges are exerting some important influences, but that there are significant new things which the colleges can do to become more effective in leavening the lump in the future.

2. THE COLLEGE AS A CATALYST
FOR EDUCATIONAL REFORM

Higher education in India is in a state of flux, searching for roots and efficacious means for nourishing first-class education. The many governmentally appointed commissions for studying education attest to this groping after an educational policy which can effectively meet the philosophical, political, economic and social requirements of the new India. Among other things, colleges and universities are caught between utilitarianism and classical types of education, between quantitative extension to meet personal yearnings and political demands and the desire to maintain or develop quality in education, between the desire to break out of the straight-jacket of traditional pedagogy and the realistic recognition that material and human limitations preclude swift and fundamental changes in this respect. Indian higher education is in a malaise which often extends from the top levels of administration right down to the first or second year student.

If the educational structure of a nation is intimately linked with the country's capacity to develop, as we have argued, constant educational reform is necessary. Where education is not meaningful, relevant and efficient, it is unconscionably squandering the scarce resources of a developing country. India cannot afford the luxury of an aimless educational system. Colleges and universities are strategically situated to promote educational reform; they can set the tone for what happens at other educational levels. Perhaps this is especially true for Christian colleges because of the number of Christian secondary and elementary schools.

Everyone talks of the need for reform; what are Christian colleges doing to achieve it? Undoubtedly they are in a position to exert influence far out of proportion to their numbers, even though this influence may be partly undermined by jealousies and suspicions from both the outside and inside. Christian colleges are among the oldest and most respected colleges in the country, with a reputation for academic superiority and service which has endeared them to broad sections of the population. Many non-Christian Indian leaders have graduated from these institutions and send their children and grandchildren to them today. This reputation for excellence may have become tarnished in some places, but generally speaking the legacy has not been squandered.

A second strength is that Christian colleges are dispersed throughout the country. Diversity of background often makes it difficult for these colleges to become deeply engaged with one another, but at the same time it opens up the possibility that through collaboration narrow perspectives will be chastened by a larger vision of education and service in the country. That Christian colleges are found in all parts of the country (North and South, villages and cities, frontiers and metropolitan centers) and in a variety of types of education (teacher-training, agricultural, medical, liberal arts, etc.) gives them a potential multiple perspective from which to see educational problems. No other single group of colleges is so large, and no other group enjoys the same national dispersion and character.

Another factor favoring Christian colleges as educational reformers is their large network of secondary and primary schools — larger than any other single non-governmental group. While we do not have adequate statistics for the large Protestant efforts, there were, in 1964, 4,877 primary schools, 1,229 middle schools, and 899 high schools under Roman Catholic auspices. Protestants also have a network of schools, probably almost as large. Administrators in these institutions are in an excellent position to reflect upon the relationships between the different levels of education, and to consider changes which could bring mutual advantage.

Beyond seeing the problems, moreover, joint actions for reform are possible. As both schools and colleges are subject to regulations from the outside, such joint action will be primarily in exerting pressure on the real decision-makers. This has seldom been done effectively, partly because the churches, and their institutions, have not learned efficacious means for lobbying (and lobbying could be dangerous for a small minority already under pressure from nationalists and right-wing champions of a Hindu state). Beyond this more formal level of reforming, however, are the many imaginative and internal reforms which can be made without violating the directives which come from outside. Of crucial importance, naturally, are the kinds of attitudes inculcated in future teachers at schools and colleges, through the large number of teachers in Christian schools and colleges who have themselves graduated from Christian colleges.

Christian colleges can also profit from their often superior physical equipment and general facilities, even though Christian college principals constantly complain of inadequate resources. In many cases they have developed superior libraries, playing fields, laboratories, hostels, and other facilities. And not the least important asset enjoyed by these colleges is their often superior faculty. Unfortunately, the superior facilities of many Christian colleges are used as arguments against them — arguments against additional subsidy until poorer institutions attain the same level. But the fact remains that with superior facilities Christian colleges are freed to innovate and experiment to a far greater degree than their weaker sisters.

Furthermore, special relationships with organizations and people outside India (Mission Boards, Foundations, Christian colleges abroad) frequently stimulate improvements in these colleges, through financial and other incentives. This special contact and relationship with agencies outside the country is fraught with perils. At the same time it affords opportunities for creativity and stimulation not open to the average private college in India.

There are liabilities as well, some of which are inherent. Christian colleges face a self-image and a public image problem. The self-image danger is to see the college as a confessional institution, thus corrupting education for ecclesiastical and religious gain and making too frequent and large concessions to the churches or Christian community. There is sometimes a tendency for a college to act like a church. The public image needs constant re-focussing because Christianity and its institutions are suspect in a religious and social milieu to which it is, despite all disclaimers, something of an alien. Communalism must be constantly battled both within and without.

In addition, there are problems of pre-eminence and success, along with special relationships outside the country. The Christian college is sometimes envied by sister institutions and/or politicians; it is also feared. What some Christian colleges attain is often not yet possible for other private colleges, like the gap between the have-more and have-less countries, and this limits the potential innovative influence of Christian colleges and their role as demonstrators of good education.

Indeed, the whole concept and psychology of 'demonstration' projects (in agriculture, education, community development) is widely resented because it so insidiously suggests that some people have answers which they patronizingly share with others. More acceptable and useful are modest efforts at joint experimentation and discovery in line with the possibilities and problems of each situation. Therefore, Christian colleges can influence educational reform by being first-class educational institutions. But not all the things which are possible in one Christian college are possible, or desirable, in other colleges.

What could be most useful, perhaps, would be for the Christian colleges to develop pragmatic, problem-solving ways to meet their own problems, bringing many perspectives into the decision-making process, rather than relying on formalistic patterns. This the colleges have seldom done. Our evidence is that teaching staff have been so tangentially and peripherally related to the decision-making process of the college. A major reason for the poverty of ideas in Indian Christian colleges is that teachers have not been brought into the decision-making process.

Christian colleges also have practical liabilities as education reformers: the proliferation of Christian colleges has strained and drained their resources; competition rather than co-operation still characterizes relationships between colleges of even the same Christian denomination; money and personnel from outside the country are diminishing; some non-Christian colleges now attract some of the very best students; governmental and community resources are not readily forthcoming for Christian institutions; Christian colleges themselves are seeking a profound reformulation of their objectives in modern and secular India. Despite all these problems, it remains clear that Christian colleges in India are in a strong position to influence educational policy and promote educational reforms.

Have the Christian colleges been wielding this reforming influence? Have they realized the strengths of their special position and taken advantage of them? In some measure, 'yes'; in large measure, 'no'. More often than not their policy has been one of reaction rather than initiation, of grumbling compliance rather than resolute and co-ordinated opposition to pressures which compromise educational advance.

How have they promoted reform? Many have set outstanding examples. Christian colleges are among the best in the country; they are among the pace-setters. Examples? Their pass-percentage far surpasses the national pass-percentage average; they have been and continue to be pioneers in education for tribal groups, lower economic groups, and women; they have responded to the need for science training far more dramatically, and in an expensive way, than any other single group of colleges; they provide more facilities, from library to playing field, for the students; they are at the forefront in the development of student services such as placement programs and guidance; they have a relatively high proportion of hostels for students and housing for teachers on campus, etc. Without doubt, Christian colleges have been among the *avant-garde* in new educational practices. The influence of this kind of example on others who want to either compete or emulate should not be minimized.

Another positive note is that some Christian colleges have been pushed to critical self-examination by their own constituencies, their supporters both within and outside India, and by political and educational developments in the country as a whole. This has led to a growing movement toward self-criticism in the Christian colleges, expressed in study circles, faculty retreats, and college self-studies. Notable examples of self-study efforts are at Wilson College, Bombay (annual staff retreats with important consequent publications) and Madras Christian College (with a well-articulated analysis and development plan for the coming years).[6] While this movement has not gathered much momentum yet, it augurs well for the future, especially if several colleges from the same region collaborate in the self-evaluations.

It is equally encouraging that individual colleges are beginning to look at their own performance in the light of the recent Education Commission Report, which thrusts upon the colleges large questions of philosophy as well as strategy. The Jesuit Educational Association has promoted a series of conferences to discuss the implications of this Report for the future work of the Christian colleges. The Consultation of Christian College Principals in 1966–7 showed that the principals were keen to understand how the Report would affect their own work. The Report also helps colleges to think more relevantly and concretely about how individual colleges can participate in Indian development as a whole. At the above Consultation the vision was extended beyond individual institutions, or even regional groups of institutions, to the broad questions of the relation between Christian colleges as a species and national development.

The spirit and quality of this self-criticism was clear when a Protestant principal complimented Roman Catholics for their very high pass-percentage. The Catholic principal responded that high pass-percentages worried him because it might indicate that too many sacrifices of sound pedagogy were being made in the interest of high examination scores. If the examination system itself was so deplorable, could one take comfort in succeeding at it? He was generous enough to attribute the lower examination success of Protestant institutions to a stricter observance of sound pedagogy. Similar exchanges on student behavior and methods of discipline often evoked probing questions about the responsibility of colleges to create an environment for responsible decision-making. Should colleges pride themselves in their reputation for discipline when discipline is external rather than progressively internalized? Further, what is the place of non-Christian religions and religious practice on the Christian college campus? Can it be Christian to encourage non-Christians not to practice their own worship and deepen their own faith? What conception of religion and community does this suggest? These, and related questions, go to the very foundations of the nature and purpose of Christian colleges in India today.

It is a sign of vitality that these issues are prominent in the minds of many Christian college administrators in India, and that they are increasingly being considered in an ecumenical rather than a narrowly sectarian framework. This is a most significant way for Christian colleges to contribute to their own reform, and to reforming education as a whole in the country. This is the more important since prominent Christian college educators serve on important government bodies, such as the Education Commission, and on university committees. In this way the vitality of individual Christian colleges, or groups of Christian colleges, can be fed into the larger education debate.

Yet Christian colleges could be much more effective in educational reform. They have failed in their potential impact partly because of their preoccupation with the problems of single institutions. Such narrow preoccupations are almost inevitable, given the circumstances of many colleges in India; they are fighting for survival. There is no time to think about broader issues and wider contacts. There also has been a certain defensiveness about communalism which has encouraged some principals to concentrate only on internal problems of church and college. What is needed, above all, is a clarification of the self-image of each particular Christian college and Christian colleges as a group. This self-image must be realistic about what only 130 Christian colleges (or 150) spread over the whole country, and only 5 per cent of the total number of colleges, should be expected to accomplish. But at the same time there should not be too much modesty; there is need for a larger conception of sharing in, and contributing toward, the entire educational enterprise. It will be pitiful if these goals are defined too broadly, as they have tended to be in the past (broad affirmations which have little biting edge for the development of ongoing strategy and policy); it will be scandalous if they are defined too narrowly (as, for example, the protection of the Christian community, or to provide education for Christians who would not get into college elsewhere). More pathetic than either of these is that they should not be refined or re-formulated at all.

Self-conscious ecumenical endeavor could help alleviate these problems. This ecumenism could get its impulse from both practical and philosophical considerations. A recognition that competition and isolation are too costly in terms of money and influence might be the first stage of awareness; a second could be a deepening consciousness that the ecumenical perspective enriches most kinds of decision-making. Certainly Christian colleges are open institutions in some respects, in some colleges less than 10 per cent of the students and 25 per cent of the staff are Christian, but they are closed and ingrown in others. We have already alluded to a few examples of ingrownness: on the Boards of Governors there is a heavy preponderance of educators (49 per cent), with few businessmen (2 per cent); twenty-seven per cent of the teachers have graduated from the institutions in which they now teach, etc.

That there is little co-ordination between institutions is clear from the fact that a Protestant Christian Colleges Association was founded only in 1962 (there had been one under the National Christian Council earlier), up to 1967 it had not met since the Constitution was first formulated. On the Roman Catholic side the Xavier Board of Higher Education was formed in 1957, but it has not developed much of a co-ordinating function. Further, there is clear evidence that some of the 36 Christian colleges in Kerala were started in order to compete with already existing Christian institutions, sometimes of the same denomination. This competition still shows little sign of abating, with the establishment of almost 10 new Christian colleges in Kerala since the first draft of this study.

Examples of lack of co-ordination and parochialism could be multiplied, but the basic point is that if Christian colleges are to become influential educational reformers, they must evolve a system of communication and co-ordination. This is true for two reasons. The first is that without this network of communication and cross-fertilization of ideas, thinking about reform in Christian colleges will tend to be parochial and 'gimmicky', seldom raising fundamental questions about premises or terms of reference.

The second imperative for co-ordination of effort is to make power or influence felt where it counts, not for narrow Christian interests. Christian colleges have developed little sophistication about how to use their power to influence educational decisions. Individual principals and teachers have had influence; some have been very creative and powerful persons. But church colleges have done little thinking about a *strategy* of influence.

They need to develop well defined, agreed goals on which common action would be possible, and strategically important. They also must forge the organizations necessary to implement these common concerns. It is too much to hope that a common agreement can be reached soon on a philosophy of the Christian college, although the tendency will be to start the discussion at that stage. What is more urgently needed is strategic thinking, i.e. about what are some of the obstacles to achieving in the colleges and in higher education what almost everyone agrees should be accomplished: reform of the examination system, more involvement of teachers in the operation and decision-making of the college, more services for students, more freedom from the prescribed curriculum and all its consequences, less political influence in the university. Can Christian colleges unite on these points and make their corporate weight felt? Can they enlist the support of non-Christian colleges and principals? In short, can Christian colleges work together to define limited areas for priority action, without trying to cover the waterfront? Can they concentrate their energies in a clear action program to achieve these objectives? This will require being very *concrete* about objectives and *specific* about means for attaining them. They must take a politician's perspective. Such strategic thinking and acting can maximize the potential influence of the Christian college in a way which has not been envisaged in the past.

We now shift attention from collaboration between Christian colleges to the individual college. While some institutions are alert and innovative, many are blinded by their own past habits (euphemistically called traditions). One often hears the excuse that certain changes are not tried because of university regulations or lack of money. What strikes the outsider (who does not have to deal with problems in the concrete!) is how much could be improved *within* the existing limitations of university policy and admittedly short funds. Money and freedom are rare; even more rare in some situations is imagination and flexibility.

For example, it is clear that one real bottleneck in Indian higher education is the shortage of books. Students seldom have

184 THE CHRISTIAN COLLEGE IN DEVELOPING INDIA

money to buy books even if they are available for sale, which they often are not. In such a situation, library resources must be maximized; usually they are not. Christian college libraries are open on an average of four and a half hours per day, and this almost always when students are either in class or laboratory. Almost never is a library open in the evenings, even though almost a third of the students are resident. What makes the situation even more baffling is that libraries are so frequently treated like museums, with librarians as curators. In over 35 per cent of the libraries books are not circulated, and seating capacities overall range between 5 per cent and 25 per cent of the student body. Libraries are not thought of as laboratories where students may browse or follow their moods; rather they are psychologically cramped places. The mood of exploration is stifled rather than quickened. Would it cost much money to expand the hours of the library, to encourage the use of the collections both in the library and outside? Would it not be useful to have some students involved in the operation of the library, under proper guidance and control? Books in India are precious, but this is all the more reason for making them accessible.

What of the tutorials on which many Christian colleges pride themselves? Some are shabby affairs, where the student is imposed upon with extra hours of classes but where no creative work is done. In general, there is a tendency to apotheosize classes, and too little time or incentive is given for individual students to explore or work on their own, and too little organization and crystallization of thought and expression through the writing of papers. Would it cost money to reform tutorials so that they provide dynamic interplay of ideas with teachers and other students? If this cannot be done, should tutorials be abandoned altogether?

A third internal change could be the provision of more services for the student. Admittedly this would cost money, but undoubtedly a moderate amount in view of the advantages gained. Few Christian colleges have orientation programs, and few provide other kinds of help, as indicated in Table 59. Colleges could make a modest beginning to provide some of

TABLE 59

Services provided for students
(by number of colleges)

Service		Catholic	Protestant	Syrian	Total
Orientation program	Yes	10	18	—	28
	NA	10	6	2	17
Vocational & aptitude testing	Yes	5	2	—	6
	NA	22	13	3	39
Psychological testing	Yes	4	2	—	6
	NA	25	10	3	39
Staff advisors for each student	Yes	19	14	2	35
	NA	21	11	4	36
Tutorials	Yes	33	25	2	61
	NA	1	2	—	2
Placement program	Yes	7	6	—	13
	NA	14	8	4	25
Guidance counsellor for counselling service	Yes	14	5	—	19
	NA	7	5	1	13
Speakers about vocational choices	Yes	31	20	4	53
	NA	10	7	2	18
Chaplain	Yes	40	15	2	57
	NA	4	3	—	7
Doctor/Nurse	Yes	41	25	5	71
	NA	4	2		6
Doctor on campus	Yes	16	13	—	29
	NA	7	5	1	13
English improvement program	Yes	45	26	4	77
	NA	6	6	1	13
Hindi improvement program	Yes	17	8	2	27
	NA	9	9	2	19

these services without huge expenditures, and it is crucially important for them to do so in view of the wastage and stagnation of talent which results partly from students' unrealistic aspirations and lack of guidance. Because students start college at fifteen or sixteen years old, they need more special guidance.

We have alluded above to the centralization of administration in Christian colleges. There are principals who personally review approximately 2,000 admission applications every year, along with their other extremely heavy work load. They have not adjusted to the fact that their college has grown too large to take minute personal interest in every student, at least in the same ways that this was done in the past. Few principals have adequate secretarial staff to carry on even the routine correspondence and, unlike some colleges and universities in the West, the administrative wing of buildings is often hard to find! This centralization of administration chains principals to puttering business, allowing little time for reflection on the larger issues of the college.

More important, however, is that it stultifies the sense of community and participation by the teaching staff whose involvement in committees could quicken the life of the whole community. One of the most valuable resources of the college, its teachers, is relatively untapped. Channels of communication for new ideas and improvements in the college have not been functionally developed. Estrangement between teachers and administration is almost inevitable in such an arrangement, but more so when administration is done entirely through a religious order. Perhaps most significant in the long run is the loss of the insight and perspectives of those teachers who see different dimensions of the college, and who are in constant contact with the student.

Further, is there any reason why students themselves could not be worked into the organizational aspects of the college, thus also strengthening their sense of involvement? Certain areas are particularly relevant for students' involvement — the religious and assembly program, the running of hostels, development of extracurricular and community oriented programs. Perhaps students could even be given a share in the upkeep of buildings and grounds, college farms etc. Among other things it would give them a modicum of experience in manual labor. Far more important would be the sense of responsibility and community it would evolve.

One improvement which would cost money, but which appears essential for the overall development of a college, is the keeping of records. It has been a shocking experience to discover how little attention is paid in Christian colleges to maintaining good, standardized records. Our own search for empirical information revealed that some institutions could not give basic enrollment information for even a few years before, although this would have been submitted as a matter of course to the university (university registrars, too, are very protective of their records!). Even current enrollment totals were often obscure. It took us almost one year to be reasonably certain that we had found all the church-related university colleges in India. The Xavier Board admitted that the statistics on enrollments which they submitted were woefully inaccurate (as they were!), and the composite records for enrollment in Protestant institutions were already ten years old. Yet almost half of the institutions covered in the study reported that they did have master plans for development! We found only two situations where, in reality, there was a long-range and quite specific development plan.

It is inconceivable that colleges can make their maximum contribution to students, the college's own future, or to educational reform in the university, without empirical information about their evolution. Institutions tend to grow like Topsy, muddling their way through problems, reacting to pressures and finding short-range solutions to pressing needs. Certainly no one has the wisdom to plan far ahead in Indian higher education because the pressures change so often. Yet it cannot but impair good education to have a college wallowing along without clear empirical information about where it has been, where it is, and where it would like to go. Spongy thinking cannot provide adequate direction for good education.

One of the gravest needs on the Indian college campus today is for principals, who play the central role in Indian colleges, to be given training for their jobs — a training which includes a large dose of how to develop and delegate responsibility, and how to develop the records so essential to long-term rational planning of the evolution of a college. A series of short-term (five-week) summer institutes for college principals would be a major contribution to the improvement of Indian higher education.

Finally, Christian colleges could do much more to maintain lively contacts with their alumni. While most colleges claim to have current information about their alumni, our study revealed that information was neither current, nor nearly complete in most cases. Most alumni had no active relationship with their *alma mater*. Our survey of 3,200 graduates of both Christian and non-Christian colleges confirmed that graduates have little continuing relationship with their college, even though most of them continue to live in the same general community. Overall 41 per cent of the respondees reported never having returned to the college campus (a higher percentage for most Christian colleges' graduates) and an additional 36 per cent reported have returned once or twice, with Christian colleges about the same as non-Christian colleges. Only about 5 per cent reported frequent visits to the college. Fifty-four per cent reported never having contact with their former teachers, and only 8 per cent as often or now and then, with little difference between graduates of Christian and non-Christian institutions.

We are not concerned here about the financial help which the colleges may forfeit by not keeping closer relationships to alumni, but with the intellectual and psychological loss to both the college and alumni. An active relationship with alumni could give the college an important channel of influence in society at large, a channel which is particularly important on the Indian scene where there are so few organizations or institutions which can sustain an alumnus in his reflection of the directions of goals of society. Through such contact the college could also have its own work made constantly alive by developments in 'the world'. Because India is in rapid social change, colleges have a special responsibility to keep apace with these changes through contact with their alumni. The college needs the alumnus, in order to be relevant and in order to activate an important channel of communication with the world at large ; the alumnus needs the college to help him understand and interpret the vast and often rapid changes swirling around him.

If Christian colleges begin to see their broader tasks, to alumni as well as to current students, and to the community at large as well as to its own clientele, it cannot but become a more effective catalyst in educational reform, at all levels of education. This can be one of its most significant contributions to Indian development.

3. THE COLLEGE AS A PARTICIPANT
IN THE LOCAL COMMUNITY

The American Land Grant College concept has aroused widespread interest in India — the university as an educational center for the development of an entire region. In contrast, universities and colleges in India have little effective inter-relationship with the larger local or national community. This is tragic in a nation which so desperately needs the resources of the college, and which invests so much of its scarce resources in college education.

Christian colleges hardly do better than their sister institutions in this respect, although they think of themselves as servants of the community at large. This was clear from the statement of goals of Christian college principals in Table 21 ; service to society as a whole rated the highest as the 'objective' of the colleges. The establishment of many colleges was, in the first place, largely prompted by a desire to serve a specific locale, as was obviously the case with the recent founding of St. Mary's College (Shillong), Maris Stella College (Viajaya-wada), Union Christian College (Shillong), Ahmednagar College (Maharashtra) and St. John's Medical College (Banga-lore). These were self-conscious efforts to upgrade areas where no college for the same purposes was already in existence. Despite the fact that many colleges are in cities, and that there are concentrations of Christian colleges in certain areas, duplicating one another's energies, many colleges are clear responses to real community needs. In several instances Christians were asked by non-Christians to found a college to serve in sparsely Christianized areas.

What is abundantly clear, however, is that usually colleges have narrow conceptions of how they can be involved in a community. Their function is conceived as preparing students to pass their examination. If the 'town' and 'gown' cleavage is strong in Western countries, it is even more pronounced on the Indian scene. Why is it, for instance, that local business and community leaders are so seldom found on their Boards of Directors or governing bodies? Why are there so few non-Christians? Why does the college plant lie for weeks on end like an unsown field - - a major resource being squandered during evenings, innumerable holidays and long vacations? This impoverishes both the college and the community in which it is located. Why are there not actively cultivated programs of social research and social service from the college in the community? Why are community members not invited to many college functions?

How do Christian colleges try to relate to the local community? Raising money for needy causes was the most prominent activity, with social service societies ranking second. Our reservations about the latter already have been voiced, but it is also obvious that unless imaginatively used, raising money for needy causes hardly promotes dialogue, and may result in estrangement instead of deeper understanding. When we come to more potentially meaningful relationships, a much smaller number of Christian colleges are engaged in them: night school courses 16 per cent; demonstration programs 33 per cent; participation in cultural and educational events at college 37 per cent; staff research on community and national issues 17 per cent. Fifty per cent of the teachers reported doing no research at all, with another 24 per cent not answering the question. It is interesting to note that Protestant institutions tend to be more involved than Roman Catholic ones in community relations: 25 per cent as against 10 per cent for night school programs; 40 per cent as compared with 21 per cent with college staff serving on community affairs programs; 22 per cent compared with 14 per cent with staff involved in community or national research. More striking, however, than the differences between Protestant and Catholic colleges is that all are less involved in their local communities than the situation would seem to warrant. We have no basic of comparison with non-Christian colleges.

Further confirmation of this lack of involvement in the community at large is suggested in Table 60, based on the question, 'Approximately how many times per month does the principal speak to groups outside the college?'

TABLE 60

*Principals' speaking engagements outside college**

Number of times per month	RCW	RCM	RCD	PS	PU	S	Total
Nil	22 (62)	2 (10)	4 (20)	1 (7)	5 (16)	—	34 (27)
1-2	2 (6)	10 (50)	7 (35)	6 (48)	12 (38)	4 (59)	41 (32)
3-4	1 (3)	2 (10)	2 (10)	2 (15)	4 (13)	—	11 (9)
5 +	—	3 (15)	5 (25)	2 (15)	7 (23)	1 (14)	18 (14)
NA	10 (29)	3 (15)	2 (10)	2 (15)	3 (10)	2 (29)	22 (18)
Total	35	20	20	13	31	7	126

* Only 126 of the 130 college principals are included.
  Numbers in brackets indicate percentages.

Considering that the non-respondents would be heavily weighted on the side of 'no speaking engagements', we find that almost half of the college principals do not speak to community groups, or even to other college or educational groups on an average of even once a month. Only about a third of the principals seem to be active speakers outside the college. Protestant college principals are involved in these extra-college affairs far more than Roman Catholic college principals. This may reflect the fact that more Protestant principals are laymen, and there is a lower percentage of women principals. It is not likely that Sister principals would receive many invitations to speak outside of the college. Only 28 per cent of the Christian college principals reported having published articles, with one-third reporting 'one or two' and another third 'over ten'. Protestant principals were significantly more active in both speaking and publishing, even considering only the co-educational and men's institutions.

Teaching staff showed basically the same pattern of lack of involvement in the community. Fifty-six per cent of the staff reported never speaking outside of the college, with another 12 per cent not answering. Of the remainder, only 10 per cent reported speaking frequently or often. As one could expect, teachers in Roman Catholic women's colleges were the least involved in speaking-type activities, with 72 per cent reporting 'nil' and another 17 per cent not answering. About one-quarter of this outside speaking was for religious groups, about half for academic or student situations, about a quarter for civic and socio-cultural occasions, and almost none for professional groups. Teachers in Roman Catholic men's colleges and in United Protestant colleges seemed to be the most active speakers off-campus.

Further, teachers are little involved in social service programs in the community. Overall, 45 per cent of the teachers interviewed said that they spent no time in social service activities, with another 26 per cent not answering the question. Fifteen per cent reported spending one or two hours per week in social service programs, while approximately 15 per cent were involved for three or more hours per week. It was not easy to discern any significant differences between teachers in one or another kind of institutions. It is also interesting to note that less than 30 per cent of the teachers reported reading vernacular papers. While this hypothesis has not been tested, it could well be that this suggests an intellectual involvement of teachers in the broader social issues of the nation, but less direct involvement in the affairs of their local community.

The following table shows staff readership characteristics. It should be remembered that 62 per cent of the Christian colleges are in the South, and that Protestant colleges are less concentrated in the South, helping to account for the good showing of the *Hindu* and the *Indian Express*.

The teachers' conception of the function of a college, and the low status accorded community service, is reflected in answers they gave on why colleges could be considered strong. This evidence is somewhat more significant because it is intentionally indirect. Teachers were asked to select the seven best colleges they could think of, and were later requested to enumerate *why* these were the best colleges. 'Training for

TABLE 61

Staff newspaper readership
(by sponsorship)*

Newspaper	RCW	RCM	RCD	PS	PU	Total
'The Indian Express'	85 (30)	75 (30)	37 (33)	47 (24)	87 (32)	331 (30)
'The Hindu'	68 (24)	60 (24)	19 (17)	14 (7)	77 (29)	238 (21)
'The Mail'	21 (8)	7 (3)	1 (1)	2 (1)	27 (10)	58 (5)
'The Statesman'	8 (3)	16 (6)	—	15 (8)	7 (3)	46 (4)
'Blitz'	—	—	—	3 (1)	2 (1)	5 (1)
'The Times of India'	8 (3)	6 (2)	2 (2)	37 (19)	5 (2)	58 (5)
'The Hindustan Times'	9 (3)	2 (1)	—	16 (8)	6 (2)	33 (3)
'Amrita Bazar Patrika'	1 (—)	6 (2)	—	12 (6)	2 (1)	21 (2)
Vernacular	51 (18)	54 (21)	46 (42)	32 (16)	33 (12)	216 (19)
Other	18 (7)	19 (8)	2 (2)	17 (9)	17 (6)	73 (7)
NA	10 (4)	9 (3)	3 (3)	2 (1)	6 (2)	30 (3)

* There were insufficient number of responses from Syrian college staff included in this table.

Numbers in brackets indicate percentages.

discipline and character' was rated highest (19 points on a scale of 100), and 'good examination results' and 'good staff' seemed about equally important tests of a quality college (14 points). 'Producing leaders for society' was named for only 4 points while 'relevance to society's needs' was weighted for only 3 points. When these same teachers were asked to evaluate the strengths and weaknesses of the college where they were presently teaching, only in rare cases was mention made of the college's role as a servant to society as a whole, or to the community. If this narrow conception of the role of a college is characteristic of teacher's attitudes, it is small wonder that colleges are little related to the communities in which they are set.

A further substantiation of this view comes from the alumni questionnaire. When alumni were asked what were the most important things their college had given them, the three highest scores were given to what might be called personal gains: self-discipline 18; knowledge 23; self-reliance and self-respect 17. What might be called social values scored much lower. 'A sense of social responsibility' scored 13. On this item there was no difference between graduates of Christian colleges and those of non-Christian institutions. In fact, the only area in which there was a perceptible, and perhaps significant, difference between the graduates of Christian and non-Christian institutions was in 'ethical and moral values', with scores of 10 and 6 respectively.

Obviously there are some colleges conscious of community service and relations, and perhaps the most dramatic of these is Ahmednagar College, purposely founded in a depressed rural area with no other colleges nearby. Its Rural Life Development and Research Project was initiated in 1961, although the seeds of the program had been planted with social service activities before that. This Project, described by Professor Hulbe in Volume II of this series, is not totally extra-curricular, but an attempt to integrate community work into the curriculum itself. The program is so unusual that certain points warrant repetition. The basic motivations are described as follows:

(1) to meet the ever-growing demand of our nation for responsible citizenship, effective leadership, efficient, well-informed and motivated personnel to undertake responsibilities in the field of community development and co-operation;

(2) to make education more substantive by confronting students with practical economic and social problems of our rural society;

(3) to participate in the process of nation-building by direct involvement in the developmental program of the rural surroundings; and

'What has your college given you?'
(Alumni, by sponsorship)

Benefit	Christian colleges			Non-Christian colleges			Overall		
	Total w.f.	First place 1,181 respondents	%	Total w.f.	First place 1,948 respondents	%	Total w.f.	First place 3,130 respondents	%
Good job	1,423	112	9	2,473	234	9	3,896	346	9
No rank		687			1,146			1,833	
Ethical/moral values	1,621	100	10	1,689	83	6	3,310	183	8
No rank		586			1,293			1,879	
Self-discipline	3,217	285	19	4,478	319	17	7,695	604	18
No rank		252			531			783	
Friendships	787	28	5	1,541	68	6	2,328	96	5
No rank		873			1,355			2,228	
Knowledge	3,566	332	22	6,175	624	23	9,741	956	23
No rank		188			276			464	
Self-reliance and self-respect	2,631	117	16	4,604	225	17	7,235	342	17
No rank		322			482			804	
Association with distinguished teachers	868	30	5	1,737	39	6	2,605	69	6
No rank		825			1,258			2,083	
Sense of social responsibility	2,177	82	13	3,659	169	13	5,836	251	13
No rank		355			582			937	
Degree only	1		—	17	2	—	18	2	—
No rank		1,180			1,944			3,124	
Other	75	5	—	136	9	1	211	14	—
No rank		1,147			1,888			3,035	
Nothing really significant	178	30	1	445	70	2	623	100	1
No rank		1,138			1,843			2,981	

w.f. = weighted frequency.

(4) to bridge the gap between the college and its surrounding community.[7]

The program consists of three spearheads — study, research and participation, and is being done outside of the normal patterns established by the university (at the same time attracting widespread attention from other colleges and government). Starting initially with 13 villages around the college, it has been already extended to include 100 villages — working in 'all aspects of development such as agriculture, co-operation, education, social education, adult literacy, health and industries.'[8] The nature of some of the studies is revealed in their titles:

1. 'Socio-economic Survey of Nine Villages in Ahmednagar Taluka'
2. 'Socio-economic Study of Kolhewadi'
3. 'Theory and Practice of Community Development with Special Reference to Ahmednagar Community Development Block'
4. 'The Working of Multi-purpose Service Co-operative Societies in Ahmednagar Taluka'
5. 'Patterns of Leadership'
6. 'The Story of Wells'
7. 'Tensions of Socio-economic Progress' etc.

'Over the past six years the Project has initiated a programme of soil conservation covering the total agricultural area of four villages . . . introduced new and scientific methods of cultivation in these villages . . . been responsible for spreading the use of improved seeds, fertilizers, and insecticides in the villages . . . has organized four farmers' conferences which drew a tremendous response from both official circles as well as farmers from the rural population of the district as a whole. These conferences have been responsible for highlighting some of the acute problems of rural areas and have encouraged us to make bold experiments in finding ways to solve them . . . in the field of co-operation the Project has been responsible for starting four societies: a credit society, a co-operative farming society, a co-operative poultry society, and a co-operative processing society. The co-operative processing society is a novel experiment in organizing human and material resources for progress. Its uniqueness lies in the fact that the society aims to take up total responsibility for the development of all villages. An organization at this level is one step below the Panchayat Samiti and one step above the Panchayat is capable of planning more effectively and precisely for development. . . . An example of the potentialities of such an approach is the manner in which these villages were able to raise Rs 15,000 within a period of two months for the society despite near famine conditions in the area . . . . Another aspect of these activities is the opportunity provided for the emergence of new leadership from among the rural population . . . . These activities thus provide us with useful research opportunities and provide some indicators on how best to implement a successful agricultural extension programme.

'In the field of education the Project has participated actively in the adult literacy drive and the GRAM GAURAVA programmes. The Project has also been instrumental in mobilizing the resources of the people for school buildings, equipment, and libraries . . . film unit . . . two weekly clinics which would in due time be self-supporting. . . . The work of the Project among the tribals has attracted a lot of attention . . . succeeded in rehabilitating an ex-criminal tribe . . . . Project was also able to get the Land Development Bank of the District to finance reclamation and land development work. . . . The achievements of the Rural Life Development and Research Project are many. But it must be emphasized that the role of the college is to act as a catalytic agent. By no stretch of the imagination can it be assumed that an arts and science college, such as Ahmednagar College is, is the repository of all expertise essential to solve the problems of rural India. But there is no doubt that a college or university is favourably situated to draw upon available resources and expertise available through the various government and private sources of the district. The problem of development, in most instances, can be reduced to that of the organization of communities to avail themselves of the various opportunities extended through the government development schemes and to ensure their proper utilization. The colleges and universities are ideally situated to organize the village people towards this end . . . . The Project has also drawn an unbelievable response from the rural folk. This is an indication of the degree to which the college has been able to integrate itself with the community. This may be considered as a pre-condition for successful programmes of university extension.'[9]

Ahmednagar is not the only Christian college relating itself effectively to the community, but it is a marvelous example of the kind of creative work that possibly can be duplicated in other institutions. The Government of India has found the work so interesting that it is considering subsidizing similar efforts elsewhere. Other Christian colleges have various kinds of involvement with their local communities. The Institute for Social Service, Nirmala Niketan, in Bombay, has a strong social work and welfare program; Stella Maris College in Madras is developing a most interesting community service center on a voluntary basis; Madras Christian College and Loyola College in Madras also have active community service programs; the medical schools at Vellore and Ludhiana run a great variety of social and community service projects, being models of what medical colleges can become; the School of Journalism at Hislop College in Nagpur attempted to develop contacts with other agencies in the community in order to make journalism realistic; Loyola Institute of Sociology in Trivandrum is stimulating empirical research on the situation in the local community. What is important about these various efforts is their emphasis on pragmatic experimentation, their conception of catalytic actions, and their conviction that benefit comes to the college as well as to the community at large. In general, however, Christian colleges are not integrally related to their local community, nor active in promoting concern for national issues.

4. THE COLLEGE AND MANPOWER NEEDS

Indian educators are increasingly convinced that a manpower approach to education is essential. Reliance on the market is too expensive, both with respect to actual educational costs for many who do not bring returns into the economy, and increasingly in social costs for unemployed and poorly employed secondary school and college graduates. India cannot afford the luxury of an uncontrolled education which has spiralled menacingly. Arts graduates often find no other employment than teaching additional arts candidates, thus perpetuating and intensifying the problem. The reservoir of educated unemployed is growing rather than diminishing. Thus the Education Commission Report, following several previous manpower studies, gave major attention to the need for planned educational growth. A 'Minute of Supplementation' was added at the end of the Report, dealing with manpower considerations.[10]

The major points of the Report relating to manpower considerations may be summarized as follows.

1. There is widespread and growing interest in relating education to estimates of manpower needs over the long term. As education is a long-term investment, such targets must be developed beyond the short range of five-year plans. Gopala-swami has made his targets conditional upon certain attainments in the economy, and anticipates that these could be achieved by 1975.

2. There are several approaches to manpower planning, but it is patently inadequate to project needs only on the basis of the current distribution of educated people in the various fields, and to measure only probable population increases and consequent employment pressures. Considerations relating to the level of educated people are also inadequate by themselves. Two important elements, together, are *levels* and *area* of need. Table 63 shows these two items in relation to one another.

3. A major and unresolved problem in educational planning for manpower needs in India has been that, until now, there has been no body authorized to implement or enforce even the best plans, especially on the national level. The educational structure of India is so localized that jurisdiction over education cannot be controlled. The Report suggests that to correct this difficulty, areas of need critical to development

TABLE 63

Estimated requirement of matriculates and above by industry group:
India (1960–1 to 1985–6)
(in thousands)

Industry group	1960–1 (actual)			1975–6			1985–6		
	Matriculate	Intermediate	Graduate	Matriculate	Intermediate	Graduate	Matriculate	Intermediate	Graduate
Agriculture	381	46	67	681	83	120	984	120	174
Mining	67	5	6	282	20	27	632	45	61
Manufacturing	436	90	102	2,880	584	707	6,681	1,355	1,642
Construction	99	30	19	503	150	97	1,131	367	218
Trade & commerce	452	100	92	1,181	262	240	2,565	570	522
Transport and communications	318	80	94	1,200	301	354	2,608	654	769
Services (other)									
Public services	723	245	296	1,299	441	533	1,923	652	789
Education at services	467	102	290	2,123	463	877	3,041	668	1,728
Medical and health	124	27	47	379	82	175	1,139	248	360
Other services	195	30	132	357	54	169	574	85	279
Total	3,262	755	1,146	10,874	2,440	3,299	21,278	4,734	6,542

SOURCE : I S I/L S E Paper (Education Commission Report, p. 94).

should be defined and education to meet them should be put under Union or Central Government control. The Report does not advocate subsuming all higher education under the Center. Further, the Report foresees the establishment of central organizations responsible for developing manpower in particular segments of the work force, similar to those which have been so successful in rapidly providing training facilities for top-level engineers in the country. There is still a shortage of higher-level teachers of engineering, and too few technicians of the middle range, but the Report is confident that the infra-structure for the training of engineers is now adequate. Indeed, there is a danger that politicians will want to start engineering schools which are no longer necessary. The Report suggests that in the teaching of medicine and agriculture there may be similar concentrated and centralized efforts. The National Council for Educational Research and Training is an example of the kind of co-ordinated effort which can be set up in other areas.

4. In terms of sheer quantity at the various levels, there are enough graduates to meet present demands. Too many gra-duates are in the wrong fields, and the economy is unable to absorb them. Furthermore, quantitative expansion has seriously undermined quality all down the line. This situation will get worse if left uncontrolled. In the arts there are already probably sufficient numbers of graduates for the whole Fourth Plan period (1966–71). Stringent admission policies must be vigorously enforced, despite strong pressures to maintain a freer system of entrances. Curtailment of admissions, coupled with attention to educational reforms guaranteeing improve-ment in quality, would make it possible to invest in the areas of greatest need for the economy.

5. Relating education to manpower needs is not a simple process of creating more seats for prospective students in the various faculties. Mindful of the huge wastage in and beyond the system, the Report urges attention to screening, guidance programs, and all efforts designed to assist individual students to choose vocations suitable to their talents and appropriate for the nation's needs. It is estimated that only

63 per cent of those educated were actually in the labor force (there was a large volume of educated and unemployed house-wives).[11] Adult education programs, re-training facilities, extension education for secondary school graduates were mooted. There was a need to move beyond the classical classroom concept of education.

6. Most of the educated have gone into service employment, notably government service. On the basis of projections it is predicted that there will be a dramatic increase in the need for higher educated persons in industry, which could not have been foreseen simply on the basis of extrapolating present manpower patterns. The services will need no accelerated inputs. The Gopalaswami Minute says that this future need for people educated for industrial work has not yet been seen by educational planners. This growing need is not only for large new numbers of more highly trained people, but also there is an acute need for revision of the existing curriculum.

7. One of the most critical manpower needs is for properly trained teachers. Not only is there a shortage of qualified teachers (almost half of the present primary-school teachers are not officially qualified), but preparation of teachers even in some teacher-training institutions is considered inferior. Of the four major areas of manpower needs,[12] teaching is still the least popular vocation. Quality teachers for higher education are in short supply in fields of specialized science, engineering, medicine, and pedagogy itself. Specific recommendations were made that salary revisions would help to attract better people to teaching, that special attention be given to providing teachers for the rural and backward areas of the country, and that preparation in different areas of the country relate as directly as possible to projected area needs. Obviously, there was no need for an additional input for arts teachers in higher education. The current reservoir must first be absorbed and the number of arts students curtailed.

8. While it was generally contended that science education had to be vastly expanded, and that all students regardless of their particular course should be exposed to science subjects,

the manpower study made no specific recommendations in this area. Professional science needs were divided into Agricultural-Veterinary, Health-Medical, and 'Other' groups. While no predictions or targets were set, it was assumed that big new increases in the first two were needed, and that these needs should be met through a concerted effort similar to that which had been made to improve engineering education.

9. Public administration traditionally found no place in the manpower studies made prior to the Education Commission Report, and indeed it was only in the 'Minute of Supplementation' that it was urged that re-thinking should be done about how administrators are trained. The Minute noted that more graduates are taken into the services than into any other field, and that it generally has been assumed that no special administrative training was required.

To be sure, there have been a certain number of commerce graduates, and a limited number of public administration graduates on a sub-professional level. Gopalaswami argues, however, that this is not adequate, and that attention to training cadres of managerial-administrative manpower is of the first order of importance. Administrative expertise is particularly needed now for three basic reasons:[13] the best talent is being drained off into other more promising and attractive types of career; emphasis on development requires new kinds of skills and new attitudes among administrators (a 'law and order' mentality is not sufficient); and to develop and maintain standards of administration a professionalization of the cadres is essential. In making these points he urged special professional education for public administration.

10. Education, too, must be vocationalized (not in any narrow sense), to counteract the 'pedagogical-academic' trend. This vocational emphasis is especially relevant at the secondary stages, with vocational emphasis also valuable for agricultural and technical training in the university. Agriculture, of course, was one of the most crucial areas for advanced university training and research, but it was recognized that at present most graduates in agriculture were divorced from the rural scene.

11. Finally, there were some additional suggestions about relating education to manpower needs: scholarship programs should be vastly expanded, guaranteeing that at least those in the top 15 per cent of the secondary class will receive higher education; in the scholarship program preferential treatment should be accorded to girls; there should be special provisions for training handicapped children; there must be 'deliberate and sustained effort to assist the less developed areas to come up to at least certain minimum levels'; and education for the backward classes and tribals must be broadly extended.

Manpower considerations, then, point to the need for new emphasis in certain *subject areas* (industry, teacher-training, science, agriculture, public administration), in *levels* of education (secondary and vocational), in certain *parts of the country* (rural and depressed), and among certain *groups of people* (women and depressed classes). To what extent do Christian colleges meet these needs?

Regarding levels of education, since Independence there have been 50 new colleges and a number of secondary and primary schools, as well as the new vocational schools. Statistics are not available about the increase in the number of schools other than colleges, but there is no doubt that it has been sizeable. New Christian colleges are a direct response to the felt need for more higher education places in the country.

In addition to the new colleges, there has been significant numerical growth in those institutions which already existed in 1948. An illustration of this growth is reflected in the ten-year span between 1956 and 1966 (we have data for only 37 Protestant colleges). During this period 5 colleges were reduced in size, but the overall gain in these particular colleges was 57 per cent for the teaching staff (1,432 to 2,112) and 42 per cent for the student body (26,481 to 37,529). Given the fact that the expansion of existing Roman Catholic colleges was roughly comparable, we assume, and that about one-half of the Roman Catholic colleges were founded since Independence, Christian colleges have responded dramatically to the quantitative pressures for entrance into college. On the other hand, they have greatly decreased as an overall proportion of the number of private colleges in the country. Yet, about 7 per cent of the total university-level student body are in Christian colleges.

A fairly large number of the Christian colleges offer post-Bachelor's degrees, with 26 per cent of the colleges offering Master's programs and 9 per cent offering Ph.D.s. In addition, about 160 fully-trained doctors graduate every year from Christian medical colleges. The Education Commission Report urges that post-graduate education be done in the universities because of the weak programs in so many colleges, but it is clear that, for the present, many Christian colleges are making a very important high-level manpower contribution above the Bachelor's degree. In centers like Bombay there would seem to be no compelling reason to take the Ph.D. programs out of the colleges, except that from the colleges' point of view it is a very expensive type of education, in some fields three or four times the cost for a Bachelor's degree student. Obviously medical education is prohibitively expensive.

Education for women has also accelerated. Since 1948, 17 new colleges have been started exclusively for women, and 25 were co-educational. Only 8 of the new colleges are for men only. These additions have significantly expanded the number and percentage of women in the Christian colleges. In 36 Protestant colleges for which we have enrollment figures for 1956, there has been an increase in women students of a little more than 100 per cent in that time span, which is considerably more than the overall expansion rate in those colleges. In line with the recommendations of the manpower Minute of Supplementation, Christian colleges are accelerating their investment in women's education, an acceleration started years ago.

We have indicated that new Christian colleges tend to be concentrated in the South, with 38 of 50 post-Independence Christian colleges having been placed in Kerala, Mysore, Madras and south Andhra. The first three of these four states are educationally more advanced than many other parts of the country. Should this kind of consideration be taken into account when new Christian colleges are founded? On the other hand, new colleges in Assam are clearly in depressed areas, providing facilities for those who would not otherwise attend college. Again, the motivation to serve Christian communities is obviously high, with almost 100 per cent of the students and teachers in the Assam Christian colleges being Christian.

In line with the Minute's recommendations, many of the new Christian colleges have a vocational orientation; most obvious are the 13 newer teacher-training colleges. Three professional schools also have been added to the 5 previously existing ones. Yet, while there has been a new interest in vocationalized education, the arts and science colleges still receive the most attention. In a few instances there have been attempts to put teacher-training in arts and science colleges, thus moving in the direction of the Education Commission's recommendation that there be a closer integration between teacher-training and the other faculties of college and universities. We believe, however, that it would be a questionable policy for Christian educators to divert too much attention to areas of urgent professional education, as it is likely that these will be met on a priority basis by government. Teacher-training, however, seems to be a special case where Christian institutions can make an important contribution.

Perhaps as significant as any other development is the provision for science instruction. While on the national average there are many more arts than science students (and Gopala-swami contends that the disadvantaged position of the sciences is getting even worse), Christian colleges, especially Roman Catholic ones, have developed science facilities and teaching to a level much higher than the national average. Not only are enrollments in science subjects high, but libraries are generally relatively well-stocked in the physical and natural sciences. The only areas with a higher average are English and langua-ges. Laboratories are being developed; in a sample of liberal arts colleges we found an average annual investment of approxi-mately Rs 35,000 (at that time $8,000) in laboratories, and total expense on laboratories was just below that for hostels and residences over a five-year period. There has been more growth in the number of natural and physical science depart-ments over the past ten years than in any other departments.

These are evidences of the continuing strong support given to the natural and physical sciences in Christian colleges.

Christian colleges are also prominent in attempts to provide student guidance and services, although the picture is still bleak. Wastage in education is scandalous, both for the individual and for the national economy. Aptitude and psychological tests are almost never used, but are being developed at Ewing Christian College and Loyola College, Madras. It can be expected that these programs will be significantly expanded in the near future. Adequate records of students' performance and addresses, along with continuing contact with alumni, partly through a placement service, are urgent needs. While Christian colleges are probably better in this respect than most others, they still have failed appallingly. Our study of graduates of Christian and non-Christian colleges revealed no significant difference in length of unemployment, change in jobs, training related to jobs, and types of jobs currently held. While this material needs further refinement, our tentative conclusion is that Christian colleges are not doing a better job than non-Christian colleges in preparing students for jobs for which they are particularly suited and for which there are openings.

More glaring failures are in the fields of agriculture and empirical social service. There is one agriculture college, but many of those associated with the institution claim that its graduates enter only administrative jobs. College education estranges graduates from manual labor, and it is clear that the Christian agriculture college, despite its long history and good standing, is not succeeding appreciably any better than other agriculture colleges in turning out practicing agriculturists.

Similarly, Christian colleges have not pioneered the way in the empirical social sciences, despite their connections with the West (British universities also have been traditionally weak in sociology). Economics has been an important and popular subject of study, but often it has been too classical and theoretical to be relevant to problems on the rapidly changing Indian scene. It would seem appropriate for Christian colleges, with their concern for the social and human dimensions of education, to invest heavily in first-class social science education, as it is this kind of perspective and skill which will become an increasingly critical importance as the new India find its own ethos and authenticity. In a fundamental sense, this type of education is as important to India's development as the natural and physical sciences. One major obstacle, naturally, is that there is a dearth of teachers for this kind of work, with many of the better ones being taken by government and the universities themselves.

Finally, one of the major development needs is for competent administrators. It is startling that, despite the emphasis on training teachers, educational administration has been so neglected. Christian colleges have done poorly in this respect, notwithstanding their many teacher-training colleges. The Education Commission Report concludes that the need for administrators will grow only in arithmetical proportion, but that there is need for professionalizing the stock of administrators coming along. This is more than ever true among educational administrators, as the principal plays such a dominant role in the temper and program of the whole institution. If he lacks imagination and administrative ability, even the best reforms initiated by the university and large sums of money cannot transform the college ; with imagination and ability the college can be largely transformed without changing the university and without large amounts of new money.

Christian colleges are doing much to meet critical manpower needs in India, but there are also many ways in which their efforts could be more efficacious. It would be as much a mistake to tailor the program of Christian colleges exclusively to meet current manpower assessments as it would be foolish and wasteful not to make energetic efforts to relate the work of Christian colleges to general manpower considerations. In making judgments about the proper balance of these two elements, the purposes of the colleges, the Christian ethos, the institutional capacities and limits of the churches, and long-term reflections on where Indian society is going and ought to go, must all play their part.

5. THE COLLEGE AS STIMULANT FOR
NEW KNOWLEDGE AND VISION

Bishop Newbigin's provocative address at the ISS-FERES Principals' consultation referred to the confusion of aims among Christian college administrators, and pointed out that while there is a growing emphasis on development as a normative standard for a college in India, this norm has acute limitations. Development is a fluid concept which, like progress, needs constant clarification or even re-interpretation in the light of more permanent ideals. Furthermore, development as a concept has to be broken up into its constituent elements for clarity's sake. There is also danger that preoccupation with development will lead to narrow and utilitarian education. The Commission Report itself notes this danger, and calls the university ' to seek and cultivate new knowledge, and to engage vigorously and fearlessly in the pursuit of truth, and to interpret old knowledge and beliefs in the light of new needs and discoveries.'[14] While Christian colleges should promote national development, they must never confuse development with larger goals. Bishop Newbigin's warning was timely and cogent in view of the general mood of the Education Commission Report. But the current need is that Christian college leaders should become more deeply conscious of how their institutions can be made more relevant to development.

One major contribution which the colleges can make is to stimulate and contribute to a lively dialogue about, not the technical aspects of development alone, but the governing ideas of society as a whole. In the early years of Christian colleges in India there was a conscious attempt to promote dialogue with the highest elements of Hinduism; while colleges were often developed to uplift the poor, there was never a shrinking away from the very best in Hindu society. Indeed, that society would be penetrated by confronting it at its best and letting this influence seep down to other levels. That Christian colleges in India today do not actively promote this conversation about values suggests confusion about their own purposes and perhaps too much defensiveness.

The self-confidence of Christian leaders has vanished; many are uncertain of their ground and reluctant to engage revived Hinduism directly. This changed mood has been wrought by theological developments, by resurgent nationalism expressed in a sometimes hostile Hinduism, new conceptions of and roles for the state as such, the shift from missionary to local leadership, etc. The question is partly one of how best to fully identify the Christian community with the Indian community's hopes — how to demonstrate to themselves and others that Christianity is not an alien import unrelated to authentic Indian aspirations and life. The question is only partly how Christian *institutions* should relate to the larger development efforts, but more fundamentally now Christians themselves, as a community, define their relationship to the non-Christian majority among which they find themselves. In short, the confusion of goals in relation to the purposes of Christian colleges is a symptom of a deeper malaise, viz. the nature and character of the Christian community's presence in independent India.

Many Christians find a secular state attractive as a barrier against Hindu hostility, but at the same time have not developed a philosophy which fits a secular state into traditional Christian teachings. Paul Devanandan and M. M. Thomas' study, *Christian Participation in Nation Building*,[15] was a very important contribution to this philosophy. The discussion needs to be pushed further, and with broader participation from the Christian communities. That Christian colleges should find a compelling *raison d'être* is acute not only for the continued vitality of the colleges themselves, but as a Christian contribution to a deeper understanding of the place of religions in a pluralistic society, given the special problems of national integration and political cohesion. The comparatively easy pluralism of Western countries, where it does exist, may be irrelevant for countries plagued by fissiparous tendencies. In Western countries national myths have been evolved which provide a basic unity; diversity is possible and useful. In many developing countries, like India, diversity (even if covered with a veneer of unity based on anti-colonialism, a military dictatorship, a common enemy) is given, and the problem is to find coherence and unity. Christian colleges, symbolizing a funda-mental religious cleavage in Indian society, have a special obligation to contribute, on philosophical and practical levels, to a more comprehensive and adequate idea of Indian society. This can be fostered by what a college *says*, what it *does*, and what it *is*.

The ethos of Christian colleges would suggest concern for developing and promoting a philosophy of society. It does not appear that Christian colleges are doing this, perhaps because colleges are hypnotized by their minority position, or perhaps because education in India today tends to be overwhelmingly utilitarian. Young people are not attracted to philosophic and religious studies. What religious or philosophical learning there is tends to be moralistic and individualistic, symbolized in the 'Moral and Religious Instruction Programs'. This is difficult to believe of a nation steeped in speculative religious and philosophical reflection, and known throughout the world for its systems of thought. In moral and religious instruction, there is almost no attention to social issues and structures, no attempt to question the assumed values of society or the institutions of society on the basis of religious norms. It is a moralism without roots in intellectually challenging and satisfying foundations. Vigorous philosophical and religious inquiry just does not often happen on the Christian college campuses.

In many colleges philosophy and religion departments do not even exist; where they do exist they usually are weak sisters. Only 6 out of 1,800 students in our survey were found to be studying religion and philosophy! What can colleges do when students are not willing to take these courses, and where state-aided institutions cannot require philosophical and religious instruction? Three main avenues are left open: to make the optional religious and moral instruction broader and more compelling, to develop an attractive, not superficial, extracurricular religious program, and to encourage teachers to be attentive to this dimension in their teaching, insofar as it is consistent with the internal character of their subject matter.

Attempts are being made in a few institutions to deepen the study of religion. The Henry Martin Institute of Islamic Studies (not a university-related college) is one attempt to deepen conversation across religious traditions, but even this program has not developed very significantly. A more recent effort has been the establishment of a school of Sikh studies at Baring Union Christian College, nestled in the Punjab among the Sikh community. A third venture, still not finalized, is the establishment of a Radhakrishnan Chair of Philosophy at Madras Christian College. But these are exceptions.

What a college does with its Christian and non-Christian staff and students, its *implicit* religious policy, is another important aspect of an attempt to gain and communicate a larger vision of society. Can the college become, in microcosm, the kind of community it aspires for the whole nation? Can relations between the religious groups on campus be used to deepen the staff and students' experience and thinking about the nature of a pluralistic and secular India? Ultimately these experiments may be more influential than formal philosophical and religious courses, though the latter should not be minimized.

As we have seen in Chapter IV, there is partiality toward Christian staff and students. Non-Christians are generally tolerant of this partiality because it is a Christian institution. It is interesting that non-Christian teachers, and all kinds of teachers in their forties, seem most convinced that there is a strong preferential treatment accorded to Christians. Perhaps they are feeling the pinch, if they are non-Christians, in promotions, residences of campus, and other perquisites. Younger teachers, whether Christian or not, tend to more strongly resent this partiality. Here the question arises whether the younger teachers are more indignant at alleged partiality or whether years of experience at the college convinces teachers that preferential treatment is accorded less often than they once suspected.

Partiality toward Christians is felt to be stronger among teachers in Roman Catholic institutions than in Protestant ones. Here, again, we are speaking about feeling, and not judging objective reality. Twenty-four per cent of the teachers in Roman Catholic institutions felt that there was strong partiality for Christians, while the figure for teachers in Protestant colleges was 15 per cent. Overall, 18 per cent of the teachers felt that there was over-protection at either the staff or student level. The feeling that Christians were over-protected was stronger in the South than in the North, which may be related to the fact that more of the Roman Catholic colleges are in the South, and that the Protestant colleges in the North are in a more precarious position in recruiting Christian staff and students. On the other hand, teachers in Kerala colleges felt much less opposed to preferential treatment for Christians.

There is some evidence of partiality, and perhaps the most pernicious aspect of special treatment relates to the promotion policy for teachers. Some teachers, in Roman Catholic institutions particularly, expressed frustration and discontent. But partiality towards Christians in promotions does not come out very strongly in the empirical evidence. Principals almost universally state that the major consideration in making promotions is years of service, followed in order by teaching ability, and degrees. Religion, and being a member of the management's religion, did not rate high. These priorities are basically the same for both graduate and post-graduate instruction. On the other hand, there are a few more Christians in the higher teaching ranks of the Christian colleges.

Regarding staff tenure, there is no appreciable difference between the length of stay for Christian and non-Christian teachers. The percentage of those having taught under one year is about the same, ranging between 9 and 12 per cent, for Roman Catholics, Protestants, Syrian Christians, and Hindus. The percentages for Muslims and others is insignificant because the numbers were so small. Similarly, if one takes the number of teachers who have been at a college for up to five years, the percentages are again very close for the three main groups of teachers: Protestant (41 per cent), Roman Catholic (44 per cent), and Hindu (46 per cent). This is hardly a trace of a difference, and is statistically irrelevant. Looking at the other end of the scale, at those who have served for more than ten years, again the percentage of teachers from the various religious backgrounds is almost the same: Roman

Catholic (33 per cent), Protestant (33 per cent), and Hindu (30 per cent). There are slight differences which could reflect some discrimination, but it is only slight. (We are speaking here of tenure, and not of the better chance that Christians may have to become teachers in the first place.)

Christians are hired with less teaching experience than Hindus; 66 per cent of the Protestants who responded were in their first college, while 64 per cent of the Catholics were in their first, and 57 and 50 were the respective percentages for Hindus and Muslims. Also, almost twice as many (by percentage) Hindu teachers have their Ph.D., 11 and 6 per cent respectively; a slightly smaller proportion of non-Christians have only Bachelor's degrees. It is natural that a higher percentage of Christian staff should reside on campus; the figures are actually 48 per cent for Christian staff and 26 per cent for non-Christian staff, in a sample of 232 teachers.

Naturally there are a large number of Christian students, but a much lower percentage than is often thought. Preference for Christian students is partly reflected in a study of the school-leaving position of students, showing that there is a considerably higher percentage of Christians from the lower echelons of secondary school examinations. For example, 20 per cent of the Christians received first-class degrees, while 28 per cent of the enrolled non-Christians had received a first-class in their secondary examinations.

As for residence during the college year, Table 23 shows that a higher percentage of Christian students, especially Protestants, live in college hostels. The differences are not as great as one would expect, however. These figures suggest a normal partiality for Christian staff and students, but still enough to cause unrest and frustration among a small percentage of those who were also dissatisfied on other matters.

Scholarship statistics, inadequate as they are, offer some insights into possible special treatment policies. Scholarships are used here to describe all kinds of financial aid, and not just that due to a student's aptitude and academic performance. These figures are based on those who did receive scholarships of some kind, or 406 respondees. About 68 per cent of the respondees (1,800) reported receiving no scholarship help at all, with an equal percentage for Christians and non-Christians.

Government scholarships were the most numerous, with 74 per cent of the scholarships having come from government. Christians do not appear to be discriminated against in government scholarships.

TABLE 64

Sources of financial aid for students
(406 respondees)

Source	Catholic	Protestant	Syrian	Hindu	Muslim	Total
Government	47 (61)	66 (69)	5 (71)	164 (80)	17 (80)	299 (74)
Colleges	18 (24)	11 (12)	0 (0)	31 (15)	1 (5)	61 (16)
Religious institutions	9 (11)	13 (14)	2 (29)	1 (—)	1 (5)	26 (6)
Community	2 (2)	2 (2)	0 (0)	2 (1)	1 (5)	7 (1)
Private	1 (1)	1 (1)	0 (0)	2 (1)	1 (5)	5 (1)
Other	1 (1)	2 (2)	0 (0)	5 (3)	0 (0)	8 (2)
Total	78 (100)	95 (100)	7 (100)	205 (100)	21 (100)	406 (100)

Numbers in brackets indicate percentages.

The average annual income for Hindu students' families was higher than that for Christian students: Protestants Rs 3,739; Roman Catholics Rs 3,376; Syrian Orthodox Rs 3,365; Hindus Rs 4,528; and 'Other' Rs 4,506. Colleges and religious institutions award few scholarships. Less than 5 per cent of the students in Christian colleges receive financial help from one or other of these two sources, while only 22 per cent of the scholarship recipients received money from the college or a church. It is natural to anticipate that Christian students should receive a higher proportion of the specifically church-related scholarships, but Hindu students actually received, in proportion, almost as many college scholarships as did Christian students. This indicates an open policy, based upon merit and need.

Another question is whether the colleges are living on the frontiers of new knowledge. Do they stimulate creative, relational and sythesizing thought? Do they encourage unorthodox and critical questioning? Indian teachers are famous for their conversations, but does it have a biting edge and is it systematic and sustained? There is not much evidence of this kind of involvement of the colleges in current and cutting-edge issues. While there are noteworthy exceptions, the extracurricular programs of most Christian colleges are not creatively stimulating. Few teachers belong to professional associations. Many do belong to teachers' organizations which operate more like unions to protect teachers' rights than as professional groups. Despite the Lindsay Commission's strong advocacy of research, reiterated many times by the University Grants Commission, and lip-service paid to it by almost everyone, few teachers appear to be actually doing research. Fifty per cent reported doing no research at all, with 24 per cent not marking the question. We conclude that at least three-fourths of the teachers are not engaged in research at all. Another 11 per cent reported spending between 1 and 5 hours per week on research, with 15 per cent reporting spending more than 6 hours per week at it. Protestant institutions seemed to have a higher percentage of research than Roman Catholic ones.

How long do teachers spend in preparing for their classes? More than 50 per cent spend less than twelve hours a week in preparation for classes, or less than one hour per classroom hours. Three per cent of the teachers reported spending no time in preparation for classes. Teachers in Roman Catholic Women's (auspices) colleges and in those under Protestant United sponsorship appeared to spend considerably less time in class preparations. Fourteen per cent of the teachers had had refresher courses of some kind, with the highest percentage of these being in Protestant United colleges. Eleven per cent of the teachers reported purchasing no books in a year, with about half of the teachers purchasing between 4 and 12 books per year. Five per cent of the teachers own no books, 37 per cent own fewer than 50 books, and 55 per cent own under 100 books.

Almost 60 per cent of the teachers never speak to groups outside the college, and another 22 per cent reported seldom speaking.

Mass communication, urbanization, industrialization, and even education itself are eroding the traditional foundations of Indian society. Colleges must become equipped to contribute to the emergence of broad-gauged, compelling, and internalized values to sustain Indian society as it gropes toward its authentic character. To this process the Christian college can contribute if it is itself engaged in a search for coherence and authenticity — a search which is not only theoretical (that also!) but reflected in and transmitted through college policies (as, for example, in the treatment of non-Christians on campus) and college internal life (as the kind of community it attempts to develop in the hostels, or the relationships it fosters between teachers and students).

We do *not* mean that colleges should be purveyors of dogmatic Christianity, but they should join with others in an active search for the truth that makes men free. A college can join this search only if it grubs in the facts of history and contemporary society, seeking in them a greater truth and a greater meaning. Christian colleges have not yet discovered the full meaning and necessity of this existential involvement; until they do, they will be living, as most colleges in India do today, on the periphery of Indian life.

VI

GENERAL ASSESSMENT OF
PERFORMANCE

In recapitulating here strengths and weaknesses, we unfortunately reiterate some of the argument, and a little of the information, already given above. Yet it seems justified not primarily to give emphasis, but to present a brief synopsis of the major features of the college in this different framework.

I. STRENGTHS

Since our intent here is to present a synoptic view of the diverse material presented in various sections above, and not to develop new arguments, it is not possible to go into detail on the several points to be made.

In general, Christian colleges in India are among the superior institutions in the country. This quality is widely recognized, and as a species, the colleges deserve their continued good reputation; it is not based solely upon past performance. Some allege that Christian colleges have slipped from their past standards, and it would be only natural if, under the heavy pressures of the day, this were the case. We have not tried to determine whether the colleges have slipped, but whether in terms of their own aspirations, the Education Commission Report, and widely accepted pedagogical norms, they are measuring up. Further, we have explicitly avoided comparison with other particular groups of colleges; instead we have compared Christian college performance with national averages and patterns, where that type of information was available.

Were it politically possible to do, and it is clearly not possible, probably a selection of the 50 best colleges for a degree of autonomy, as urged by the Education Commission, would result in the naming of 15 to 20 Christian colleges for this privilege — far out of proportion to the percentage of Christian colleges to the total in the country (about 5 per cent). This quality of Christian colleges is reflected in several concretely discernible aspects.

A telling indication of the position of Christian colleges is the performance of their students on the Bachelor's and Master's degree examinations. Since all students within a university, and within a given faculty, sit for the same examination, examination results are a good indication of the quality of students attracted to the various colleges, and the quality of the colleges' instruction. External examiners do not know either the student or the college being graded. Many Christian colleges have a Bachelor's pass percentage of between 80 and 100 per cent, while the national average is about 50 per cent for the B.A. Were Christian colleges not included in the national computations, of course, the national average would be discernibly lower. The pass percentage at the Master's level is correspondingly higher in Christian colleges, and the number of first and second classes awarded to students of Christian colleges further attest to the superior performance of graduates of Christian institutions. Certainly success in examinations is not an unmixed blessing ; it should not be taken completely on its face value. But it would be equally foolish to denigrate examination results as showing nothing about the quality of colleges. (See Tables 65 and 66).

Christian colleges seem to make a significant impression upon its students in value formation and in building self-discipline. Roman Catholic colleges rate somewhat higher on this point, particularly in relation to discipline. Strong emphasis is placed on discipline in the Roman Catholic colleges. However, there is considerable evidence to suggest that the values imparted are more personal and private, rather than social and community ones. We do not pretend that we have been able to scientifically measure the college's contribution, if any, to values ; we refer above only to what various people associated with the college, including alumni, think of the college, and believe the college has given them as individuals.

One of the most frequent claims made for Christian colleges is that they promote close teacher-student relationships. Does this stand the test of empirical evidence? The evidence so far is not clear. We have three sources of empiricial information about teacher-student relationships, but the information is not uniform.

In a study of 1,800 students in Christian colleges throughout India, chosen in a scientifically developed random sample, more than 85 per cent of those responding felt strongly that their teachers were interested in them, while only 3 per cent had a definite feeling that their teachers were uninterested. On another question the same students were asked whether, in their experience, the generalization that 'Indian teachers have little interest in their students' was true. Approximately one-third felt the statement was true, while two-thirds felt it untrue. Further, about 15 per cent of the students reported consulting with their teachers often or very often on personal problems, another 45 per cent spoke of occasional meetings with teachers on personal problems, and 35 per cent said that they never had contact with their teachers on such matters.

In our study of 3,200 alumni of both Christian and non-Christian colleges it was clear that one of the most appreciated and remembered things about college life was the students' relationships with their teachers. This was a spontaneously mentioned feature in many cases where additional information was volunteered in an open-ended question. It was interesting to note, however, that graduates of Christian colleges did not mention this more frequently than did graduates of non-Christian institutions. Christian colleges should not too easily assume that they have better staff-student relations than non-Christian colleges. The information needs considerable more refinement.

In a small preliminary study of 232 college staff, from 79 Christian colleges, teachers were asked to assess their colleagues' dedication to student welfare. About 50 per cent thought interest in student welfare was high and only 5 per cent termed it poor. Christian teachers were more generous in their assessments of colleagues on the question. In addition, 23 per cent of the non-Christian teachers, and 16 per cent of the Christian teachers, thought there was over-protection of Christians on both the student and staff levels.

TABLE 65

Profile of High Pass-Percentage Institutions
(Bachelor's degree)

Pass %	Sponsors								Total	Kind		
	RCW	RCM	RCD	RC Total	PS	PU	P Total	S		LA	TT	Other
To 29%	—	—	—	—	1 (8)	—	1 (3)	—	1 (1)	1 (1)	—	—
30–39%	—	—	—	—	—	—	—	—	—	—	—	—
40–49%	—	—	1 (6)	1 (1)	—	—	—	—	1 (1)	1 (1)	—	—
50–59%	3 (9)	1 (6)	—	4 (6)	2 (17)	2 (7)	4 (10)	—	8 (7)	7 (8)	1 (5)	—
60–69%	—	3 (18)	1 (6)	4 (6)	1 (8)	2 (7)	3 (8)	—	7 (6)	7 (8)	—	—
70–79%	9 (26)	—	1 (6)	10 (15)	3 (25)	10 (37)	13 (33)	2 (29)	25 (22)	23 (25)	2 (11)	—
80–89%	10 (28)	4 (23)	7 (44)	21 (31)	4 (34)	8 (30)	12 (31)	2 (29)	35 (31)	32 (35)	3 (16)	—
90–100%	13 (37)	9 (53)	6 (38)	28 (41)	1 (8)	5 (19)	6 (15)	3 (42)	37 (32)	21 (22)	13 (68)	2 (100)
Total	35	17	16	68	12	27	39	7	114	92	19	2

TABLE 65 (continued)

	Type			Founding date				Region		
	Male	Female	Co-ed.	Pre-1900	1901–1948	1949–1960	1961–1967	North	Center	South
To 29%	—	—	1 (2)	—	—	1 (3)	—	1 (3)	—	—
30–39%	—	—	—	—	—	—	—	—	—	—
40–49%	—	—	1 (2)	—	1 (3)	—	—	1 (3)	—	—
50–59%	2 (9)	—	4 (8)	4 (11)	1 (3)	—	1 (17)	2 (6)	—	4 (6)
60–69%	2 (9)	2 (5)	5 (10)	5 (13)	2 (6)	2 (5)	—	4 (13)	2 (17)	3 (4)
70–79%	5 (23)	7 (17)	13 (26)	10 (26)	9 (27)	5 (14)	1 (17)	8 (25)	3 (25)	14 (20)
80–89%	7 (32)	14 (34)	13 (26)(a)	11 (29)	11 (34)	12 (32)	1 (17)	8 (25)	2 (17)	25 (36)
90–100%	6 (27)	18 (44)	13 (26)	8 (21)	9 (27)	17 (46)	3 (49)	8 (25)	5 (41)	24 (34)
Total	22	41	50	38	33	37	6	32	12	70

(a) 1 NA

TABLE 65 (continued)

	Percentage of Christian staff						Number of students					
	Under 20	21–30	31–40	41–50	51–60	61+	Under 300	301–500	501–1,000	1,001–1,500	1,501–2,000	2,001+
To 29%	—	—	—	—	—	—	—	—	—	—	1 (5)	—
30–39%	—	—	—	—	—	—	—	—	—	—	—	—
40–49%	1 (10)	—	—	—	—	—	—	—	—	—	—	—
50–59%	1 (10)	1 (8)	1 (7)	3 (18)	—	2 (5)	2 (7)	1 (10)	1 (4)	1 (5)	3 (18)	1 (8)
60–69%	2 (20)	2 (15)	1 (7)	—	—	1 (2)	—	—	1 (4)	2 (8)	3 (18)	3 (23)
70–79%	4 (40)	2 (15)	5 (34)	6 (35)	—	7 (16)	3 (11)	1 (10)	10 (38)	6 (29)	2 (12)	3 (23)
80–89%	1 (10)	4 (31)	4 (26)	3 (18)	8 (73)	14 (32)	4 (15)	5 (50)	7 (27)	6 (29)	6 (35)	7 (54)
90–100%	1 (10)	4 (31)	4 (26)	5 (29)	3 (27)	20 (45)	18 (67)	3 (30)	7 (27)	5 (24)	2 (12)	2 (15)
Total	10	13	15	17	11	44(a)	27	10	26	21	17	13

(a) 1 NA

TABLE 65 (concluded)

	Library volumes per student						No. of Jesuits	No. offering Ph.D.
	Under 10	11–25	26–50	51–75	76–100	101+		
To 29%	—	1 (2)	—	—	—	—	—	—
30–39%	—	—	—	—	—	—	—	—
40–49%	1 (4)	—	—	—	—	—	—	—
50–59%	—	5 (9)	3 (12)	1 (20)	—	—	—	1 (9)
60–69%	1 (4)	4 (7)	1 (4)	—	—	—	2 (15)	1 (9)
70–79%	7 (29)	13 (24)	4 (17)	—	—	1 (25)	2 (15)	2 (18)
80–89%	11 (46)	18 (33)	6 (25)	—	—	—	3 (23)	5 (46)
90–100%	4 (17)	14 (25)	10 (42)	4 (80)	1 (100)	3 (75)	6 (47)	2 (18)
Total	24	55	24	5	1	4	13	11

Numbers in brackets indicate percentages.

TABLE 66

Profile of High Pass-Percentage Institutions
(Master's degree)

	Sponsors									Kind		
	RCW	RCM	RCD	RC Total	PS	PU	P Total	S	Total	LA	TT	Other
30–39%	—	—	—	—	—	—	—	1 (50)	1 (3)	1 (3)	—	—
50–59%	—	—	—	—	—	1 (10)	1 (7)	—	1 (3)	1 (3)	—	—
60–69%	—	1 (17)	—	1 (6)	—	1 (10)	1 (7)	—	2 (6)	2 (6)	—	—
70–79%	—	—	1 (17)	1 (6)	—	2 (20)	2 (14)	1 (50)	4 (12)	4 (13)	—	—
80–89%	1 (20)	1 (17)	—	2 (11)	—	1 (10)	1 (7)	—	3 (9)	3 (9)	—	—
90–100%	4 (80)	4 (66)	5 (83)	18 (77)	4 (100)	5 (50)	9 (65)	—	22 (67)	21 (66)	1 (100)	—
Total	5	6	6	17	4	10	14	2	33	32	1	1

15

TABLE 66 (continued)

	Type			Founding date				Region		
	Male	Female	Co-ed.	Pre-1900	1901–1948	1949–1960	1961–1967	North	Center	South
30–39%	—	—	1 (6)	—	—	1 (14)	—	—	—	1 (4)
50–59%	—	—	1 (6)	—	1 (7)	—	—	—	1 (25)	—
60–69%	—	—	2 (11)	2 (15)	—	—	—	1 (17)	1 (25)	—
70–79%	1 (14)	—	3 (16)	3 (23)	1 (7)	—	—	—	—	4 (18)
80–89%	1 (14)	2 (25)	—	—	3 (24)	—	—	—	—	3 (13)
90–100%	5 (72)	6 (75)	11 (61)	8 (62)	8 (62)	6 (86)	—	5 (83)	2 (50)	15 (65)
Total	7	8	18	13	13	7	—	6	4	23

TABLE 66 (continued)

	Percentage of Christian staff						Number of students					
	Under 20	21–30	31–40	41–50	51–60	61+	Under 300	301–500	501–1,000	1,001–1,500	1,501–2,000	2,001+
30–39%	—	—	—	—	—	1 (6)	—	—	—	—	1 (17)	—
50–59%	1 (50)	—	—	—	—	—	—	—	—	—	—	1 (9)
60–69%	—	1 (33)	—	—	—	1(a) (6)	—	—	—	—	1 (17)	1 (9)
70–79%	—	—	—	1 (100)	1 (17)	2 (13)	—	—	—	1 (13)	1 (17)	2 (18)
80–89%	—	—	—	—	2 (33)	1 (6)	—	—	1 (25)	—	1 (17)	1 (9)
90–100%	1 (50)	2 (67)	5 (100)	—	3 (50)	11 (69)	3 (100)	1 (100)	3 (75)	7 (87)	2 (32)	6 (55)
Total	2	3	5	1	6	16	3	1	4	8	6	11

(a) 1 NA

TABLE 66 (concluded)

	Under 10	11–25	26–50	51–75	76–100	101+	No. of Jesuits	No. offering Ph.D.
			Library volumes per students					
30–39%	1 (14)	—	—	—	—	—	—	1 (9)
50–59%	—	1 (6)	—	—	—	—	—	—
60–69%	—	1 (6)	1 (17)	—	—	—	1 (25)	2 (18)
70–79%	2 (28)	1 (6)	1 (17)	—	—	—	—	1 (9)
80–89%	1 (14)	1 (6)	1 (17)	—	—	—	1 (25)	1 (9)
90–100%	3 (34)	14 (76)	3 (49)	1 (100)	—	1 (100)	2 (50)	6 (55)
Total	7	18	6	1	1	1	4	11

Numbers in brackets indicate percentages.

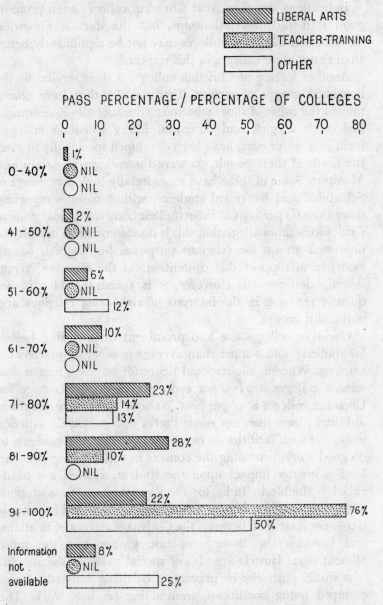

Figure 10. BACHELOR'S DEGREE PASS-PERCENTAGE IN CHRISTIAN COLLEGES (BY TYPE OF INSTITUTION)

Indications are, then, that Christian colleges often promote good staff-student relationships, but the data is somewhat uneven, and Christian colleges may not be significantly better than many other colleges in this respect.

Another feature of Christian colleges is their service to the depressed groups of society. Traditionally they have championed the cause of those who were educationally disenfranchised, such as girls and outcastes. Many Christian colleges, including newer ones, have been developed specifically to meet the needs of these people, as were the colleges in Assam and Manipur. Some of these have an especially high percentage of Scheduled and Backward students, with 7 colleges reporting more than 60 per cent of their student body from these groups. Critics sometimes allege that this is done in order to exploit the depressed groups for religious purposes, but there is scanty evidence to support this contention, as the abortive Niyogi investigation proved. However, it is a charge which is frequently renewed in the interests of right-wing religious and nationalist groups.

Christian colleges are also prominent in providing hostels for students, and a more than average number of quarters for teachers. Whereas the national figure for hostelers in arts and science colleges is 21·5 per cent, the overall percentage for Christian colleges is 31 per cent. Naturally, the mere provision of hostel places does not *ensure* that a college will do superior work, but such facilities do enhance the capacity of students to do good work, providing the context in which college life can have a greater impact upon the student. Hostels are particularly valuable in India for the development of associations and understandings between the various traditional communities — not least of all between the Christians and non-Christians, and between the lower economic groups and the more affluent ones. Hostels are also of special value to the student who would otherwise be prevented, by tiring daily travel and cramped living conditions, from doing his best work. The provision of more hostels has been a constant emphasis of the University Grants Commission and also of the recent Education Commission Report. The Education Commission recommends that 25 per cent of Bachelor's degree students should live in hostels, while the national average is presently half of that total. On this score, Christian colleges are taking the lead.

The University Grants Commission and the Education Commission both stress the importance of providing for more women's education. The Education Commission Report noted that 'shortages of educated women available for taking up positions of directional and organizational responsibilities in various professions and occupations . . . point to the need for special efforts to expand women's education at the college and university stage.'[1] The proportion of women students in the country has increased from 13 per cent in 1955 to about 21 per cent in 1966. But the Commission recommends that the percentage be increased to 33 per cent over the next ten years. Important strides have been made by both non-Christians and Christian colleges over the past several years in meeting the need for women's higher education. Thirty-five per cent of the students in Christian colleges are women, already beyond the target set by the Report for the next ten years, and the difference between the Christian and non-Christian institutions would be markedly greater were not the former included in the national average.

The Report argues that there are directional and organizational posts which need to be filled by women, but they have omitted the fundamental argument that women, as wives and mothers, impart important cultural and educational values to their families. Further, it is not at all clear that educated women are taking up these directional and organizational posts even when they are educated. Statistics on the wastage in education suggest that most women graduates are marginal to the employment market; women's education tends to be for consumption rather than an input into development. There are many educated women in the South, but traditional conceptions of the role of women in South Indian society make it difficult for even educated women to be brought effectively into the work force.

The Education Commission stresses the need for more science and fewer arts candidates. Arts students are more numerous for many reasons, among them is the fact that it costs more to provide facilities for science instruction, and many colleges have not been willing, or able, to make the necessary investment. Science education costs about Rs 375 per student, as compared with Rs 300 per student for arts candidates, as calculated for the period of the Third Plan. Compared with the national average, Christian colleges are training far more than their share of science students, with 38 per cent enrolled in arts and 48 per cent enrolled in science. On the national level, the percentage is reversed in favor of arts students, with 31 and 42 per cent respectively.[2] Were we to consider liberal arts colleges only, the percentages of the total would be higher, but the basic relationships between science and arts students would remain as described above. It is significant that no less than one-fourth of all science degree earners have studied in a Christian college.

Roman Catholic colleges, especially the men's and diocesan institutions, provide a relatively large number of places for science students, while Protestant colleges, especially those under single denominational control, are weaker in this respect. A further index of Christian college concern to develop science education is their heavy expenditure for fresh laboratory equipment. Over the past five years a great deal of money has been so invested. It is clear that Christian colleges are in the forefront of scientific and professional education. Some Christian college administrators are beginning to fear that there is now too much preoccupation with science and teaching, and too little attention to the humanities.

Christian colleges also stand out above the national average in expenditures per student. The Education Commission calculated that *per capita* student costs in arts and science colleges was Rs 231 per annum in 1950–1, but has gone up to Rs 328 in 1965–6.[3] It is expected that these expenditures will rise sharply during the next twenty years, with teacher costs bringing the largest increase.[4] While our figures are not complete, it appears that *per capita* annual expenditure in Christian colleges was Rs 459 for recurring expenditures. At a time when finance is probably the most difficult problem for Christian

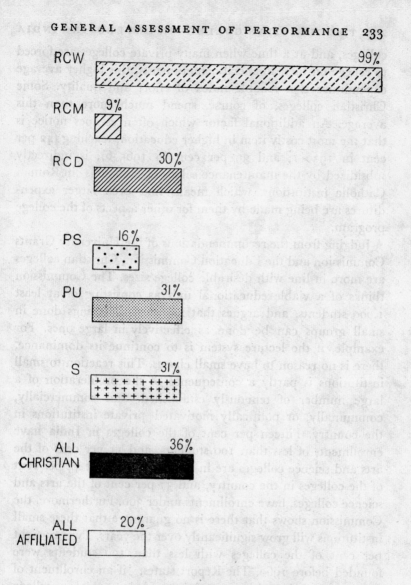

Figure II. WOMEN STUDENTS
IN AFFILIATED COLLEGES (BY SPONSOR)

colleges, and at a time when many private colleges are forced to renege on their financial commitments, this higher average expenditure is a reliable index of effort and quality. Some Christian colleges, of course, spend much more than this average. An additional factor which often escapes notice is that the most costly item in higher education, teaching (42 per cent in 1950–1, and 39 per cent in 1965–6), is indirectly subsidized by the maintenance salary of 'religious' in Roman Catholic institutions, which means that even larger expenditures are being made by them for other aspects of the college program.

Judging from the recommendations of the University Grants Commission and the Education Commission, Christian colleges are more in line with desirable college sizes. The Commission thinks of a viable educational unit as consisting of at least 1,000 students, and argues that many of the things done in small groups can be done as effectively in large ones. For example, if the lecture system is to continue its dominance, there is no reason to have small classes. This reaction to small institutions is partly a consequence of the proliferation of a large number of tenuously established, and commercially, communally, or politically motivated private institutions in the country. Fifteen per cent of the colleges in India have enrollments of less than 100 students, and 11 per cent of the arts and science colleges are in this range. Almost 44 per cent of the colleges in the country, and 37 per cent of the arts and science colleges, have enrollments under 300. Furthermore, the Commission shows that there is no guarantee that these small institutions will grow significantly over the years. Twenty-eight per cent of the colleges with less than 100 students were founded before 1960. The Report states, 'if an enrollment of 500 is regarded as the very minimum below which a college may tend to be uneconomic and inefficient, about 60 per cent of the affiliated colleges are below this level.'[5] The conception of what makes an economically and educationally viable college is changing.

Christian colleges tend to be larger than non-Christian institutions. While violating the Lindsay Commission norms,

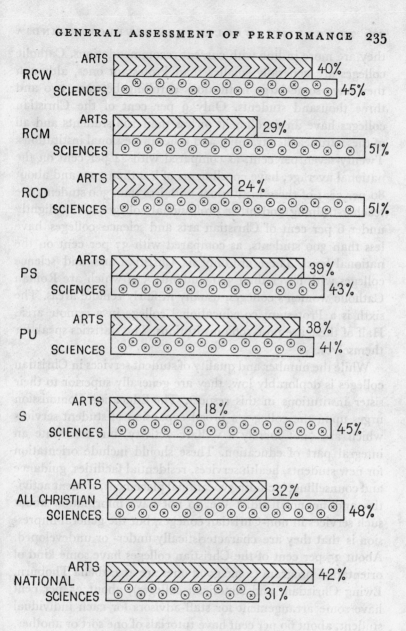

Figure 12. ARTS AND SCIENCES:
ENROLLMENT IN PERCENTAGES (BY SPONSOR)

they are more in line with current recommendations. Catholic colleges are generally smaller than Protestant ones, although they have some large institutions enrolling between two and three thousand students. Only 9 per cent of the Christian colleges have an enrollment of less than 100 students and all of these are teacher-training and other professional institutions. Twenty-seven per cent, as compared with 44 per cent on the national average, have enrollments of less than 300, and about 80 per cent of these institutions with less than 300 students are teacher-training and other professional colleges. Only slightly under 6 per cent of Christian arts and science colleges have less than 300 students, as compared with 37 per cent on the national level. There are only six Christian arts and science colleges with fewer than 300 students, 5 of which are Roman Catholic women's colleges, usually in fairly remote areas. The sixth is a Protestant co-educational college in a remote area. Half of these are post-1960 institutions. The statistics speak for themselves.

While the number and quality of student services in Christian colleges is deplorably low, they are generally superior to their sister institutions in this respect. The Education Commission urges upon the colleges a broad expansion of student services which are 'not merely a welfare activity, but constitute an integral part of education. These should include orientation for new students, health services, residential facilities, guidance and counselling, including vocational placement, student activities and financial aid.'[6] We do not have information about such services in non-Christian colleges, but the general impression is that they are characteristically under- or undeveloped. About 25 per cent of the Christian colleges have some kind of orientation program (some good ones are at Isabella Thoburn, Ewing Christian, and American colleges), about 35 per cent have some arrangement for staff-advisors for each individual student, about 60 per cent have tutorials of one sort or another, about 75 per cent have special English improvement programs (less than 30 per cent have special Hindi improvement programs!), about 75 per cent have doctors or nurses on campus. On the other hand, only 6 per cent have some

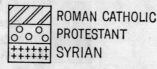

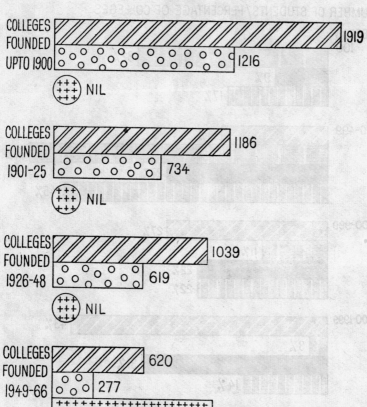

Figure 13. AVERAGE NUMBER OF STUDENTS IN COLLEGES
(BY DATE OF FOUNDING)

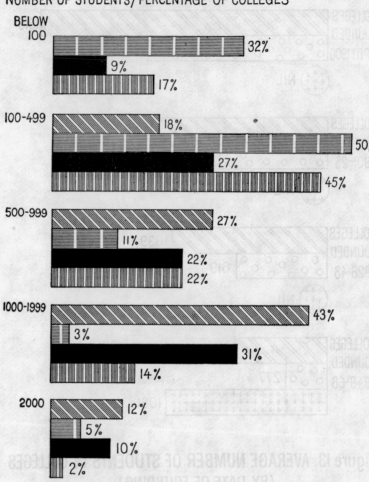

Figure 14. INSTITUTIONAL SIZE: CHRISTIAN AND NATIONAL

kind of vocational or aptitude testing (Ewing Christian College is developing very good testing instruments and programs for this kind of work), 6 per cent have some kind of psychological tests, 13 per cent are developing placement and vocational guidance programs, and 20 per cent have some guidance and counselling service.

Christian colleges also tend to have superior facilities. Many Christian colleges are endowed with large campuses (70 per cent of them have more than 6 acres; 44 per cent have more than 15 acres; 30 per cent have more than 25 acres), reflecting the fact that they were sometimes established when more land was available. It also reflects the fact that those responsible have made an important place for playing fields, hostels, general extracurricular affairs, and potential development. Christian colleges have made a large investment in the physical plants, which is reflected not only in acreage but also in the generally good quality and maintenance of buildings, and the grooming of the campus.

Other facilities are also good, such as the laboratories and libraries. These are strong features not only in the older institutions, but also in many of the newer ones. It is unfortunate that more books are not available, but considering the general situation of colleges in India, facilities at Christian colleges are unusually good. Whether they will remain significantly better, as their own funds dwindle and as government and other private colleges receive heavier investments, is a matter of conjecture. One would hope that other colleges would come as quickly as possible up of at least the same standard.

Extracurricular activities are also strong. On most Christian arts and science college campuses there are large numbers of clubs, athletic teams and extracurricular activities. We have noted above that several kinds of student responsibility and initiative need to be developed — student courts, newspapers, etc. — but there are many programs nevertheless. Athletic programs are often strong, resulting from a conscious policy of blending physical exercise with intellectual effort. These extracurricular programs give depth and fullness to the

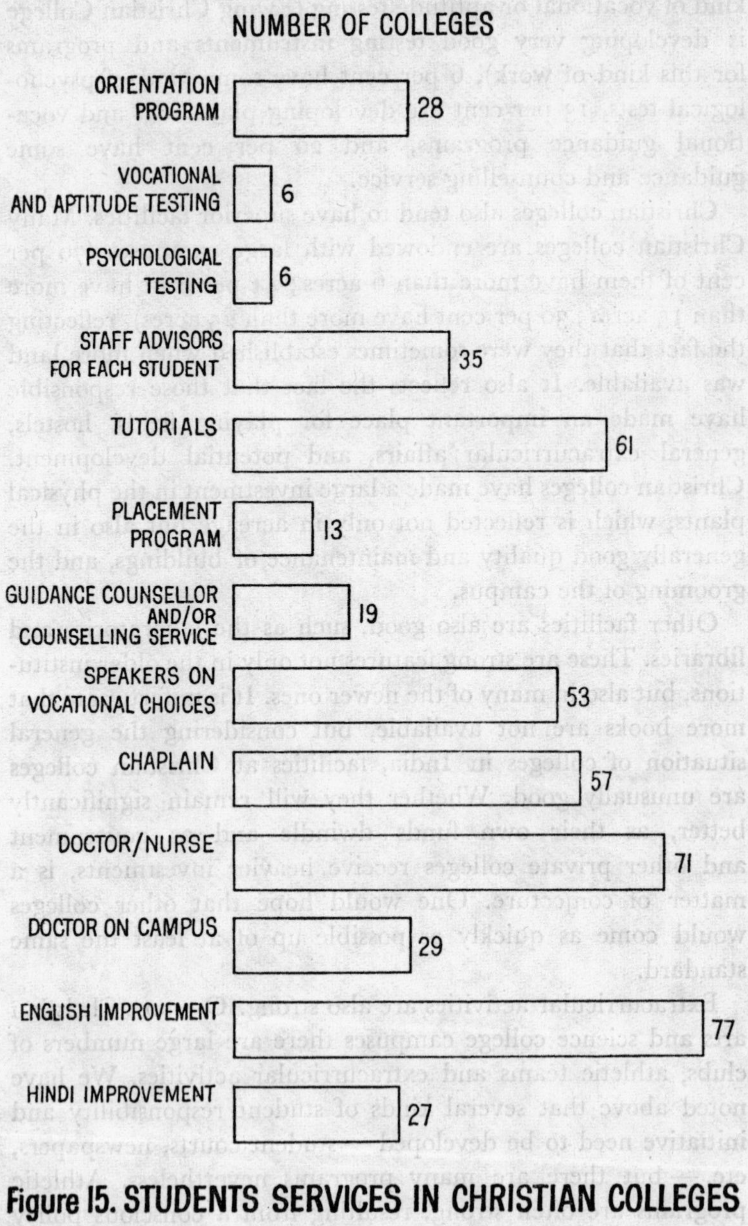

NUMBER OF COLLEGES

ORIENTATION PROGRAM — 28

VOCATIONAL AND APTITUDE TESTING — 6

PSYCHOLOGICAL TESTING — 6

STAFF ADVISORS FOR EACH STUDENT — 35

TUTORIALS — 61

PLACEMENT PROGRAM — 13

GUIDANCE COUNSELLOR AND/OR COUNSELLING SERVICE — 19

SPEAKERS ON VOCATIONAL CHOICES — 53

CHAPLAIN — 57

DOCTOR/NURSE — 71

DOCTOR ON CAMPUS — 29

ENGLISH IMPROVEMENT — 77

HINDI IMPROVEMENT — 27

Figure 15. STUDENTS SERVICES IN CHRISTIAN COLLEGES

college experience, contributing to an *élan* which carries over into the years after college.

Christian colleges are increasingly strong in their vocational emphases. Since Independence about one-third of the new colleges under Christian sponsorship have had a vocational orientation. The importance of teacher-training colleges, for example, is pointed up by the inferior qualifications of many of the primary and secondary school teachers in the country. The Commission Report noted that in 1950–1 only 10 per cent of those teaching in lower primary grades, and only 47 per cent of those teaching in higher primary grades had the minimum qualifications (secondary school certificate). By 1955–66 the percentage had risen to 51 and 60 per cent respectively. The situation in secondary schools is equally difficult. Further, these untrained teachers are not the older ones, but large sections of the younger teacher group. The situation is not likely to be radically improved in the near future, particularly with the large new increases in primary and secondary school enrollment expected over the next few years.

One disconcerting thing about the new Christian teacher-training colleges, however, is that 80 per cent of those founded since Independence are in Kerala and Madras, where already 93 and 97 per cent of the teachers are fully qualified. States like Assam and West Bengal, with only half the number of trained teachers in lower and higher primary schools, have not had any new Christian teachers' colleges; indeed, there is only one full-fledged Christian teacher-training college in these states.

There are a few other initiatives to develop professional education, but most of these do not consist in the establishment of new institutions. At Stella Maris College, Madras, a new course in social work has been added to the college program. The four post-Independence professional schools, other than teacher-training, are Nirmala Niketan (social work, Bombay), Mar Athanasius College of Engineering (Kerala), St. John's Medical College (Bangalore), and Loyola Institute of Sociology (Trivandrum)— three out of four in the South.

Christian colleges continue to experiment and innovate, even though under difficult financial limitations and university regulations. We continue to think that most colleges have not been imaginative enough, either for their own institutions or in their relationships with others. Nevertheless a few examples will demonstrate that some Christian colleges are trying bold and unorthodox innovations: Madras Christian College has just completed an impressive self-study and is preparing to launch a development program; Ahmednagar College's experiments in community involvement have already been mentioned; Stella Maris College, Madras, is developing an impressive fine arts program, concentrating on India's culture and art forms; St. Xavier's College, Bombay, has one of the finest biological science collections and programs in the country; Loyola College, Madras, has developed a school of social psychology and social work with something of an empirical orientation; Baring Union College, Batala, is developing a program of Sikh studies; at Madras Christian College a Hindu studies program is being planned in honour of President Radhakrishnan; Isabella Thoburn College has worked out an impressive orientation program; Ewing Christian College has built up a promising and high quality program for educational testing and to be used not only on its own campus, but on others as well; Union Christian College, Barapani, is experimenting with a student self-help program; Hislop College, Nagpur, developed one of the first schools of journalism in the country; Xavier Labor Relations Institute (not officially a college), Jamshedpur, is working on studies and training in that field; Christian Medical College, Vellore, is engaged in truly exciting remedial and preventive health work in Madras State; Union Christian College, Alwaye, is a major center for post-graduate university work in the physical sciences and has a very interesting approach to revolving college administration on a non-denominational basis; St. Stephen's College, Delhi, continues to have one of the most impressive tutorial programs in the country; Wilson College, Bombay, has an exciting program of faculty retreats to discuss current issues in education, both within and outside of the college. These are examples that come readily to mind; obviously others could be cited.

Finally, an intangible, but notable, feature of many Christian colleges is the spirit of dedication and deep motivation among many of their staff. Among many, there is a concern for student welfare which is grounded in religious commitment. It would be ridiculous to claim that this is true of all individual teachers, and equally true of all colleges. But when rapacious practices are so characteristic of many private colleges in the country, and when so many institutions are in the business of higher education as a commercial venture, the clear service motivations of most Christian institutions gives them a mark of special quality. This desire for service makes important contributions to the staff-student relations, the provision of suitable equipment, financing, and even staff-student relationships — indeed, to the whole life and character of the college. It also shows itself clearly in the open and questioning manner in which many Christian colleges are planning their future — where time and again the dominant question is not self-preservation, but how to become more effective in public service. The Madras Christian College self-study, the Wilson College staff retreats on national integration, the discussions of the Consultation of Christian college principals on the Education Commission Report, are all examples of this deep concern. Government has often recognized this concern and called upon Christian institutions to pioneer in programs of social service. This trust in Christian colleges' excellence gives them greater responsibility than those not yet so fully attuned to national service.

We have not attempted here to give an exhaustive list of the strengths of Christian colleges, and it has not been our purpose, basically, to make a case for the Christian college. We have tried to get a broad general perspective on the work of the colleges, mostly in connection with the Education Commission Report. While we believe the Report excellent in most respects, we do not concern with all of its recommendations. There are other strengths, or possible strengths of the Christian colleges on which we would have liked to comment, but for which there is no significant or reliable comparative data. We have shown that in many respects Christian colleges are among the

244 THE CHRISTIAN COLLEGE IN DEVELOPING INDIA

strongest in the nation. That there is still much room for improvement is our next concern.

2. WEAK FEATURES AND OPPORTUNITIES

Despite these evidences of strength, however, many opportunities for improvement are open. Here we are not intent upon making a complete list, but to illustrate the general situation. Again, there is some duplication here of material already discussed, but here in briefer form.

Perhaps the most crucial need is for the clearer specification of goals. These goals need to be both concrete for specific situations, and cast into a broad or integrated general framework. At present stated goals tend to be nebulous and diffuse, offering little concrete guidance for hard administrative decisions which must be made over the next ten or fifteen years. There is a tendency to assume that vaguely phrased goals, like 'social service', justify and give direction and life to a college. Each college should evolve, as a top priority responsibility, a clear idea of what it wants to achieve in the specific locale and milieu in which it is set. Thinking about the actual social situation in which the college is located will help a college become a more effective instrument of service. Without priorities for specific kinds of action, a college will become a blunted and ineffectual instrument.

But even before these concrete objectives can be finalized, and in the midst of trying to finalize them, more fundamental questions about the nature and purpose of Christian colleges need to be tackled. To what extent are Christian colleges intended to be instruments of evangelism, and what kind of evangelism? To what extent are Christian colleges connected with, and extensions of, the Churches which they represent and in the midst of whom they are set? What is the relationship between evangelism and disinterested service? What, if any, is the special obligation of the Christian college to the members of the existing Christian community? What should be the relationship of a Christian college to national development? These questions are all related to one another in a fundamental sense, meaning that decisions about one involve tacit decisions about others. We would argue strongly, on the basis of evidence from our study, that perhaps the fundamental weakness of Christian colleges is that they cannot give clear and convincing (even to themselves) answers to this question.

This kind of broad-gauged and fundamental thinking can seldom be done effectively by single institutions because they tend to be preoccupied with local problems. Studies in single institutions might get them off the diving board and into the water. But there needs to be much more communication between and among institutions — perhaps starting with Christian colleges but gradually including others — about what they are doing and what they should be doing. This could pave the way for more co-ordinated action. There are instances where several colleges are within the same city and within a few kilometers of one another, but with little or no interaction between them, save that several colleges may have considerable overlapping in the Boards of Governors. In re-thinking goals and in re-structuring action there is much to commend a co-operative and, if possible, ecumenical approach.

Another glaring weakness of Christian colleges is their inattention to records and empirical information about their operations. This dearth of information is most noticeable in relation to finances, but is true in most other areas as well. Admittedly, staffs are small and much overworked in tiny offices, and it *is* a healthy sign that most Indians have not been poisoned with the passion for statistics which afflicts so many in the West. Yet it is clearly impossible to make sophisticated evaluations and mature plans without a basic network of systematically organized data about the evolution and present condition of fundamental aspects of the college. Perhaps it would be useful for a group of colleges to devise the same basic information patterns so that there could be relatively easy exchange of information.

Administration in the Christian colleges is definitely a weak link, notwithstanding the several competent, and the many deeply dedicated, principals in Christian colleges. Most principals have no penchant for administration, and no particular training. Most are heavily overworked, yet tend to centralize responsibilities in their own hands. It could be of great service to the colleges if a series of summer training institutes or some other type of administrative training program were inaugurated. And it should help, further, if some system whereby trained and efficient college administrators could work for a short time, on location, with new college principals, helping them to develop their own administrative skills.

We have contended that Christian colleges probably have superior staff-student relationships. In general, however, the talents of the teachers are not sufficiently used. Too many teachers are permitted to remain peripheral and increasingly indifferent to the college's total life. It is vaguely hoped that they will be responsible and do superior work, but they are given little incentive to improve themselves, aside from exhortations. There is hardly a place for them to do serious work, except perhaps in libraries, and often no suitable place even to meet students. Opportunities for refresher work are limited, and usually too costly; participation in professional associations is not actively promoted. Despite these limitations caused by lack of financial resources, we feel that more important in enervating teachers is their divorce from the important decision-making machinery of the college. This is further exacerbated by the fact that the college itself is cut off from the centers of power at the university. A sense of creative responsibility can develop more readily if teachers are given a genuine opportunity to influence, or even take, decisions. Too often, in the Christian college as well as in others, the teacher is something of a second-class citizen.

In line with this, but as a separate point, we feel that new entrants work under particularly difficult handicaps. All young teachers are thrust into very difficult situations, but in Indian colleges it is particularly difficult. Teachers have seldom any training in the philosophy or techniques of education; they are often hardly separated from their students in years or degrees; they will have no voice in whether the student finally passes the examination or not; except insofar as he is able to inspire or guide; the examination system and traditions of education in the country almost totally deprive him of a sense of engagement with students and creative dealing with the subject because it is not *his* ideas and insights which pay off on the examination. If more needs to be done to orient the student to college life, a great deal more also needs to be done to initiate the neophyte teacher into the profession. Why is it that fresh teachers often get the biggest classes, the heaviest loads, and the drudgery responsibilities? Is it fair? And is it calculated to make the teacher a strong teacher, and the college a strong community?

Christian colleges also tend to be ingrown and localized, and there are obvious reasons for this. There are obviously strong arguments for making concerted efforts to break out of a narrow geographic and religious base — fewer teachers who are graduates of the college, more students and teachers from other parts of the country, more vigorous efforts to attract Muslim students and teachers, concerted efforts to expand the kinds of background experience in the Boards of Governors. These are but a few possible ways of expanding the value and intellectual horizons of the college.

What is the Christian college's role in national integration? With their particular ethos and sociological position Christian colleges should be in an enviable position to promote national integration. A fundamental obstacle to India's development is the persistence of highly volatile, deeply divisive communal feelings rooted in caste, race, religion, and area of the country. These divisions and frictions are probably as crucial as are any economic impediments to India's development. It is all the more urgent that a Christian college, which in the mind of many people symbolizes separateness and exclusiveness, and for some a threat to the unity of India, should adopt open and clear policies of fostering national integration. In their life they should stand for an inclusive community of mutual respect and mutual search for truth and fulfillment. Christian colleges could recruit students and staff from all over India ; they could use hostel facilities and staff residences for the promotion of genuine community ; they could re-think their policy of opposition to non-Christian religious expressions on campus. In short, they should strive to demonstrate in their daily life and in their organization that a religiously-oriented college does not have to be communally divisive. National integration is an area of overwhelming need, and one to which Christian colleges can play a distinctive and leading part, but there is painfully little aliveness to this challenge and possibility.

Christian colleges are deplorably weak in their philosophical and religious training. We have already noted some of the reasons for this. It is a thorny question. Yet it is of great urgency that this kind of instruction be given more scope, both for the spiritual maturity of individuals who pass through and work in the college, as well as for activating the dialogue between the religious traditions of the country — so important to the nation's self-identity. Madras Christian College and Baring Union College have tried to strengthen philosophy and religion. What is needed, however, is not only centers or special departments for philosophical and religious studies, but a permeation of the curriculum with at least some philosophical questioning. This is an instance where Christian educators should formulate a position and develop a strategy for changing existing university practices; they cannot afford to be timid on this point.

It is not useful to review the religious situation on Christian college campuses, nor to make specific recommendations for improving it. However, we cannot avoid remarking that one of the shockingly unsuccessful aspects of Christian college life is the religious program itself. Unfortunately there is not much to be learned from most Christian colleges in the West. It is small wonder that few graduates of Christian colleges feel religious vocations a compelling option. Having made these negative remarks, it is frustrating not to make positive suggestions. One thing that must be energetically sought, however, is a formulation of philosophical and religious issues in terms of how they impinge on the social and moral questions arising out of students' daily life and contemporary social situations. One gets the feeling that a hiatus exists between theological formulations and concrete personal experiences. Perhaps the most important reformulation of the religious program will come through the sponsorship of imaginative discussion-type

1 RAISING MONEY FOR NEEDY CAUSES
2 WORK EXPERIENCE WITH ACADEMIC
3 TRAINING COURSES AND REFRESHERS
4 NIGHT SCHOOL
5 DEMONSTRATIONS PROGRAMS FOR COMMUNITY
6 PROFESSIONAL AND VOCATIONAL MEETINGS
7 VOLUNTARY SOCIAL SERVICE
8 ENCOURAGE STUDENTS ASSIST LOCAL COMMUNITY ORGANIZATION
9 STALL CONSULTATION
10 FOCUSSING ACADEMIC WORK ON INDIAN PROBLEMS AND STUDIES
11 STALL RESEARCH NATIONAL ISSUES
12 INVITING COMMUNITY TO COLLEGE EVENTS

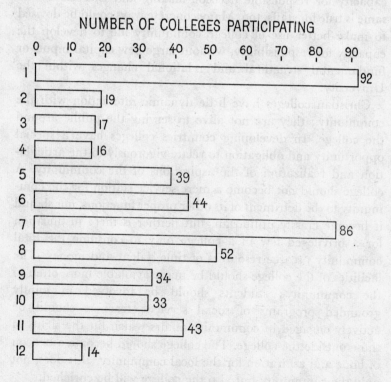

NUMBER OF COLLEGES PARTICIPATING

Figure 16. COMMUNITY SERVICES

programs, later evolving, for some, into more formal and ritualistic expressions.

Christian colleges do appallingly little to train students and staff for responsible citizenship. In India, college is one of the few places where this kind of experience is so pregnant with possibilities. Most students come from traditional home and community patterns which minimize private decisions; many will return to that pattern of relationship in their family and job after the college years. A democratic India needs young people with decision-making capacity, but there is little done in the colleges — from syllabus, classrooms and examinations to extracurricular and living conditions — to cultivate the capacity for responsible decision-making and execution. The same is true for staffs, too. Many concrete ways could be devised to make better use of college community life to develop the capacity for responsibility, without large new capital inputs or fundamental structural and relational changes within the University.

Christian colleges have little dynamic interaction with the community; they are not alive to serving the public around the college. In developing countries colleges have a special opportunity and obligation to relate vigorously to the articulation and realization of the aspirations of the community. A college should not become a mere service station for the community to the detriment of its other proper functions, nor should it become crassly utilitarian. But neither is there justification for a privileged few in a college only to consume the total community's scarce resources of time, talent and money. The facilities of the college should be made available more often to the community; students should be involved in jointly grounded programs of social service; teachers should be actively engaged in community affairs which lift the sights of those outside the college. The college should become a beacon of hope and aspiration for the local community. If it does, not only the community but also the college will be enriched.

We have alluded to the potential role that Christian colleges could play in educational reform; they have been weak in developing this role. What is needed is for a group of colleges

— more than just Christian ones — to identify the acute and particular problem areas which are log-jams in the whole educational complex. If a group of colleges could agree to work on a limited number of specific fulcral issues, and then develop a common strategy of attacking these problems, they could be instrumental in getting flexibility and action into the whole field of university education. What is needed most is a concentration on limited and well-defined objectives — changes at structurally critical points.

The Education Commission also has urged that special efforts be made to develop empirical social sciences, recognizing that this is a deplorably weak area in all Indian higher education. No other area of study is potentially more explosive, or creative, in the Indian environment if it is grounded in a dedication to be relevant and to serve the whole country. Should not Christian colleges pioneer in this development in view of their concern for the social and human sciences, and in view of their commitment to first-class education?

Finally, Christian colleges are obliged to expand their services to students, especially because many enter college at fifteen or sixteen years, and because there are almost no other institutional sources of help and guidance. That this is an acute need is evident from the shocking wastage in education — the number of drop-outs and failures is more than actually pass in any given year ; graduates not finding employment for months or years ; or graduates taking employment which does not use their skills. Some illuminating studies have been made on these problems.[7] While about half of the Christian colleges provide some sort of orientation program for students, few offer vocational guidance, psychological and aptitude tests, and placement services. Admission tests are probably never administered. If records about the students are kept at all, they are usually cursory. Counselling services are unprofessional and unsystematic. Several colleges do have some kind of tutorial program, but most of these are in a narrow academic structure and do not develop into personal guidance on vocational matters. It is clear that a meaningful service to students needs much more effort and imagination.

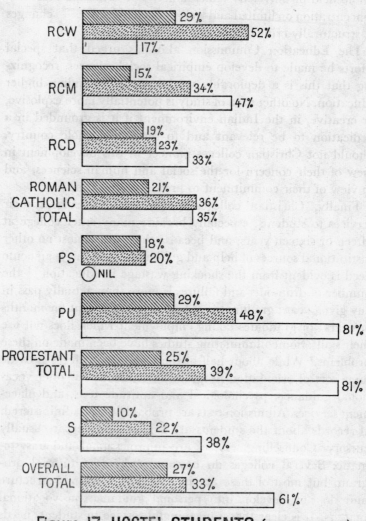

Figure 17. HOSTEL STUDENTS (BY SPONSOR)

These are but a few of the many ways in which Christian colleges may become alive to their opportunities for service and for contributing significantly to Indian national development. The colleges are in difficult financial straits and injections of financial support can be of critical importance in properly selected key situations. But it is also clear that much can be done even without big new financial investments and even without radical changes in the structure of university education, important as such changes are. Major gains can be made through imaginative leadership, pooling of information and efforts, training in administrative competence, fuller involvement of staff in leadership decisions and responsibilities. Christian colleges must be dedicated to relevant education and to excellent education. To be relevant and excellent demands a long-overdue and deep questioning of just what the Christian college has to offer in concrete situations.

VII

TOWARDS THE FUTURE

CHRISTIAN colleges are not in a vacuum; they exist amidst the pressures of other institutions and social forces. What they are is determined by not only what they would like to be, but by what others think they should be. Colleges are not abstractions, but concrete realities forged in the interplay of aspirations on the one hand, and specific situations and pressures on the other. Many of these pressures are beyond the power of individual or groups of colleges to control, although they may influence them. But neither is a college a passive clay that can be formed and moulded at the will of those on the outside; it can and should be an active agent in the interplay of forces, thus helping to define and determine its own roles, and contributing to the formation of the character of other institutions as well. We have argued throughout that Christian colleges can play this creative role only if they have articulate and clear goals, both in terms of general principles and concrete achievements to be made in particular locale. We have argued that there is much muddled thinking about overall principles and specific localized objectives. Straightening out this muddle should have the highest priority.

We believe that this fuzzy thinking about goals can be overcome, not so much by elaborating a new theology or philosophy of Christian higher education in India, but by considering the functional relationships with the various 'publics' to which Christian colleges must relate: the government (i.e. the *Indian* government), the Church (the *Indian* Christian community, primarily), the rest of the educational system, the national and local communities to be served, the leaders and teachers of the colleges, and the students. We would put 'finances' also as one of the publics simply because it is so influential in what a college seeks to do and can do. We contend that reflection on these relationships will help to force a more dynamic and relevant theology or philosophy for the Christian college in

254

India. Furthermore, for practical as well as ideological reasons we believe that reflection about how colleges should relate to these other institutions should be done not only by individual colleges (but done by them, at any rate) but by groups of colleges having different denominational discussion — to be a catalyst — and not to propose answers. Answers from the outside would likely be wrong, but more certainly would remain dormant.

Christian colleges and government

First, let us consider the government. Many Christians fear that they will lose the right to run schools and colleges. They think they detect favoritism toward non-Christian colleges and actual adverse pressures, especially in matters of finance. Although there is actually much to give them hope and courage, particularly in positions taken by Central Government bodies, there is a tendency for insecure Christians to be hypersensitive to anything that appears critical of, or inimical to, the Christian community. This defensiveness may have advantages in keeping the Christian community alert to potential problem areas, but it exacts a heavy price, and tends to be self-defeating. It fortifies the existing belief among some non-Christians that Christians are reluctant or equivocal in their support of the government. For example, Christians were quite critical of the Sri Prakasa Report on moral and religious instruction in colleges. While some of these reservations were well-grounded, such reactions, often played-up by the militant nationalist and Hindu groups, reinforce the impression that Christians are exclusivistic and not fully Indian.

There is among many churchmen a fear that pressure — political or financial — will force the closing of Christian institutions. However, there are three bulwarks against the closing of Christian institutions: constitutional, practical, and social. As for the first, India is an avowed secular state, with constitutional guarantees for the freedom of religious groups within the state. In relation to the colleges, the important constitutional provisions are the following Articles:

Article 15 (i):

'The State shall not discriminate against any citizen on grounds only of religion, race, caste, sex, place of birth or any of them.'

Article 16, No. 2:

'No citizen shall, on grounds only of religion, race, caste, sex, descent, place of birth, residence . . . be eligible for, or discriminated against in respect of any employment or office under the State.'

Article 19:

'All citizens shall have the right to freedom of speech and expression, to form associations or unions; to acquire, hold, dispose of property; and to practise a profession, or to carry on any occupation, trade or business.'

Article 26:

'Subject to public order, morality and health, every religious denomination or any section thereof shall have the right: (a) to establish and maintain institutions for religious and charitable purposes; (b) to manage its own affairs in matters of religion; (c) to own and acquire movable and immovable property; and (d) to administer such property in accordance with the law.'

Article 30, No. 1:

'All minorities, whether based on religion or language, shall have the right to establish and administer educational institutions of their choice.'

No. 3:

'The state shall not, in granting aid to educational institutions, discriminate against any educational institution on the ground that it is under the management of a minority, whether based on religion or language.'

These are clear constitutional guarantees for the freedom of Christians to run their own schools and colleges.

In addition there is a practical argument. Christian colleges are a sizeable portion of the total higher education effort (5 per cent of the institutions and 10 per cent of the student bodies). At the primary and secondary levels they are also very active. While most of the money for running these colleges comes from fees and government, there are sizeable additional inputs, teaching and money, from specifically Christian sources, some of it from abroad (it has been recently estimated in Parliament that Christian groups import Rs 30 crores per year, or about $40,000,000, in hard currency) for all types of Christian-sponsored programs in the country. Furthermore, it would be difficult to justify shutting down Christian colleges but no other private colleges, and all private colleges together comprise 85 per cent of the affiliated colleges in the country. To assume responsibility for all of these would impose a very heavy additional financial and administrative burden on government.

The social consideration is that, despite the numerous attacks against Christians and Christian institutions (for example, the Niyogi Committee), the general populace in most areas of the country, and dominant elements in the leadership of the country, could be counted on to oppose such an anti-Christian move. Christian colleges have a fine reputation — so fine that in some places there is considerable pressure from non-Christian sources to establish new Christian colleges — and it is widely believed, or recognized, that to permit government to take over Christian schools and colleges would impoverish education and threaten other private institutions as well. Enlightened public opinion supports the continuation of Christian colleges, and this is likely to remain a deterrent to extremist groups even in a time of resurgent and militant right-wing Hinduism.

Notwithstanding these constitutional and practical guarantees, Christians often feel defensive and threatened, and there is scattered evidence to lend credence to their fears. Some allege discrimination against them for the better government positions, that their children are not given equal opportunities in the government-run schools and colleges, in either seats or scholarships, that their institutions are not supported in proportion to their merit. Churches are very occasionally burdened; religious sensibilities are sometimes offended; some newspapers do print anti-Christian articles; certain political leaders do harangue against the Christian community; there are party platforms which attack the very existence of the Christian community; there are efforts to change the Constitution to make India a Hindu state; there are unwarranted and sometimes vitriolic attacks against the Christians even for their good work — as in the 1966-7 food crisis. It is difficult to overlook these attacks, scattered as they may be; the Christian community in India is tiny, and it can never completely forget the spectacle of recent religious turmoil between Muslims and Hindus.

One area where Government policy is frequently criticized by Christians relates to visas granted to missionary workers. In the post-Independence period the Government has stringently curtailed the number of foreign workers under church auspices, whether they are specifically evangelists or not. Some have argued that the Constitutional freedom to propagate the religion of their choice applies only to Indians, while others wish to change the Constitution itself. Pothacamury showed that while the number of approved requests for visas for Roman Catholics declined between 1947 and 1956, between 1956 and 1960 there was a dramatic reversal of the trend. Whereas in 1956 only 10 visas were granted (with 14 refused and 21 pending), in 1960, up to October, 128 visas had been granted (with 50 refusals and 12 pending).[1] On the Protestant side, Government has urged churches to channel visa requests through the National Christian Council, thus helping the Government to assess the various entry requests. But the National Christian Council is itself sometimes subjected to attack because it depends on overseas support for more than 90 per cent of its operating budget, although it has an Indian staff.

Since 1960 there seems to have been a hardening of the Government position on visas, as also on financial support from outside the country. This stiffening was accelerated by the results of the 1967 election which greatly weakened the power and influence of the Congress Party and dramatically strengthened the traditionally right-wing Hindu groups. It is probable that anti-Christian sentiments and activities may intensify. As I write these lines, there is rumor that the Government has made a firm policy not to renew visas for any foreigners working in India for the church, which would mean that within a year the work of many Christian groups in India would be radically altered, and some of the financial support might be withheld. The factual truth or falsity of the rumor is perhaps not as important to our argument as the fact that many Christians feel it to be true.

In the Education Commission Report itself there is some equivocation on the role of private institutions in the total educational picture. The Report acknowledges that some 'private education has played an important role in the development of education in modern India, [and] that a large proportion of our good institutions are in the private sector ... the State should ... make all possible use of the assistance that can come from the private sector for the development of education.'[2] But it would be a 'mistake to show any over-dependence on private enterprise which is basically uncertain; private enterprise can only have a limited and minor role.' As for those institutions which receive financial support from the State, 'these should be gradually assimilated with the system of public education.'[3] Such statements raise many questions and fears among Christians, many of whom think of their institutions as a necessary protection of the Christian community against the encroachments of the non-Christian majority.

If these fears are expressed about the Central Government, they are frequently felt much more keenly on the state level, where the churches and their institutions are subject to more severe local and parochial pressures. In some states, where Christians are an extremely small minority (such as Madhya Pradesh, Bihar, Uttar Pradesh, Jammu and Kashmir), these pressures often are felt directly and personally. Because states are responsible for education within their boundaries, Christian institutions are particularly vulnerable to such pressures where they may exist. When the Communist government assumed power in Kerala in 1961, it tried to undermine the churches' influence in the schools, but the attempt 'boomeranged' for several reasons, not the least important of which was the size and influence of the church in the state. In other states, however, the churches are too small to wield this kind of power.

Parel makes this point strongly in his assessment of the churches' position in India, noting that in the centers of political influence, Christianity — numerically, psychologically, institutionally — counts for practically nothing. The areas of Christian strength are not the centers of political power.

Given these hard realities, the churches need to work on at least three major points.

1. They must articulate a conception of society, and the State as an expression of that society, which not only tolerates secular pluralism, but which accepts it as the basis of meaningful community in the modern era.

2. They must develop as cogently as possible a philosophy for Christian institutions, and especially educational institutions of certain types, in such a society. This *raison d'être* should be not only in terms of broad theoretical principles, but also including well-reasoned guidelines for what kinds of education Christians should sponsor and where they do not intend to make an effort. What are the reasons and conditions for Christians' involvement in certain kinds of education, and not in others? If Christians in India could clarify this question they would not only be able to enunciate operational guidelines, but would not feel so threatened at every new initiative of the state. Indeed, they could rejoice if and when the state system of education becomes so comprehensive and so good that by its very quality it poses a threat to the status and continuation of the Christian schools and colleges.

3. They need to evolve effective organizational means for focussing issues and concerns, and to make these concerns felt in the corridors of power.

We are not talking here about vague new organizations of unity and verbal collaboration, which are often more an admission of weakness and defeat than a reflection of inner vitality. Organizations frequently become substitutes for creative response to threats and tension. What is needed is *prismatic* organizations, located in the centers of influence and power, which can focus the diffused light of the churches in the country into heat and light in the right places at the right times. The impression given is that the churches' presence has been sporadic, often focussing only on issues which affect its life directly, and usually negative and reactive. This kind of half-hearted and unsustained effort can have little impact.

Christian colleges and the university

Affiliated colleges are at the mercy of the university, and the state government behind the university. Much of what the college does is determined far from the college and by people who have little first-hand and detailed knowledge of what the college is doing. Important responsibilities, like examinations, hiring and dismissal policies, are all set by the university. Possibly, autonomous college status will be awarded some of the better Christian colleges, but most of them are likely to remain under the aegis of the university for a long time to come. Therefore it is realistic to think primarily in those terms.

It bears repetition that Christian colleges should discover and support reforms being urged by such educational bodies as the University Grants Commission and the Inter-University Board. While not all proposals can be supported, until now there has not been even an active policy of discovering what is being discussed, and participating as directly as possible in these high-level discussions. Studious awareness of current movements and proposals should not be motivated by a narrow concern to protect the Christian colleges, but by dedication to elevate the whole educational enterprise. Many college administrators have been so preoccupied with local problems that they have not taken time to understand issues on state or national levels. There are, of course, a few principals who serve on national teams of educators, and who are thoroughly conversant with national and state-wide educational issues. But there is a general tendency to see policies only in terms of whether it promotes or threatens a particular institution, or Christian institutions as a group.

Involvement in the life of the university is also of critical importance. Many reforms suggested from the Center are blocked before implementation in the different universities. Some of the most laudable educational reform proposals are stymied at the state and university level for lack of concerted effort and local pressure to put them into practice. It is conceivable, even probable, that the Education Commission's recommendation about autonomous colleges will either not be carried out, or will be emasculated by other than quality considerations in the selection of colleges for autonomous status. All educators concerned with quality reform need to be vigorously connected to the life and politics of the university, and colleges should actively encourage the principals and teachers to this kind of involvement. This will be more difficult for remote colleges than for those in the university centers, but also more important in many respects. We are not advocating a specifically Christian lobby; we are concerned more to mobilize all parties interested in quality college and university education to make their voices felt where decisions are made. This applies to broad policy matters such as in the selections of autonomous colleges, revising the colleges' sole reliance on the university examination, and devising means of flexibility in the treatment of different kinds and qualities of colleges. It relates equally to the more mundane issues of developing syllabi, setting examination questions, and similar questions.

Further, universities often are looked upon by the individual college as an imposing and powerful force, and there is a tendency to long for the curtailment of the university's scope and influence. However, within the present educational pattern in India as a whole, the autonomy of the university itself is continually jeopardized and will be increasingly threatened as states invest huge sums in university education. Individual colleges would be more subject to arbitrary and dangerous outside political interference if the university were weakened, if the educational autonomy of the university is not upheld. Individual colleges need to see their own work and relationship to the university in this broader perspective, and to support the autonomy of education *vis-à-vis* political forces wherever that becomes necessary.

We assume that the basic pattern of college affiliation with universities is a fixed element on the Indian scene for the foreseeable future. The task of individual colleges is to work for university autonomy from political influence, and for reforms and flexibility in the university's relationships to the various colleges. This requires concrete thinking about how to affect an organization, and not moral nostrums.

Finally, some contend that the answer to present university pressures is to form a Christian university. There are already a Hindu university and a Muslim university (both 'Residential and Teaching' and not 'Affiliating'), established almost fifty years ago. Those who favor a Christian university argue that only in this way can standards be maintained and the distinctive character of Christian institutions be developed. Some contend that it would facilitate administrative arrangements for contacts between various sections of the country, exchange of teachers and students, and other similar advantages. There are attractive considerations in the Christian university proposals, but there are also some basic unanswered, and perhaps unasked, questions. Perhaps the most critical question is whether Christians would cut themselves off from the total community in this way. Would it be psychologically healthy for the Christian community itself, already plagued by defensiveness and feelings of alienation from the broader national community? Do Christians want to cultivate and give credence to a public image of separateness and exclusiveness, symbolically separated through a distinct university from the public educational enterprise? If the colleges are really interested in quality education, can they best achieve it by creating enclaves of excellence which have little contact with 93 per cent of Indian higher education, or by trying to permeate the total system through an involved critical but loyal presence? To what extent could such a Christian university keep alive and relevant to the issues and needs in India, without a continuing vital contact with non-Christian institutions?

Assuming that satisfactory answers could be found for these questions, there are also practical considerations. Would the Government of India tolerate or approve such a university at the present stage? Would the university represent all of the Christian groups, and could this ecumenical venture be achieved? What kind of students would it attract over the long-haul, and what kind of teachers? Could it be assumed that such a university, presumably affiliating, would receive adequate government financing, at least for the affiliated colleges, and if not, would other sources inside India be able and willing to meet the costs? If the university were affiliating, under which state government jurisdictions would it fall, and how could the various approaches of the different states be integrated? These are but a few of the theoretical and practical considerations raised in the proposals made for a Christian university. For the most part, this suggestion is unattractive to contemporary Christian college leaders in India, but a thorough discussion of the advantages and limitations of the conception would do much to clarify the motivation for the Christian higher education enterprise in India.

Christian colleges and the churches

Clarification of the Christian colleges' relationship to the churches is also required — not only the churches in India, but those abroad. Much of what we have said already implicitly relates to the churches also. Furthermore, it is important to look at relationships with the church as an organization, and with Christians as a community. Most pre-Independence Christian colleges relied heavily on mission bodies for financing and leadership, but in the post-Independence era this has been greatly reduced, and some institutions are completely dependent upon Indian resources. It is striking that only one Roman Catholic college reported receiving money from overseas churches, while almost half of the Protestant colleges reported receiving some support, but this may partly reflect different ways of channeling money, or more reticence in giving financial information. Of the 22 Protestant colleges reporting receipt of some money from churches overseas during the past five years, about a third were under $5,000, another third were under $20,000, and almost a third were well over $20,000. These were for non-recurring expenditures. Nine Protestant colleges reported receiving aid from Indian Christian churches and 'management'. In any case, while some colleges benefit from strong mission board or church connections, their overall budget comes primarily from fees and government assistance.

As for the leadership in Christian colleges, it is overwhelmingly Indian. Boards of Governors are largely Indian, only 20 per cent of the Roman Catholic and 6 per cent of the Protestant college principals are not Indian citizens, and about 96 per cent of the teaching staff are Indians. Ninety-two per cent of the Catholic colleges have principals who are ordained or members of a congregation, while 25 per cent of the Protestant colleges are under ordained leadership. Boards of Governors are heavily weighted on the side of officials of the churches, with fully one-third of them being church functionaries.

What should be the relationship between the church and the college? We have adduced evidence that heavy reliance on members of a particular congregation or religious order creates some tensions (only 10 per cent of the Hindu teachers are Professors or Heads of Departments, while 16 per cent of the Protestants and 15 per cent of the Roman Catholic teachers are Heads of Departments and Professors). We have also argued that religious diversity on the Board of Governors could bring more vitality into the college (only 9 per cent are Hindus, and only ·004 per cent of them are Muslims). There is a constant danger that church-colleges will confuse the functions of a college with those of a church, not only in the classroom, but also in the religious life at the college. Perhaps this says something about the lack of freedom for non-Christians to have their own religious exercises on campus.

Some Christian colleges have been deeply affected by church rivalries and politics. Recently personal animosities between two church leaders led to strife and the temporary closure of neighboring Christian colleges in Kerala. These inter-church rivalries have led to the opening of colleges too ; in some areas of South India new colleges have been started on a competitive basis, between denominations, or between dioceses of the same denomination. This has contributed to the proliferation of colleges beyond the means of the local church resources to support them, and has watered down the level of teaching in some institutions because some of the better teachers have been lured to the new institutions. The time has certainly come for a moratorium on starting new Christian colleges (except perhaps for a new Jesuit college in Delhi), and freeing colleges from church politics will contribute to that end.

Yet the churches are responsible even if indirectly and weakly for the colleges; the colleges need the support which the churches can give, and vice versa. Not only is the leadership and financial support, though small, from the churches important, but connection with the churches can give, if not corrupted by petty and narrow interests, an intellectual and spiritual climate and foundation. The college could thus have one foot planted in the educational establishment and another in the church, thus giving balance in the evolution of the college. For both church and college it should be a relationship of mutual support and encouragement, but a relationship in organizational freedom.

Perhaps the most pressing practical question, with deep philosophical implications, concerns the colleges' relationship to the Christian community. Does the college have a special responsibility to cater to the felt and real needs of the Christian community? To what extent should preferential treatment be given to Christian students and staff just because they are Christians — admissions, hiring, promotions, scholarships, residences, etc.? To what extent is a college justified in establishing quota systems for members of its own religious group, and if such quotas are adopted, what does this do to the life and image of the college in the long run? Is there evidence that a college with 75 per cent or more Christian staff is better than one with under 20 per cent Christian staff, and if so 'better' judged by what criteria? There is a widespread assumption in many Christian colleges in India that they have a particular responsibility to Christians, to provide leaders for Christian institutions, and that Christian colleges will be better when they attain large numbers of Christian staff and students. Obviously, these are important concerns or arguments. But they raise serious questions on a number of levels — questions to which a number of Christian educators from different perspectives and experiences should give concerted attention. From these deliberations operational guidelines can be formulated to guide individual college administrators who are continually plagued with these questions. There is a need to examine the principles of special treatment for Christians, to test the assumption that the best education and the best way to support the Christian community is through preferential treatment, and to explore the possible educational and social consequences of acting on these assumptions.

Christian colleges and the community at large

The theme of the Education Commission Report is a testimony to the fact that colleges and universities have not sufficiently attuned their work to the nation's needs. Our own study underscored that this is true of Christian colleges as well; only a few of them are consciously striving to develop this relationship. There are many who insist that national development is only one of the objectives of education, and that there is danger of making education too utilitarian, and of putting too much emphasis on the state and consequently minimizing the individual. While these arguments are important, it is also true that many individuals have not been fulfilled or served very well because they have found their education a dead-end road, not connected to meaningful employment and not contributing to society. Further, many colleges have tended to become parasitic on an already undernourished body, using up the resources of the community without contributing to the community in return.

This alienation of the college from the community has impoverished both. For their own vigor, as well as to serve, the colleges must develop a different self-image. Among their mandates will be not only the transmission of knowledge, the creation of attitudes and skills, the discovery of new facts and interpretations of meanings, the enrichment of individual and corporate life in a spiritual way, but also the uplifting of the human community, and in particular of the community in which the college is set. This is important not only as an independent and isolated mandate, but essential for the full achievement of the colleges' other objectives as well. It is not something 'in addition', but an integral part of the whole constellation of college and university responsibilities. Yet this conception of community service has hardly affected the colleges at all, and usually then only in a peripheral and tangential way, as something not really a part of the corpus of college life.

We believe that a Christian college cannot develop a proper conception of its own *raison d'être* without serious reflection on its concrete responsibilities in and to the community, and without imaginative experimentation with techniques for weaving a wider and firmer fabric of commerce between the college and the community at large. Again, this is required not only by a sense of service and goodwill, but also by a commitment to provide dynamic and relevant education.

Christian colleges and their staffs and students

We have intentionally combined staff and students because we think of the college as a community searching together for meaning and truth, for discovering and refining skills. In addition, colleges have a responsibility for guiding students into their studies and vocational possibilities — 62 per cent of the students in a recent study said they did not know enough about qualifications needed for different kinds of jobs, and 52 per cent complained that they did not know enough about their own aptitudes for different kinds of work.[4] Concern for the teacher and student beyond the provision of formal courses of instruction is often expressed but seldom institutionalized. We have already intimated a few areas in which the colleges could better serve their staffs, and have argued strongly for the development of more suitable student services, including guidance and counselling.

If Christian colleges take these responsibilities seriously, it may have ramifications for many fundamental decisions about the running of colleges. Money will have to be channeled into the services provided and opportunities given; new patterns of organization will be called for, for both students and staff; new styles of organizing the college community will often be evolved; curricular affairs will have to lose their exclusive orientation to examination results. Reflection on these deeper elements of and purposes for the educational effort could help throw into sharper relief the purposes of a Christian college, and result in better means for achieving those objectives.

Christian colleges and their financing

Fees and government assistance make it possible for most Christian colleges to operate. Legally, a certain amount of a private college's budget must be contributed from 'private' sources, and this differs from state to state. But Christians have not the resources, through fees, contributions or endowments, to maintain first-class colleges without government assistance. The Christian community in India is financially too weak to make any sustained and significant contribution to the colleges. The proliferation of Christian colleges has further diminished the capacity of the Christian community to give full support for its institutions, and foreign support has dwindled. Alumni giving has been sparse and weak. Special gifts, from foundations, the University Grants Commission, and others, have played significant roles in improvements in some of the better institutions, but they do not carry a college's ongoing burdens. Christian colleges, therefore, must continue their dependence upon government grants, and be subject to the conditions regulating recipients of such grants. This is the given framework within which Christian colleges will have to work for the foreseeable future; efforts at modifying the conditions will be more promising than attempts to change the framework.

However, some funds may continue to trickle in from outside sources, in addition to those available from the college's own operating budget. Attention should be given to the priority areas for soliciting and using these funds. Near or at the top of the list should be the following concerns:

1. Support for self-studies of individual colleges and groups of colleges — self-studies along the lines suggested in the essay by Dirks in the second companion volume.[5]

2. Programs for special training of administrators, especially principals, either through summer institutes, experienced administrative advisors from other colleges, or similar efforts.

3. Provision of more satisfactory testing, guidance and counselling, and placement-cum-alumni programs for students and graduates.

4. Elaboration of a simple but wide-gauged records-keeping system and the staff to keep it current.

5. Provision of suitable study and/or residential accommodations for staff at the college.

6. Study of existing library resources and usage to determine ways it could be more like a workshop.

7. Development of meaningful ways of relating to, and serving, the community in which the college is located.

8. Providing leadership and modicum of facilities for creating democratic and responsible student organizations, and especially a student government with purposeful responsibilities and authority.

9. Formation of local and regional working parties from Christian colleges — later on possibly non-Christian institutions as well — to reflect on the nature and purposes of Christian colleges in India today. Perhaps these ideas could be shared in more general consultations at a later stage.

10. Programs of orientation for both new students and new teachers.

11. Evolution of channels of communications, mutual support and collaboration between and among the colleges, thereby sharing successes. These suggestions are, in a sense, picking around the edges of the problems. But we do not underestimate their importance, for it is our conviction that the two fundamental problems of Christian colleges are the lack of a compelling justification and philosophy on the one hand, and the dearth of strategic thinking on identifying and achieving objectives within the present university and political setting. Problems will not vanish until they are faced directly. It is also our firm belief that the most efficacious means of clarifying the motivations and developing a strategy is to think of the concrete situation of the colleges and how they do and should relate to those other institutions which have so much influence on what the college hopes to achieve, and can achieve. Christian colleges need a newly articulated philosophy

in a secular state; they need a philosophy specifically related to the Indian complex; they need an articulation of 'middle axiom' objectives which stand between ultimate theological principles and the tactics of year to year. If these are forged out of the give and take of solid and sustained ecumenical dialogue they could provide the compelling rationale for a regeneration of the Christian college enterprise as it seeks to serve in India.

What of the future?

At the beginning of our work we were much impressed by arguments one frequently hears in the West that the conception of a Christian college is no longer relevant or valid. This study of the role of Christian colleges in India, however, has forced a different conclusion. These colleges have played, do play, and can continue to play, over the next two decades at least, an important role in India's development, and thus in the evolution of the entire South Asia region. If men and women, properly trained, motivated, and deployed are the key to development, as increasingly we are forced to admit, higher education can be an important, even indispensable, ingredient in the development process.

Thus, in the total higher education picture in India, Christian colleges have a most significant opportunity. Here we reiterate what we have argued before. Though they are disadvantaged in some ways, they are also in a privileged position. We ignore here the specific spiritual resources of the churches and their colleges, not because they are unimportant (perhaps they are the most important asset of the colleges), but because we have been focussing on the sociological and educational aspects of the colleges.

1. Christian colleges enjoy a reputation for excellence which could enable them to influence educational policy. This reputation roots in the past, but is continually nourished by some of the finest colleges in the country today. It helps these colleges attract many of the best students in their areas; it means that innovative and unorthodox experiments at these colleges have visibility, and others are likely to make similar

experiments; teachers and leaders in the Christian colleges are often heard with respect and can wield a potentially important influence in university and educational affairs.

2. Christian colleges are found throughout the country, in a variety of settings and providing diverse kinds of education. There is no other single group of private colleges with this range and scope, nor is there another single group with as many as 130 institutions. While this dispersion could render co-ordination difficult, with imagination and effort the Christian colleges could develop and promote a national perspective on educational problems which no other set of institutions is now in a position to offer. The fact that the colleges have a strong base in the South rather than in the North, where political influence is strongest, means that special adaptations have to be made, but this is a matter of organization more than fundamental weakness.

3. The network of Christian schools and other institutions means that graduates of Christian colleges can extend into other situations any special influences the colleges have been able to impart. This is particularly true of teacher-training institutions. The problem of Christian colleges is not that they lack inherent strength or potential influence, but that they have sold this for the pottage of petty bickerings, jealousies and tensions of denominational warfare. If this warfare can be ended, Christian colleges can exert a more significant impact upon the real evils which impede India's development.

4. Finally, Christian colleges have enjoyed the stimulus of foreign connections and occasional overseas financial support. They can, to some extent, draw upon the intellectual, spiritual and financial resources of a large and dedicated Christian community, both within and outside the country. Support from outside the country may diminish, but this heterogeneity within a common heritage is something, which, if sensitively and intelligently used, can stimulate creativity.

Christian colleges have pioneered in Indian higher education, in quality as well as quantity. They have made incalculable contributions to India's self-consciousness and development. But India needs pioneers today too, men and institutions with commitment and courage to blaze new trails and 'home-stead' in unexplored lands. If Christian colleges are deeply intent upon service, to individuals and to the nation as a whole, they can be among those pioneers.

APPENDIXES

APPENDIXES

APPENDIX I
INFORMATION ON CHRISTIAN COLLEGES (1966)

State and Name of College	Sponsorship	Year of foundation	Type[1]	Highest degree[2]	Staff			Student			Staff-student ratio	% Christians	% Hostel students	% Schedule S & B	States represented	Book titles in library	Applicants admitted
					Total staff	% Christians	No. Religious	Men	Women	Total							
ANDHRA																	
Andhra Christian College, Guntur	P	1885	LA	B	92	50	Nil	1,302	253	1,555	1:17	15	23	32	1	26,000	49%
Andhra Loyola College, Vijayawada	RC	1954	LA	B	104	10	5	1,595	Nil	1,595	1:15	10	50	7	3	26,150	32%
Andhra Lutheran College of Education, Guntur	P	1965	TT	B	15	60	Nil	148	Nil	148	1:10	43	20	32	1	1,650	18%
J.M.J. College for Women, Tenali	RC	1963	LA	B	16	38	3	Nil	136	136	1:8	22	44	26	2	1,950	92%
St. Francis College for Women, Secunderabad	RC	1959	LA	B	27	51	5	Nil	441	441	1:16	23	5	17	6	4,000	74%
Maris Stella, Vijayawada	RC	1962	LA	B	36	36	7	Nil	594	594	1:16	10	21	9	4	3,015	87%

[1] LA: Liberal Arts
TT: Teacher-Training

[2] B: Bachelor's   M: Master's
Prof.: Professional

APPENDIX I (continued)

State and Name of College	Sponsorship	Year of foundation	Type	Highest degree	Total staff	Staff % Christians	No. Religious	Student Men	Student Women	Student Total	Staff-student ratio	% Christians	% Hostel students	% Schedule S & B	States represented	Book titles in library	Applicants admitted
ANDHRA (continued)																	
St. Joseph's College for Women, Waltair	RC	1958	LA	B	37	41	9	Nil	891	391	1:11	8	13	17	9	4,750	91%
St. Joseph's Training College for Women, Guntur	RC	1946	TT	B	12	50	3	Nil	130	130	1:11	46	76	50	12	7,800	65%
St. Theresa's College for Women, Eluru	RC	1953	LA	B	36	22	4	Nil	508	508	1:14	18	INA	25	2	5,920	67%
ASSAM																	
St. Anthony's College, Shillong	RC	1934	LA	B	61	21	2	1,769	93	1,862	1:31	23	45	45	6	15,040	70%
St. Edmund's College, Shillong	RC	1924	LA	B	54	20	4	1,239	25	1,264	1:23	28	8	40	3	11,500	85%
St. Mary's College, Shillong	RC	1937	LA TT	B	26	40	3	Nil	343	343	1:13	37	2	30	10	4,000	85%
Union Christian College, Barapani	P	1952	LA	B	20	90	1	114	46	160	1:8	98	100	81	4	6,300	INA

BIHAR Patna Women's College, Patna	RC	1940	LA	B	34	20	7	Nil	626	626	1 : 18	9	25	5	11	13,200	40%
St. Columba's College, Hazaribagh	P	1899	LA	B	57	INA	INA	1,402	201	1,603	1 : 28	4	9	40	INA	17,366	92%
St. Xavier's College, Ranchi	RC	1944	LA	B	72	36	22	1,883	531	2,414	1 : 33	42	38	47	5	30,000	46%
GUJARAT St. Xavier's College, Ahmedabad	RC	1955	LA	B	87	18	10	890	609	1,499	1 : 17	4	14	1	7	26,650	54%
DELHI St. Stephen's College	P	1881	LA	M	42	29	INA	703	Nil	703	1 : 16	13	36	INA	12	40,000	25%
GOA St. Xavier's College, Goa	RC	1963	LA	B	28	44	4	215	103	318	1 : 11	50	11	13	3	5,550	96%
Institute of Education, Goa	RC	1963	TT	B	6	66	2	31	22	53	1 : 8	66	Nil	2	3	2,500	76%
HIMACHAL PRADESH St. Bede's College, Simla	RC	1904	LA TT	B	8	38	2	Nil	145	145	1 : 18	14	67	INA	10	5,289	27%
KERALA Assumption College for Women, Changanacherry	RC	1950	LA	B	71	93	13	Nil	1,724	1,724	1 : 24	90	49	5	1	10,996	84%

APPENDIX I (continued)

State and Name of College	Sponsorship	Year of foundation	Type	Highest degree	Staff			Student			Staff-student ratio	% Christians	% Hostel students	% Schedule S & B	States represented	Book titles in library	Applicants admitted
					Total staff	% Christians	No. Religious	Men	Women	Total							
KERALA (continued)																	
Bishop Chulaparambil Memorial College, Kottayam	RC	1955	LA	B	72	85	9	Nil	1,698	1,698	1 : 24	69	22	11	1	7,620	56%
C.M.S. College, Kottayam	P	1816	LA	M	91	82	4	1,681	487	2,168	1 : 23	61	8	INA	INA	2,500	INA
Catholicate College, Pathanamthitta	S	1952	LA	M	85	61	5	1,317	709	2,026	1 : 23	INA	8	14	1	13,500	65%
Christ College, Irinjalakuda	RC	1956	LA	M	80	61	12	1,529	Nil	1,529	1 : 19	18	22	12	1	20,600	31%
Fatima Mata National College, Quilon	RC	1951	LA	M	112	73	5	1,642	810	2,452	1 : 22	58	18	INA	1	21,872	60%
Karmela Rani Training College, Quilon	RC	1960	TT	B	10	80	1	45	75	120	1 : 12	93	20	12	1	2,765	65%

Little Flower College, Guruvayoor	RC	1955	LA	B	52	42	10	Nil	1,119	1,119	1:22	22	45	26	2	INA	75%
Loyola Institute of Social Sciences, Trivandrum	RC	1963	Prof.	M	10	INA	4	38	33	71	1:7	33	11	INA	1	4,000	80%
Malabar Christian College, Kozhikode	P	1909	LA	M	46	39	1	671	268	939	1:24	6	48	Nil	3	11,700	31%
Mar Athanasius College, Kothamangalam	S	1955	LA	M	56	61	INA	852	510	1,362	1:24	79	13	12	1	6,000	70%
Mar Athanasius College of Engineering, Kothamangalam	S	1961	Prof.	B	49	78	INA	533	34	567	1:12	INA	38	14	1	3,447	INA
Mar Ivanios College, Trivandrum	RC	1949	LA	M	92	80	INA	1,968	219	2,187	1:24	50	19	32	2	16,500	22%
Mar Theophilus Training College, Trivandrum	RC	1956	TT	B	8	75	2	46	74	120	1:15	55	22	24	2	5,000	60%
Mar Thoma College, Kuttapuzha, Tiruvalla	S	1952	LA	M	78	92	1	1,500	340	1,840	1:24	62	10	8	1	15,000	76%

APPENDIX I (continued)

State and Name of College	Sponsorship	Year of foundation	Type	Highest degree	Staff			Student			Staff-student ratio	% Christians	% Hostel students	% Schedule S & B	States represented	Book titles in library	Applicants admitted
					Total staff	% Christians	No. Religious	Men	Women	Total							
KERALA (continued)																	
Mt. Carmel Training College, Kottayam	RC	1953	TT	B	8	88	6	Nil	120	120	1 : 15	79	53	17	1	3,600	40%
Mt. Tabor Training College, Pathanapuram	S	1960	TT	B	7	71	4	50	70	120	1 : 17	55	33	12	1	2,000	INA
Nirmala College, Muvattapuzha	RC	1953	LA	M	60	90	5	947	691	1,638	1 : 27	32	14	10	1	9,000	59%
Peet Memorial Training College, Mavelikara	P	1960	TT	B	7	100	1	39	81	120	1 : 17	55	20	14	1	1,500	12%
Providence College for Women, Calicut	RC	1960	LA	B	29	45	9	Nil	709	709	1 : 24	16	51	35	5	12,049	80%
Sacred Heart College, Thevara	RC	1944	LA	M	95	66	10	1,721	Nil	1,721	1 : 18	54	33	14	1	27,630	28%

Sahitya Deepika Sanskrit College, Bavarati	RC	1932	TT	Other	6	33	Nil	14	79	93	1 : 15	56	Nil	INA	1	4,770	INA
St. Albert's College, Ernakulam	RC	1946	LA	M	71	80	5	1,478	Nil	1,478	1 : 21	38	15	13	3	16,000	62%
St. Berchman's College, Changanacherry	RC	1922	LA	M	107	21	8	2,135	62	2,197	1 : 21	79	30	9	1	37,727	48%
St. Joseph's College, Calicut	RC	1956	LA	M	65	63	6	1,254	Nil	1,254	1 : 19	22	46	29	INA	13,500	INA
St. Joseph's College for Women, Alleppey	RC	1954	LA	B	41	78	5	Nil	849	849	1 : 21	59	20	9	3	7,559	97%
St. Joseph's Training College, Mannanam	RC	1957	TT	B	9	100	3	120	Nil	120	1 : 13	70	65	4	1	6,680	100%
St. Joseph's Training College for Women, Ernakulam	RC	1957	TT	B	11	91	6	Nil	97	97	1 : 9	54	48	6	1	2,218	INA
St. Mary's College, Trichur	RC	1946	LA	M Other	80	56	20	Nil	2,001	2,001	1 : 25	45	33	8	3	19,000	56%
St. Teresa's College, Ernakulam	RC	1925	LA	M	58	52	22	Nil	1,313	1,313	1 : 23	50	20	5	5	13,000	49%
St. Thomas College, Kozhenchery	S	1953	LA	B	49	82	Nil	892	638	1,530	1 : 13	72	8	14	1	10,920	INA

APPENDIX I (continued)

State and Name of College	Sponsorship	Year of foundation	Type	Highest degree	Staff			Student			Staff-student ratio	% Christians	% Hostel students	% Schedule S & B	States represented	Book titles in library	Applicants admitted
					Total staff	% Christians	No. Religious	Men	Women	Total							
KERALA (continued)																	
St. Thomas College, Palai	RC	1950	LA	M	112	89	13	1,949	300	2,249	1 : 20	73	10	9	2	29,000	62%
St. Thomas College, Trichur	RC	1919	LA	M	97	55	5	2,480	Nil	2,480	1 : 25	56	14	10	INA	23,262	INA
St. Thomas Training College, Palai	RC	1957	TT	B	12	100	3	58	62	120	1 : 10	81	36	2	1	3,100	68%
Titus II Teachers' College, Tiruvalla	S	1957	TT	B	8	75	Nil	39	81	120	1 : 15	83	10	4	1	3,500	44%
Union Christian College, Alwaye	P	1921	LA	Ph.D.	52	60	2	584	385	969	1 : 18	53	38	8	1	16,000	27%
MADHYA PRADESH Hawabagh Women's College, Jabalpur	P	1928	LA TT	M Other	34	71	1	Nil	264	264	1 : 8	74	70	5	10	6,260	69%
Indore Christian College, Indore	P	1887	LA	Ph.D.	30	63	2	736	190	926	1 : 31	9	10	17	9	20,900	78%

St. Aloysius College, Jabalpur	RC	1951	LA	B	19	21	1	377	103	480	1 : 25	19	Nil	14	12	5,890	69%
MADRAS American College, Madurai	P	1881	LA	M	78	68	3	1,249	21	1,270	1 : 16	23	51	57	1	3,135	31%
Auxilium College, Katpadi	RC	1954	LA	B	30	58	7	Nil	554	554	1 : 18	23	35	INA	3	13,131	100%
Christian College, Martandam	P	1964	LA	B	30	INA	1	530	Nil	530	1 : 18	41	2	47	2	1,501	74%
Christian Medical College, Vellore	P	1918	Prof.	Other	216	INA	10	480	320	800	1 : 4	48	100	Nil	12	4,857	3%
Fatima College, Madurai	RC	1953	LA	M Other	71	24	8	Nil	1,084	1,084	1 : 15	9	44	36	7	10,389	73%
Holy Cross College, Tiruchirapalli	RC	1924	LA	M	51	60	16	Nil	1,109	1,109	1 : 21	23	41	38	4	16,000	93%
Lady Doak College, Madurai	P	1948	LA	M	51	80	1	Nil	621	621	1 : 12	39	41	24	3	16,500	50%
Loyola College, Madras	RC	1925	LA	Ph.D.	115	55	12	1,931	Nil	1,931	1 : 17	25	34	23	10	26,500	30%
Madras Christian College, Tambaram	P	1865	LA	Ph.D.	108	48	6	1,404	134	1,538	1 : 14	34	40	29	9	45,104	35%

APPENDIX I (continued)

State and Name of College	Sponsorship	Year of foundation	Type	Highest degree	Staff			Student			Staff-student ratio	% Christians	% Hostel students	% Schedule S & B	States represented	Book titles in library	Applicants admitted
					Total staff	% Christians	No. Religious	Men	Women	Total							
MADRAS (continued)																	
Meston Training College, Madras	P	1937	TT	M	10	100	1	76	8	84	1 : 8	33	56	17	4	8,764	59%
Nirmala College for Women, Coimbatore	RC	1948	LA	B	43	35	4	Nil	711	711	1 : 17	16	21	1	2	5,350	99%
Pope College, Sawyerpuram	P	1962	LA	B	27	90	Nil	470	Nil	470	1 : 18	20	80	65	2	4,500	80%
Sacred Heart College, Tirupattur	RC	1951	LA	B	31	51	5	538	Nil	538	1 : 17	81	49	Nil	4	10,442	26%
Sarah Tucker College, Palayamkottai	P	1896	LA	B	45	56	Nil	Nil	843	843	1 : 19	63	60	23	1	11,008	INA
Scott Christian College, Nagercoil	P	1893	LA	B	70	76	Nil	1,091	419	1,510	1 : 22	64	11	44	3	26,014	INA

St. Christopher's Training College, Madras	P	1923	TT	M	13	85	Nil	Nil	80	80	1:6	79	58	14	3	10,495	46%
St. Ignatius Training College, Madras	RC	1957	TT	B	7	100	3	Nil	60	60	1:9	77	58	60	2	1,812	50%
St. John's College, Palayamkottai	P	1878	LA	B	60	80	2	1,130	Nil	1,130	1:19	52	65	Nil	1	12,210	INA
St. Joseph's College, Tiruchirapalli	RC	1859	LA	Ph.D.	105	37	11	2,031	Nil	2,031	1:19	49	62	40	6	60,367	14%
St. Mary's College, Tuticorin	RC	1948	LA	B	35	71	8	Nil	755	755	1:21	50	50	28	2	9,236	99%
St. Xavier's College, Palayamkottai	RC	1923	LA	B Other	61	70	4	1,160	Nil	1,160	1:19	37	69	55	2	21,000	14%
St. Xavier's Teachers' Training College, Palayamkottai	RC	1950	TT	B	7	55	1	62	Nil	62	1:8	60	75	76	2	4,000	26%
Stella Maris College, Madras	RC	1947	LA Prof.	M Other	70	39	17	Nil	1,434	1,434	1:20	18	14	7	15	22,000	31%
Stella Matulina Training College, Madras	RC	1961	TT	M	11	66	3	Nil	82	82	1:7	38	56	16	4	4,126	68%
Voorhees College, Vellore	P	1898	LA	B	48	46	2	1,028	Nil	1,028	1:21	8	19	43	2	13,450	75%

APPENDIX I (continued)

State and Name of College	Sponsorship	Year of foundation	Type	Highest degree	Total staff	Staff % Christians	Staff No. Religious	Student Men	Student Women	Student Total	Staff-student ratio	% Christians	% Hostel students	% Schedule S & B	States represented	Book titles in library	Applicants admitted
MADRAS (continued)																	
Women's Christian College, Madras	P	1915	LA	M	45	71	Nil	Nil	489	489	1 : 11	52	46	10	12	16,000	INA
Y.M.C.A. College of Physical Education, Madras	P	1932	Prof.	Other	12	84	Nil	24	15	39	1 : 3	18	100	18	10	5,700	57%
MAHARASHTRA																	
Ahmednagar College, Ahmednagar	P	1947	LA TT	M	75	20	2	2,113	367	2,480	1 : 33	10	20	62	10	35,000	100%
Hislop College, Nagpur	P	1883	LA Prof.	B Other	83	26	1	1,461	442	1,903	1 : 23	5	5	16	5	20,539	63%
Nirmala Niketan, Bombay	RC	1955	Prof.	Other	13	23	3	Nil	46	46	1 : 3	24	17	INA	5	4,500	58%
Sophia College, Bombay	RC	1941	LA	M	55	33	5	Nil	1,253	1,253	1 : 22	42	7	4	9	22,000	INA
Spicer Memorial College, Poona	P	1937	LA	—	68	98	18	305	120	425	1 : 6	98	93	INA	15	24,150	66%

Name																	
St. Francis de Sales College, Nagpur	RC	1956	LA LT	B Other	46	32	8	777	124	901	1 : 19	19	8	20	8	6,776	91%
St. Xavier's College, Bombay	RC	1869	LA	Ph.D.	116	28	14	1,558	991	2,549	1 : 21	22	5	1	9	10,100	40%
St. Xavier's Institute of Education, Bombay	RC	1953	TT	Ph.D. Other	19	31	4	68	195	263	1 : 14	INA	6	1	1	6,233	83%
Wilson College, Bombay	P	1861	LA	Ph.D.	99	INA	1	657	1,209	1,826	1 : 18	4	10	1	8	28,400	40%
MYSORE Mt. Carmel College, Bangalore	RC	1944	LA	B	48	42	13	Nil	999	999	1 : 21	17	12	INA	10	16,000	72%
St. Agnes College, Mysore	RC	1921	LA	B	37	43	10	Nil	789	789	1 : 21	47	14	12	5	17,000	85%
St. Aloysius College, Mysore	RC	1880	LA	B	51	40	6	1,050	Nil	1,050	1 : 21	37	25	34	4	24,000	68%
St. Ann's Training College, Mangalore	RC	1943	TT	B	6	84	5	Nil	46	46	1 : 8	59	40	13	4	7,700	83%
St. John's Medical College, Bangalore	RC	1963	Prof.	Other	47	51	4	139	61	200	1 : 4	83	33	Nil	15	3,000	9%
St. Joseph's College, Bangalore	RC	1882	LA	B	79	INA	8	1,594	16	1,610	1 : 20	14	11	18	10	30,000	28%
St. Philomena's College, Mysore	RC	1946	LA	B	55	49	8	1,133	109	1,242	1 : 23	14	INA	1	5	12,000	75%

APPENDIX I (continued)

State and Name of College	Sponsorship	Year of Foundation	Type	Highest degree	Staff			Students			Staff-student ratio	% Christians	% Hostel students	% Schedule S & B	States represented	Book titles in library	Applicants admitted
					Total staff	% Christians	No. Religious	Men	Women	Total							
MYSORE (continued)																	
St. Philomena's College, Puttur	RC	1958	LA	B	26	27	1	356	74	430	1 : 16	18	20	1	2	5,500	INA
Teresian College, Mysore	RC	1966	LA	B	19	58	3	Nil	181	181	1 : 9	11	42	Nil	5	4,000	100%
ORISSA Christ College, Cuttack	P	1944	LA	B	40	INA	Nil	960	Nil	960	1 : 24	3	8	16	4	8,000	40%
Stewart Science College, Cuttack	P	1944	LA	B	21	12	Nil	432	Nil	432	1 : 21	1	45	2	1	2,900	INA
PUNJAB Baring Union Christian College, Batala	P	1944	LA	M	47	43	4	754	138	892	1 : 19	5	6	10	2	15,000	50%
Christian Medical College, Ludhiana	P	1894	Prof.	Other	100	52	Nil	150	150	300	1 : 3	85	100	1	12	10,000	4%

Sacred Heart College, Dalhousie	RC	1952	LA	B	9	33	3	Nil	108	108	1:12	5	84	Nil	10	1,900	44%
RAJASTHAN Sophia Girls' College, Ajmer	RC	1919	LA	B	16	38	2	Nil	168	168	1:10	35	8	6	16	6,140	90%
UTTAR PRADESH Allahabad Agricultural College, Allahabad	P	1910	LA Prof.	M Prof. Other	60	50	Nil	471	51	522	1:9	INA	80	INA	13	30,000	INA
Christ Church College, Kanpur	P	1892	LA	Ph.D.	63	17	Nil	932	318	1,250	1:20	5	8	2	8	30,000	60%
Ewing Christian College, Allahabad	P	1902	LA	B	52	47	1	813	108	921	1:18	6	27	10	9	30,000	88%
Isabella Thoburn College, Lucknow	P	1886	LA TT	B Other	44	52	Nil	Nil	420	420	1:10	22	50	Nil	INA	32,365	33%
Loreto Convent College, Lucknow	RC	1956	LA	B	17	47	2	Nil	320	320	1:19	5	30	Nil	10	4,500	73%
Lucknow Christian College, Lucknow	P	1889	LA Prof.	B Other	49	37	Nil	817	Nil	817	1:17	9	24	3	5	24,250	53%
St. Andrew's College, Gorakhpur	P	1899	LA Prof.	B Other	58	14	Nil	964	49	1,013	1:17	1	5	7	4	19,068	80%
St. John's College, Agra	P	1850	LA	Ph.D.	59	37	2	381	342	1,223	1:21	7	18	27	16	31,872	60%

APPENDIX I (continued)

State and Name of College	Sponsorship	Year of foundation	Type	Highest degree	Staff			Students			Staff-student ratio	% Christians	% Hostel students	% Schedule S & B	States represented	Book titles in library	Applicants admitted
					Total staff	% Christians	No. Religious	Men	Women	Total							
WEST BENGAL																	
Bankura Christian College, Bankura	P	1903	LA	B Other	49	16	1	INA	INA	1,152	1 : 24	2	26	4	5	10,814	79%
Loreto College, Calcutta	RC	1912	LA TT	B Other	28	43	7	Nil	497	497	1 : 18	18	12	Nil	10	5,500	56%
Loreto College, Darjeeling	RC	1961	LA	B	13	15	3	Nil	116	116	1 : 9	13	40	INA	8	4,000	100%
Scottish Church College, Calcutta	P	1857	LA TT	B	104	10	Nil	872	742	1,614	1 : 16	14	13	2	12	58,000	4%
Serampore College, Serampore	P	1827	LA Prof.	B Other	60	28	9	764	427	1,191	1 : 20	21	13	3	12	38,000	89%
St. Joseph's College, Darjeeling	RC	1927	LA	B	28	21	12	490	60	550	1 : 20	INA	34	63	9	96,000	93%
St. Paul's Cathedral Mission College, Calcutta	P	1865	LA	B	57	19	Nil	875	Nil	875	1 : 15	5	18	75	9	20,815	87%
St. Xavier's College, Calcutta	RC	1862	LA TT	B	92	24	12	2,354	Nil	2,354	1 : 26	12	70	INA	16	65,000	43%
Union Christian Training College, Berhampur	P	1941	TT	B	9	44	4	90	30	120	1 : 13	5	70	38	16	6,000	9%
Women's Christian College, Calcutta															16		

ROMAN CATHOLIC STATISTICS

Parishes and Q. Parishes	3,701		
Primary schools	4,877	Catholics	402,157
		Non-Catholics	430,319
		Total	832,475
		Boys	55%
		Girls	45%
Middle schools	1,299	Catholics	151,155
		Non-Catholics	174,321
		Total	325,476
		Boys	55%
		Girls	45%
High schools	899	Catholics	203,466
		Non-Catholics	174,321
		Total	491,315
		Boys	52%
		Girls	48%
Hostels	467		
Orphanages	526		
Hospitals & Nursing Homes	205		
Priests			
Diocesan	4,781		
Indian	1,739		
Foreign	1,211		
Brothers			
Indian	1,727		
Foreign	332		
Nuns			
Indian	22,554		
Foreign	2,115		

APPENDIX 3

ROMAN CATHOLIC JUNIOR COLLEGES

College	Staff						Students					
	Priests or Religious	*Lay Catholics*	*Total*	*Other Christian communities*	*Non-Christians*	*Grand total*	*Catholics*	*Other Christians*	*Hindus*	*Muslims*	*Others*	*Grand total*
1. All Saints College, Trivandrum	4	12	16	5	10	31	149	109	394	40	2	694
2. Alphonsa College for Women, Arunapuram P.O., Kerala	1	31	32		2	34	587	19	231	4		841
3. Bharatha Matha College, Thrikkakara, Kakanad P.O.	5	24	29		2	31	249	64	298	56		667
4. Bishop Kurialacherry College, Athirumpuzha	8	5	13	2		15	169	35	60	3		267
5. Deva Matha College, Kuravilangad												
6. Kuriakos Elias College, Mannanam P.O., via Kottayam	4	17	21	1	3	25	376	31	216	8		631
7. Mercy College, Palghat	6	4	10		13	23	25	29	495	26		575
8. Newman College, Thodupuzha	9	39	48	1	2	51	631	48	222	34	37	972
9. Nirmalagiri College, Koothuparamba P.O., Malabar	9	28	37	1	13	51	76	5	635	68		781
10. St. Aloysius College, Edathua	1	17	18	2	1	21	171	131	159	1		462
11. St. George's College, Ariuvithura		21	21			21	351	50	81	20		502

APPENDIX 3 *(continued)*

College	Staff						Students					
	Priests or Religious	Lay Catholics	Total	Other Christian communites	Non-Christians	Grand total	Catholics	Other Christians	Hindus	Muslims	Others	Grand total
12. St. Dominic's College, Kanjirapally												
13. St. John's College, Anchal	6	15	21	7	4	32	80	210	434	123		817
14. St. Joseph's College for Women, Irinjalakuda	10	10	20	4	6	30	191	10	404	24		629
15. St. Paul's College, Kalamassery	3	6	9		12	21	141	28	193	68		430
16. St. Stephen's College, Uzhavoor P.O., Kottayam	3	19	22	3	4	29	369	92	230			691
17. St. Xavier's College for Women, Alwaye	3	8	11	4	8	23	182	83	271	21		557
18. St. Xavier's College, Trivandrum	6	11	17	2	1	20	175	54	170	59		458
19. Carmel College, Goa	11	4	15		5	20	73	1	3	1	1	79
20. St. Xavier's College, Goa	4	8	12		20	32	194		200			394
21. Holy Cross College, Nagercoil												
22. Jyothi Nivas College, Bangalore												
23. Providence College, Coonoor	2		2	1	3	6	6	4	20	1		31

APPENDIX 4 GENERAL INFORMATION ON UNIVERSITIES

University	Year of foundation	Type	No. of affiliated colleges	Medium of instruction	Student advisory group	Enrollment 1962-3						
						Total	Total 1964-5	Total graduates	Men	Women	% women	Foreign students
1. Agra	1927	Affiliating	127	English and Hindi	Yes	56,384	54,005	12,739	47,500	8,884	15.8	24
2. Aligarh Muslim	1921	Residential & Teaching	0	English (Urdu & Hindi (a))		5,047	4,907	648	4,454	593	11.7	61
3. Allahabad	1887	Residential & Teaching	0	English & Hindi	Yes	10,791	8,686	2,257	8,885	1,906	17.7	32
4. Andhra	1926	Teaching & Affiliating	52	English	Yes	32,617		1,038	28,212	4,405	13.5	23
5. Annamalai	1929	Residential & Teaching	0	English (regional language (a))	Yes	3,182	3,762	423	2,911	271	8.5	82
6. Banaras Hindu	1916	Residential & Teaching	4	English & Hindi	Yes	8,410	6,975	1,167	7,152	1,258	15.0	72
7. Bhagalpur	1960	Teaching & Affiliating	33	English & Hindi		19,194		1,153	18,194	1,000	5.2	
8. Bihar	1952	Teaching & Affiliating	37	English Hindi, Urdu & Bengali		29,237	28,743	1,335	28,235	1,002	3.4	200
9. Bombay	1857	Teaching & Federal	0	English	Yes	53,902	56,653	3,583	38,809	15,093	28.0	629
10. Burdwan	1960	Teaching & Affiliating	35	English & Bengali		21,159	23,900	508	17,626	3,543	16.7	3
11. Calcutta	1857	Teaching & Affiliating	116	English	Yes	117,248	117,072	5,062	87,368	29,880	25.5	368
12. Delhi	1922	Teaching & Affiliating	13	English & Hindi	Yes	25,149	23,659	2,791	16,739	8,410	33.4	255
13. Gauhati	1948	Teaching & Affiliating	43	English	Yes	34,976	31,634	1,166	30,270	4,706	13.5	22
14. Gorakhpur	1957	Teaching & Affiliating	30	English & Hindi	Yes	14,884	3,547(b)	1,273	14,182	662	4.5	

(a) In a few departments.   (b) Does not seem comparable to 1962-3 total enrollment

APPENDIX 4 *(continued)*

University	Arts	Science	Professions	Education	Technology (d)	Commerce	Agriculture (e)	Other	No. of titles	Including affiliated colleges
1. Agra	26,279 / 17,188	15,047 / 12,587	2,782 / 2,671	2,273 / 2,208	619 / 591	4,445 / 3,354	4,939 / 4,263	Nil / Nil	890,424	No
2. Aligarh Muslim	1,159 / 472	1,773 / 926	607 / 455	Nil / Nil	1,197 / 551	287 / 111	Nil / Nil	24 / 18	200,000	NA
3. Allahabad	5,319 / 3,337	2,493 / 1,819	706 / 685	791 / 764	288 / 288	658 / 459	178 / 150	358 / 162	295,259	NA
4. Andhra	5,915 / 3,390	18,309 / 7,893	2,793 / 2,643	254 / 250	1,798 / 1,557	2,271 / 1,800	581 / 581	666 / 202	552,097	No
5. Annamalai	559 / 217	893 / 420	Nil / Nil	155 / 105	870 / 837	222 / 191	227 / 211	256 / 21	142,638	NA
6. Banaras Hindu	2,802 / 1,501	1,650 / 784	625 / 545	112 / 94	2,119 / 1,625	446 / 361	353 / 223	305 / 13	352,374	No
7. Bhagalpur	13,230 / 7,655	4,218 / 2,377	300 / 300	Nil / Nil	337 / 337	744 / 475	365 / 305	Nil / Nil	143,473	No
8. Bihar	17,566 / 10,342	8,177 / 4,505	1,209 / 1,102	Nil / Nil	509 / 509	1,496 / 980	280 / 280	Nil / Nil	243,201	Yes
9. Bombay	19,064 / 6,665	18,979 / 3,855	6,512 / 5,421	559 / 275	2,693 / 1,470	5,921 / 1,352	174 / 149	Nil / Nil	993,735	NA
10. Burdwan	10,753 / 7,323	7,367 / 4,637	Nil / Nil	119 / 119	366 / 366	2,564 / 2,082	Nil / Nil	Nil / Nil	191,532	Yes
11. Calcutta	52,822 / 34,287	30,639 / 19,387	7,912 / 7,168	1,428 / 1,428	2,580 / 2,209	21,580 / 16,673	241 / 209	44 / Nil	1,571,433	
12. Delhi	16,535 / 13,101	2,750 / 2,205	2,616 / 1,524	246 / 144	1,885 / 1,254	1,098 / 1,031	Nil / Nil	16 / Nil	622,020	No
13. Gauhati	22,668 / 13,470	6,986 / 2,952	1,500 / 1,380	235 / 200	751 / 751	2,204 / 1,214	632 / 410	Nil / Nil	320,088	No
14. Gorakhpur	8,122 / 7,096	2,710 / 2,360	550 / 550	1,214 / 1,189	Nil / Nil	863 / 693	1,412 / 1,412	Nil / Nil	199,913	No

(c) Top number = total, bottom number = degrees awarded. (d) Including Engineering. (e) Including Farm Sciences.

APPENDIX 4 (continued)

University	Year of foundation	Type	No. of affiliated colleges	Medium of instruction	Student advisory group	Enrollment 1962-3						
						Total	Total 1964-5	Total graduates	Men	Women	% women	Foreign students
15. Gujarat	1950	Teaching & Affiliating	90	Gujarati, Hindi, English	Yes	47,208	37,077(f)	2,736	38,222	8,986	19·0	6
16. Indira Kala Sangit Vishwa-vidyalaya	1957	Teaching & Affiliating	29	Hindi, Marathi, English		92(g)	150		55	37	41·1	2
17. Jabalpur	1957	Teaching & Affiliating	20	English & Hindi	Yes	10,600	9,525	1,435	8,777	1,823	17·2	3
18. Jadavpur	1955	Teaching & Residential	0	Bengali & English		3,587	3,500	585	3,091	496	13·8	23
19. Jammu and Kashmir	1948	Teaching & Affiliating	33	English		10,997	7,727	342	7,446	3,551	32·3	
20. Jodhpur	1962	Teaching & Residential	0	English & Hindi	Yes	5,299		376	4,447	852	16·1	
21. Kalyani	1950	Teaching & Residential	0	English		471		102	432	39	8·3	
22. Kameshwar Singh Darbhanga Sanskrit Vishva-vidyalaya	1961	Teaching & Affiliating	20	Sanskrit, English, Hindi, Maithili, Bengali		5,216		457	4,979	237	4·5	
23. Karnatak	1949	Teaching & Affiliating	39	English	Yes	17,121	21,710(h)	984	15,566	1,555	9·1	51
24. Kerala	1937	Teaching & Affiliating	89	English	Yes	56,038	44,511	1,563	38,394	17,644	31·5	31
25. Kurukshetra	1956	Teaching & Federal Residential	0	English, Hindi, Punjabi		797	1,273	159	605	192	24·1	
26. Lucknow	1921	Teaching & Residential	0	Hindi (a)	Yes	17,492	12,928	2,305	13,749	3,743	21·4	27
27. M.S. University of Baroda	1949	Residential & Teaching	0	English (a) English	Yes	10,106	11,191	811	8,118	1,988	19·7	213

APPENDIX 4 (continued)

University	Enrollment 1962-3 By course of study (c)								Books in library	
	Arts	Science	Professions	Education	Technology (d)	Commerce	Agriculture (e)	Other	No. of titles	Including affiliated colleges
15. Gujarat	19,940	14,588	4,056	549	1,602	6,312	126	35	610,373	No
	6,825	3,439	3,918	382	1,331	2,656	126	Nil		
16. Indira Kala Sangit Vishwa-vidyalaya									1,281	No
17. Jabalpur	2,927	2,850	863	443	1,370	1,472	675	Nil	164,874	No
	2,123	2,579	816	187	1,327	1,171	588	Nil		
18. Jadavpur	704	431	Nil	Nil	2,452	Nil	Nil	Nil	133,340	NA
	171	171	Nil	Nil	2,452	Nil	Nil	Nil		
19. Jammu and Kashmir	3,818	4,074	566	294	539	152	129	1,425	178,572	No
	1,417	989	483	294	116	85	129	234		
20. Jodhpur	1,487	1,441	313	163	1,138	712	Nil	45	73,775	NA
	807	854	313	163	1,138	517	Nil	Nil		
21. Kalyani	14	85	Nil	81	Nil	Nil	291	Nil	21,800	NA
	5	19	Nil	81	Nil	Nil	264	Nil		
22. Kameshwar Singh Darbhanga Sanskrit Vishva-vidyalaya										
23. Karnatak	6,039	4,896	2,499	327	1,600	1,283	477	Nil	329,420	No
	2,572	1,869	1,934	236	1,124	688	338	Nil		
24. Kerala	14,750	27,797	2,680	2,307	3,344	4,000	748	410	892,469	No
	6,259	15,202	2,185	2,185	3,203	2,159	468	127		
25. Kurukshetra	337	256	Nil	204	Nil	Nil	Nil	Nil	37,110	NA
	66	47	Nil	204	Nil	Nil	Nil	Nil		
26. Lucknow	6,114	3,517	6,563	205	Nil	990	Nil	103	357,250	NA
	4,623	2,887	4,026	183	Nil	720	Nil	Nil		
27. M. S. University of Baroda	1,753	1,862	1,017	262	2,812	1,620	Nil	780	288,267	NA
	959	922	810	153	1,635	1,093	Nil	149		

(c) Top number = total, bottom number = degrees awarded.   (d) Including Engineering.   (e) Including Farm Sciences.

APPENDIX 4 (continued)

University	Year of foundation	Type	No. of affiliated colleges	Medium of instruction	Student advisory group	Enrollment 1962-3						
						Total	Total 1964-5	Total graduates	Men	Women	% women	Foreign students
28. Madras	1857	Teaching & Affiliating	121(i)	English & Tamil (a)	Yes	64,091	59,635	2,231	50,593	13,498	21·1	377
29. Magadh	1962	Teaching & Affiliating	29	Hindi (a) & English		22,329		297	21,770	559	2·5	9
30. Marathwada	1958	Teaching & Affiliating	30	English		8,848	8,377	404	8,315	533	6·0	42
31. Mysore	1916	Teaching & Affiliating	53	English & Kannada	Yes	40,011	45,867	1,194	31,910	8,101	20·2	38
32. Nagpur	1923	Teaching & Affiliating	61	English, Hindi, Marathi	Yes	32,464	34,538	1,858	28,011	4,453	13·7	38
33. North Bengal	1962	Teaching & Affiliating	14	English		7,343		13	5,486	1,857	25·3	
34. Orissa	1962	Teaching & Residential	0	English		981			981	Nil	Nil	
35. Osmania	1918	Teaching & Affiliating	49	English, Hindi, Telugu, Urdu	Yes	25,430	26,821	1,019	20,957	4,473	17·6	19
36. Panjab	1947	Teaching & Affiliating	139	English, Hindi, Urdu, Punjabi	Yes	63,147	57,163	2,023	48,993	14,154	22·4	120
37. Patna	1917	Teaching & Residential	0	Hindi (a) & English	Yes	10,815	10,190	2,384	8,603	2,212	20·5	24
38. Poona	1949	Teaching & Affiliating	22	English & Marathi (a)	Yes	39,536	38,518	1,735	33,409	6,127	15·5	87
39. Punjab Agricultural	1962	Teaching & Residential	0	English		1,344		131	1,344	Nil	Nil	11
40. Punjabi	1962	Teaching & Residential	9	Hindi (a), Punjabi, English		3,605		217	2,620	985	27·3	3
41. Rabindra Bharati	1962	Teaching & Affiliating	0	Bengali & English (a)		131			90	41	31·3	0

(a) In a few departments. (i) Constituent and Affiliating.

APPENDIX 4 (continued)

University	Enrollment 1962-3 — By course of study (c)								Books in library	
	Arts	Science	Professions	Education	Technology (d)	Commerce	Agriculture (e)	Other	No. of titles	Including affiliated colleges
28. Madras	15,137 / 7,167	28,202 / 14,453	6,439 / 6,275	2,293 / 1,559	4,735 / 4,506	5,011 / 2,388	1,374 / 1,211	900 / 316	1,455,114	
29. Magadh	13,950 / 7,892	6,421 / 3,349	320	Nil / Nil	Nil / Nil	1,113 / 759	525 / 506	Nil		
30. Marathwada	3,050 / 1,478	2,592 / 1,052	983 / 545	148 / 148	567 / 192	1,146 / 511	295 / 202	67 / 17	141,960	
31. Mysore	7,709 / 4,411	20,129 / 8,270	2,432 / 2,199	606 / 584	4,517 / 4,014	3,932 / 2,326	686 / 542	Nil	789,595	
32. Nagpur	12,498 / 5,942	6,136 / 2,999	1,657 / 1,607	992 / 440	719 / 519	8,602 / 3,963	1,860 / 1,128	Nil	458,581	
33. North Bengal	4,773 / 3,519	2,017 / 1,117	Nil / Nil	207 / 207	232 / 232	114 / Nil	Nil / Nil	Nil		
34. Orissa									23,545	
35. Osmania	5,863 / 3,736	9,493 / 4,840	3,220 / 2,814	465 / 450	2,223 / 1,684	2,369 / 2,065	720 / 532	1,077 / 275	405,077	
36. Panjab	33,938 / 20,023	14,704 / 6,742	3,258 / 1,684	3,433 / 2,795	6,278 / 1,670	765 / 452	771 / 268	Nil	1,247,675	
37. Patna	5,816 / 3,146	2,014 / 857	1,466 / 1,377	289	572 / 454	639 / 375	Nil / Nil	19	240,204	
38. Poona	14,255 / 6,651	12,361 / 5,498	2,214 / 1,693	1,021 / 641	2,522 / 1,537	6,239 / 3,540	924 / 390	Nil	850,619	
39. Punjab Agricultural	Nil / Nil	Nil	Nil / Nil	Nil / Nil	Nil / Nil	Nil / Nil	1,344	Nil		
40. Punjabi	1,415 / 876	318 / 160	597 / 565	329 / 264	697 / 472	249 / 249	Nil / Nil	Nil	21,797	
41. Rabindra Bharati	131 / Nil	Nil / Nil	Nil / Nil	Nil / Nil	Nil / Nil	Nil / Nil	Nil / Nil	Nil		

(c) Top number = total, bottom number = degrees awarded.   (d) Including Engineering.   (e) Including Farm Sciences.

APPENDIX 4 (continued)

University	Year of foundation	Type	No. of affiliated colleges	Medium of instruction	Student advisory group	Enrollment 1962-3 Total	Total 1964-5	Total graduates	Men	Women	% women	Foreign students
42. Rajasthan Agricultural	1962	Teaching & Residential	0	English		1,295		38	1,293	2	0.2	0
43. Rajasthan	1947	Teaching & Affiliating	67	English & Hindi	Yes	30,649	14,625	2,340	26,430	4,219	13.8	16
44. Ranchi	1960	Teaching & Affiliating	26	Hindi (a) & English		19,705		565	17,178	2,527	12.8	18
45. Roorkee	1949	Teaching & Affiliating	0	English	Yes	1,866	1,724	104	1,844	22	1.2	60
46. S.N.D.T. Women's	1951 (j)	Teaching & Residential	9	Gujarati, Marathi, English, Hindi		4,333	8,105	211	Nil	4,333	100.0	0
47. Sardar Vallabhbhai Vidyapeeth	1955	Teaching & Affiliating	9(i)	English, Hindi, Gujarati	Yes	6,184	401(b)	403	5,710	474	7.7	28
48. Saugar	1946	Teaching & Affiliating	78	English & Hindi	Yes	20,589	13,876	1,684	18,849	1,740	8.5	0
49. Shivaji	1962	Teaching & Affiliating	37	English & Marathi								
50. Sri Venkateswara	1954	Teaching & Affiliating	23	English	Yes	9,517		337	8,339	1,178	12.4	0
51. U.P. Agricultural	1960	Teaching & Residential	0	English	Yes	678			678	Nil	Nil	7
52. Utkal	1943	Teaching & Affiliating	51	English	Yes	17,646	13,696	836	15,545	2,101	11.9	4
53. Varanaseya Sanskrit Vishvavidyalaya	1958	Teaching & Affiliating	57	Sanskrit & Hindi	Yes	710		461(k)	690	20	2.8	43
54. Vikram	1957	Teaching & Affiliating	45	English & Hindi	Yes	31,578	35,943	3,846	27,401	4,177	13.2	40
55. Visva Bharati	1951 (l)	Teaching & Residential	0	English & Bengali (a)		502	511	177	274	228	45.4	15

(a) In a few departments. (b) Does not seem comparable to 1962-3 total enrollment. (i) Constituent and Affiliating,
(j) Established in 1916 but started functioning as statutory university in 1951 under Act of Bombay Legislature, 1951. (k) 1961-2.
(l) Established in 1921 but declared institution of national importance under Act of Parliament, 1951.

Enrollment 1962-63

University	By course of study (c) Arts	Science	Professions	Education	Technology (d)	Commerce	Agriculture (e)	Other	Books in library No. of titles	Including affiliated colleges
42. Rajasthan Agricultural	Nil	Nil	Nil	Nil	Nil	Nil	1,295	Nil		
	Nil	Nil	Nil	Nil	Nil	Nil	569	Nil		
43. Rajasthan	13,136	7,319	2,027	938	949	6,033	247	Nil	823,176	No
	7,888	3,905	1,684	563	933	3,495	119	Nil		
44. Ranchi	8,760	4,314	827	Nil	3,965	1,550	289	Nil	185,908	No
	4,892	2,172	827	Nil	3,965	934	270	Nil		
45. Roorkee	Nil	70	Nil	Nil	1,796	Nil	Nil	Nil	57,195	No
	Nil	Nil	Nil	Nil	891	Nil	Nil	Nil		
46. S.N.D.T. Women's	3,700	Nil	9	275	Nil	Nil	Nil	349	85,751	No
	1,770	Nil	9	248	Nil	Nil	Nil	349		
47. Sardar Vallabhbhai Vidyapeeth	1,365	1,926	Nil	235	1,129	667	862	Nil	107,866	
	671	467	Nil	104	1,104	423	388	Nil		
48. Saugar	7,638	4,473	2,187	968	1,831	2,914	387	191	285,813	Yes
	6,426	3,979	1,358	674	805	2,779	360	145		
49. Shivaji										
50. Sri Venkateswara	2,368	4,234	643	255	1,020	217	123	230	227,177	Yes
	1,121	2,039	643	255	870	119	123	144		
51. U.P. Agricultural	Nil	Nil	Nil	Nil	Nil	Nil	678	Nil	8,788	No
	Nil	Nil	Nil	Nil	Nil	Nil	Nil	Nil		
52. Utkal	7,343	7,074	1,446	308	903	572	Nil	Nil	309,330	No
	4,061	3,508	1,392	299	903	556	Nil	Nil		
53. Varanaseya Sanskrit Vishvavidyalaya									147,259	
54. Vikram	12,777	7,948	3,016	603	2,126	3,869	1,095	144	351,095	No
	10,450	7,220	2,872	465	1,928	3,231	1,029	144		
55. Visva Bharati	258	19	Nil	74	Nil	Nil	Nil	151	224,000	No
	127	19	Nil	Nil	Nil	Nil	Nil	Nil		

(c) Top number = total, bottom number = degrees awarded.   (d) Including Engineering.   (e) Including Farm Sciences.

APPENDIX 4 (continued)

University	No. resident in hostels	No. of teachers	Staff-student ratio	No. taking B.A. examinations					Income Sources %			Total in millions of Rs.	Total expenditure in millions of Rs.
				1st class	2nd class	3rd class	Passed without class	Failed	Govt. and local bodies	Fees	Endowments and other		
1. Agra	8,028	3,360	1 : 17						55·0	40·1	4·9	28·27	29·27
2. Aligarh Muslim	2,805	421	1 : 12	16	174	115	2	177	82·2	12·7	5·1	10·32	9·92
3. Allahabad	2,552	465	1 : 23						75·7	18·5	5·8	9·78	8·46
4. Andhra	7,187	1,918	1 : 17				2,147(m)	4,174	54·7	37·1	8·2	25·14	24·78
5. Annamalai	1,829	265	1 : 12	25	55	66	Nil	87	63·1	22·2	14·7	5·18	5·02
6. Banaras Hindu	3,649	673	1 : 12	27	483	1,051	3	1,792	52·8	11·2	36·0	21·4	22·1
7. Bhagalpur	2,064	876	1 : 22	10	265	1,410	Nil	2,585	61·9	31·2	6·9	10·6	9·6
8. Bihar	3,285	1,129	1 : 26	32	410	2,136	Nil	3,489	60·6	28·6	10·8	19·0	14·1
9. Bombay	3,598	1,765	1 : 30						30·9	54·3	14·8	32·0	32·0
10. Burdwan	3,528	1,002	1 : 21	9	314	Nil	1,376	1,393	75·2	22·5	2·3	14·63	20·60
11. Calcutta	12,743	5,813	1 : 20	87	3,471	317(n)	11,116	17,532	57·0	37·2	5·8	65·14	64·45
12. Delhi	3,004	1,492	1 : 17	194	640	1,981	Nil	1,218	70·3	20·8	8·9	25·3	25·2
13. Gauhati	5,092	1,456	1 : 24						30·9	10·9	58·2	23·03	23·08

(m) Total of 1st, 2nd and 3rd classes.   (n) Distinction category (not 3rd class).

APPENDIX 4 (continued)

Salaries in rupees per month

University	Universities and constituent colleges				Affiliated colleges			
	Principal	Professor	Reader	Lecturer	Principal	Professor	Reader	Lecturer
1. Agra		1,000-50-1,500	700-40-1,100	400-30-640-40-800	800-1,200	350-800 (p)	325-625 (p)	250-500 (p)
2. Aligarh Muslim	700-40-1,000	700-40-1,000	700-40-1,000	400-30-640-40-800	650-900	300-600	275-550	225-450
3. Allahabad	1,500-50-2,000	1,100-40-1,340 / 900-40-1,140	500-30-800	350-25-600	NA	NA	NA	NA
4. Andhra		1,000-50-1,500	700-40-1,100	400-30-640-40-800	500-800 / 400-1,200 / 400-1,000 / 400-600	NA	300-600 / 250-500	200-500 / 150-300
5. Annamalai		800-1,250	500-850	250-500	NA	NA	NA	NA
6. Banaras Hindu	1,000-50-1,500	1,000-50-1,500	700-40-1,100	400-30-640-40-800	650-900	NA	300-600	225-450
7. Bhagalpur	850-1,250	850-50-1,250	350-25-650-EB-35-1,000	200-750	500-800			175-350
8. Bihar	850-50-1,250			200-20-220-25-320-EB-25-670-20-750	500-850 / 500-35-850			200-500 / 200-500
9. Bombay	600-800	350-650		250-550	NA	NA	NA	NA
10. Burdwan		1,000-50-1,500	700-40-1,100	400-30-640-40-800	500-25-700		250-10-420-15-450	150-10-
11. Calcutta	350-1,200	300-1,200	250-750	200-500	600-1,000 to 300-600	500-700 to 325-1,000	250-450 to 275-650	320-15-350 / 200-500 to 125-300
12. Delhi		1,000-50-1,500	700-40-1,100	400-30-640-40-800	800-1,150 / 600-1,000 / 350-1,600	400-850 / 350-800 / 200-600	225-600	200-600 / 200-400 / 150-250
13. Gauhati		1,000-50-1,500	700-40-1,100	400-30-640-40-800				

(p) Categories not uniform.

APPENDIX 4 (continued)

University	No. resident in hostels	No. of teachers	Staff-student ratio	No. taking B.A. examinations					Income Sources %			Total in millions of Rs.	Total expenditure in millions of Rs.
				1st class	2nd class	3rd class	Passed without class	Failed	Govt. and local bodies	Fees	Endowments and other		
14. Gorakhpur	1,597	812	1:19						49·5	43·4	7·1	7·33	6·86
15. Gujarat	6,662	2,081	1:19						51·8	38·4	9·8	21·67	21·72
16. Indira Kala Sangit Vishwavidyalaya	15	7	1:13	13(q)	65(q)	41(q)	Nil	329(q)	87·0	11·0	2·0	(r)	(s)
17. Jabalpur	2,438	603	1:18	38	493	413	13	507	73·8	19·2	7·0	8·4	8·4
18. Jadavpur	807	291	1:12	5	76	Nil	Nil	30	75·0	9·0	16·0	8·29	7·76
19. Jammu and Kashmir	919	632	1:17·5						84·1	12·2	3·7	11·76	9·69
20. Jodhpur	962	233	1:26						73·5	0·2	26·2	2·86	2·61
21. Kalyani	471	66	1:7						91·4	3·3	5·3	3·27	3·71
22. Kameshwar Singh Darbhanga Sanskrit Vishvavidyalaya		652	1:8										
23. Karnatak	3,574	1,233	1:15	63	358	982	Nil	925	65·0	33·0	2·0	19·62	18·33
24. Kerala	13,025	2,850	1:20						59·8	30·8	9·4	39·61	38·66
25. Kurukshetra	478	128	1:6	(t)	(t)	(t)	(t)	(t)	69·0	2·0	29·0	3·60	4·34
26. Lucknow	2,613	859	1:20						67·7	21·5	10·8	13·86	11·81

(q) Bachelor of Music exam.   (r) Rs 101,873.   (s) Rs 117,820.   (t) None took B.A. exam.

Salaries in rupees per month

University	Universities and constituent colleges				Affiliated colleges			
	Principal	Professor	Reader	Lecturer	Principal	Professor	Reader	Lecturer
14. Gorakhpur		1,000—50—1,500	700—40—1,100	400—30—640 —40—800	650—900	300—600	275—550	225—450
15. Gujarat		800—1,250	500—800	250—500	600—800	400—25—700	300—25—600	200—15—320—20—500
16. Indira Kala Sangit Vishwavidyalaya								
17. Jabalpur		800—1,000 1,000—50—1,500	400—800 700—40—800	225—500 400—30—640 —40—800				
18. Jadavpur	1,000—50—1,500	1,000—50—1,500	700—40—1,000	400—30— 640—40—800	NA	800—40—1,000 NA	400—25—550 —25—800 NA	NA
19. Jammu and Kashmir		1,000—50—1,500	600—50—1,000	350—30—700	500—40—700 —50—1,000	450—30—600 —40—800	300—30— 360—30—600	250—25— 350—30—500
20. Jodhpur	500—750	1,000—50—1,500	700—40—1,100	400—30— 640—40—800	NA	NA	NA	NA
21. Kalyani				400—30— 640—40—800	NA	NA	NA	NA
22. Kameshwar Singh Darbhanga Sanskrit Vishvavidyalaya				250—450				
23. Karnatak		1,000—50—1,500	700—40—1,100	400—30—640—40—800 400—30—640—EB—40—800	600—1,000 350—1,100	600—1,000 400—900	300—600	230—500
24. Kerala		1,000—50—1,500	700—40—1,100	200—500 (p) 350—25—600 to 200—400	500—800 600—700 475—700	500—800 475—700 400—700	250—500 200—400	
25. Kurukshetra	1,500—50—2,000	350—1,250(p)	250—750 (p)		NA	NA	NA	NA
26. Lucknow	500—1,500	1,100—40—1,340 900—40—1,140	600—30—900 500—30—800		NA	NA	NA	NA

(p) Categories not uniform.

APPENDIX 4 (continued)

| University | No. resident in hostels | No. of teachers | Staff-student ratio | No. taking B.A. examinations | | | | | Income | | | | Total expenditure in millions of Rs. |
| | | | | 1st class | 2nd class | 3rd class | Passed without class | Failed | Sources % | | | Total in millions of Rs. | |
									Govt. and local bodies	Fees	Endowments and other		
27. M.S. University of Baroda	2,121	432	1 : 23	54	165	390	Nil	193	59·5	25·6	14·9	11·79	13·42
28. Madras	26,585	3,978	1 : 16						54·1	30·3	15·6	60·2	62·8
29. Magadh	837	806	1 : 28						79·3	16·9	3·8	8·87	8·95
30. Marathwada	1,249	424	1 : 21	4	130	272	Nil	463	65·8	27·1	7·1	18·5	28·1
31. Mysore	4,517	1,983	1 : 20						63·9	26·3	9·8	21·9	20·3
32. Nagpur	3,104	1,336	1 : 24	69	1,086	1,087	Nil	1,229					
33. North Bengal	1,099	375	1 : 20										
34. Orissa	822	107	1 : 9										
35. Osmania	2,900	1,681	1 : 15	44	400	922	Nil	1,408	76·4	18·8	4·8	21·5	22·4
36. Panjab	12,139	3,353	1 : 19	189	938	5,834		16,174	44·8	44·3	10·9	54·16	56·76
37. Patna	5,170	590	1 : 18						70·7	27·0	2·3	10·7	8·9
38. Poona	7,207	1,652	1 : 24	39	851	1,408	Nil	2,342	53·1	37·4	9·5	28·31	27·65
39. Punjab Agricultural	719	145	1 : 9									10·19	10·19

Salaries in rupees per month

University	Universities and constituent colleges				Affiliated colleges			
	Principal	Professor	Reader	Lecturer	Principal	Professor	Reader	Lecturer
27. M.S. University of Baroda 28. Madras	600–30–900	800–1,250 450–25–850	500–800	250–500 225–10–275 –15–425	NA	NA	NA	NA
29. Magadh		850–50– 1,250	350–25–650 –EB–35– 1,000	200–20–220– 25–320–EB– 25–670–EB– 20–750	500–35–850			200–20–220– 15–340– EB–20 –500
30. Marathwada		1,000–50– 1,500	700–40– 1,100	400–30–640 –EB–40–800	400–25–700	300–20–400 –25–600	300–20–400 –25–600	200–15–380 –20–400
31. Mysore		800–50– 1,250	500–25–800	250–20–500		600–40– 1,000 400– 30–700–40– 900	300–20–400 –25–600	230–20–350 –25–500
32. Nagpur	1,250–50– 1,500	800–50– 1,200	400–40–800	250–25–500	350–1,000 to 350–25– 600	300–1,000 to 400–700	300–600 250–500	200–650 to 250–350
33. North Bengal	500–50– 1,500 to 300–10–450 1,000–1,250	400–25–700	325–1,000 300–600	275–650 to 150–350				
34. Orissa 35. Osmania		510–900 900–50– 1,250	900–40– 1,100 600–30–900	260–780 650–30–800 325–25–550 –EB–25–650	NA 600–800	NA 400–25–700	NA 300–25–600	NA 200–15– 320–20–500
36. Panjab		1,000–50– 1,500	700–40– 1,100	400–30–640 –40–800	600–40–800			200–15– 320–20–500
37. Patna		850–50– 1,250	350–25–650 –35–1,000	200–20–220 –25–320– EB–25–670 EB–20–750	NA	NA	NA	NA
38. Poona		1,000–50– 1,500	700–40– 1,100	400–360– 640–40–800	300–20–400 –25–600	300–20–400 –25–600	250–15–430 –20–450	200–15–380 –20–400
39. Punjab Agricultural	1,200–50– 1,500–50– 1,800	1,000–50– 1,500	700–40–980 –40–1,100(p)	400–30–640 –40–800 (p)	NA	NA	NA	NA

(p) Categories not uniform.

APPENDIX 4 (continued)

University	No. resident in hostels	No. of teachers	Staff-student ratio	No. taking B.A. examinations					Income Sources %			Total in millions of Rs. (u)	Total expenditure in millions of Rs. (v)
				1st class	2nd class	3rd class	Passed without class	Failed	Govt. and local bodies	Fees	Endowment and other		
40. Punjabi	998	332	1 : 11						72·4	25·2	2·4		
41. Rabindra Bharati		31	1 : 4										
42. Rajasthan Agricultural	446	146	1 : 8						86·0	2·5	11·5	2·18	1·94
43. Rajasthan	5,634	2,000	1 : 15	43	958	1,874	Nil	3,711	76·1	16·1	7·8	33·50	31·78
44. Ranchi	6,068	1,006	1 : 20				1,779(m)	1,479	71·3	23·0	5·7	15·5	11·9
45. Roorkee	1,866	183	1 : 10						84·0	12·0	4·0	6·62	7·63
46. S.N.D.T. Women's	301	272	1 : 16						32·5	57·4	10·1	3·13	3·91
47. Sardar Vallabhbhai Vidyapeeth	3,119	388	1 : 15	12	52	172	Nil	90	53·3	33·4	13·3	6·90	6·90
48. Saugar	2,758	1,452	1 : 14	34	392	1,154	23	956	72·2	21·5	6·3	12·2	13·2
49. Shivaji													
50. Sri Venkateswara	3,114	820	1 : 12	67	30	287	Nil	684	69·3	19·3	11·4	13·3	12·1
51. U.P. Agricultural	678	71	1 : 10						81·3	11·8	6·9	0·9	5·6

(m) Total of 1st, 2nd and 3rd classes. (u) Rs 552,886. (v) Rs 261,298.

APPENDIX 4 (continued)

Salaries in rupees per month

University	Universities and constituent colleges				Affiliated colleges			
	Principal	Professor	Reader	Lecturer	Principal	Professor	Reader	Lecturer
40. Punjabi		1,000-50-1,500	700-40-1,100	400-30-640-40-800	350-1,200 600-40-800		350-950 250-750	200-15-320-20-500
41. Rabindra Bharati		1,000-50-1,500	700-40-1,100	400-30-640-40-800	NA	NA	500-25-700 NA	NA
42. Rajasthan Agricultural	950-50-1,400	550-30-820-EB-30-850-50-950	285-25-510-EB-25-500-30-860-900	400-30-640-40-800 285-25-510-25-560-30-800	NA	NA	NA	NA
43. Rajasthan		1,000-50-1,500	700-40-1,100	400-30-640-40-800	800-50-1200 600-40-800	500-25-700-30-850, 400-25-700		250-15-400-25-600
44. Ranchi		850-50-1,250	350-25-650-35-1,000	200-20-220-25-320-EB-25-670-EB-20-750	500-35-850			200-20-220-15-340-EB-20-500
45. Roorkee		2,000-2,500 1,350-1,750	500-1,200	250-850	NA	NA	NA	NA
46. S.N.D.T. Women's		800-50-1,250	700-40-1,100	400-30-640-40-800			700-40-1,100	400-30-640-40-800
47. Sardar Vallabh-bhai Vidyapeeth		1,250	500-25-800	250-20-500		300-15-400		200-10-300
48. Saugar		1,000-50-1,500	700-40-1,100	400-30-640-40-800	1,000-1,250 to 350-850	350-850 300-600	350-850 to 250-400	225-600 to 215-450
49. Shivaji		1,000-50-1,500		350-350-450 380-30-590		300-20-400-25-600	250-15-	200-15-
50. Sri Venkateswara		1,000-50-1,500	600-40-100 50/2-1,150	30-770-40-850	600-40-800 400-30-700	400-25-700 250-10-400-25-500	430-20-450 300-25-600	380-20-400 200-15-320 20-500, 10-150-
51. U.P. Agricultural		1,000-50-1,400	250-25-400-EB-30-700-50-850		NA	NA	NA	10-300 NA

APPENDIX 4 (continued)

University	No. resident in hostels	No. of teachers	Staff-student ratio	No. taking B.A. examinations					Income				
				1st class	2nd class	3rd class	Passed without class	Failed	Sources %			Total in millions of Rs.	Total expenditure in millions of Rs.
									Govt. and local bodies	Fees	Endowments and other		
52. Utkal	5,857	1,136	1 : 16	44	447	1,481	Nil	1,142	62·6	18·9	18·5	13·6	14·8
53. Varanaseya Sanskrit Vishvavidyalaya	224	65	1 : 9						83·1	10·2	6·7	1·5	1·4
54. Vikram	4,237	1,747	1 : 18	30	851	2,295	21	949	77·6	18·6	3·8	18·01	18·40
55. Visvabharati	375	115	1 : 4	Nil	22	1	Nil	1	72·6	24·3	3·1	2·83	4·80

APPENDIX 4 (continued)

Salaries in rupees per month

University	Universities and constituent colleges				Affiliated colleges			
	Principal	Professor	Reader	Lecturer	Principal	Professor	Reader	Lecturer
52. Utkal		800–50–1,250 600–40–960	510–30–570 –EB–30–690 –30–780– EB–40–860	260–15–320 –20–400–30 –520–EB– 40–680–50– 780	600–40–960 600–40–800		400–25–700	300–25– 600 200–15– 320–20– 500
53. Varanaseya Sanskrit Vishvavidyalaya		1,000–50– 1,500 800 50–1,250	400–30–640– 40–800 300–20– 500–EB–25– 800					
54. Vikram		1,000–50– 1,500	700–40– 1,100 500– 25–800	300–20–600– 250–20–500	1,100–30– 1,160–40– 1,200 to 700–40–900	500–30–800 to 310–15– 340–20–500	360–15–405 –20–425–25 –550–25– 700 300– 20–600	250–25– 550 150–10– 250
55. Visvabharati		1,000–50– 1,500	700–40– 1,100	400–30–640– –40–800	NA	NA	NA	NA

Sources: *Handbook of Universities in India, 1963*, New Delhi: University Grants Commission, 1964.
United States Educational Foundation in India, *Handbook of Indian Universities*, New Delhi: Allied Publishers, 1963.
The World of Learning 1964–5, 15th edition, London: Europa Publications Ltd., 1964.

APPENDIX 5

UNIVERSITY ENROLLMENT IN INDIA: BY STATE AND FACULTY
(1964–5)

(Numbers in brackets indicate percentages)

State	Arts	Science	Commerce	Education	Engineering/Technology
Andhra	18,181 (23·1)	37,083 (47·1)	5,526 (7·0)	1,487 (1·9)	6,169 (7·8)
Assam	32,667 (67·9)	9,464 (19·6)	2,367 (4·9)	391 (0·8)	967 (2·0)
Bihar	61,253 (53·8)	31,670 (27·8)	5,774 (5·1)	1,042 (0·9)	6,632 (5·8)
Gujarat	30,966 (37·0)	24,289 (29·0)	12,329 (14·7)	1,148 (1·4)	6,019 (7·2)
Jammu & Kashmir	5,176 (39·7)	5,237 (40·2)	235 (1·8)	420 (3·2)	971 (7·5)
Kerala	28,632 (34·3)	40,978 (49·1)	3,590 (4·3)	2,450 (2·9)	4,008 (4·8)
Madhya Pradesh	36,696 (41·0)	23,226 (26·0)	10,833 (12·1)	2,326 (2·6)	6,062 (6·8)
Madras	23,002 (26·1)	41,673 (47·2)	5,697 (6·4)	1,828 (2·1)	6,580 (7·5)
Maharashtra	59,363 (35·7)	51,632 (31·1)	29,519 (17·7)	3,725 (2·2)	5,781 (3·5)
Mysore	16,703 (23·3)	29,355 (41·7)	6,058 (8·5)	1,371 (1·9)	8,340 (11·6)
Orissa	11,826 (43·5)	8,625 (31·7)	786 (2·9)	611 (2·2)	1,856 (6·8)
Punjab	39,900 (50·0)	17,749 (22·2)	1,581 (2·0)	4,069 (5·1)	7,884 (9·9)
Rajasthan	16,614 (40·9)	9,898 (24·4)	6,656 (16·5)	1,425 (3·5)	1,434 (3·5)
Uttar Pradesh	151,335 (45·3)	101,219 (30·3)	24,332 (7·3)	4,710 (1·4)	7,560 (2·3)
West Bengal	88,309 (49·2)	42,906 (23·2)	30,017 (16·8)	2,284 (1·3)	6,843 (3·8)
Delhi	20,536 (67·6)	3,229 (10·6)	2,489 (8·2)	241 (0·8)	1,008 (3·3)
Total	641,186 (42·0)	478,702 (31·2)	147,789 (9·7)	29,528 (1·0)	78,114 (5·1)

APPENDIX 5 (continued)

State	Medicine	Agriculture	Veterinary	Law	Others	Total
Andhra	6,915 (8·8)	1,181 (1·5)	626 (0·8)	1,291 (1·6)	312 (0·4)	78,691
Assam	1,117 (2·4)	391 (0·8)	246 (0·5)	527 (1·1)		43,197
Bihar	2,941 (2·6)	1,089 (0·9)	650 (0·6)	2,846 (2·5)	6	113,903
Gujarat	3,686 (4·4)	1,241 (1·5)	100 (0·1)	3,319 (3·9)	690 (0·3)	83,787
Jammu & Kashmir	650 (5·0)	334 (2·6)				13,023
Kerala	2,734 (3·3)	284 (0·4)	252 (0·3)	524 (0·6)		83,452
Madhya Pradesh	4,202 (4·7)	1,356 (2·1)	492 (0·6)	312 (3·5)	420 (0·5)	89,264
Madras	6,013 (6·8)	988 (1·1)	705 (0·8)	1,161 (1·3)	631 (0·7)	88,278
Maharashtra	6,844 (4·1)	3,909 (2·4)	361 (0·2)	5,050 (3·0)	100 (0·1)	166,334
Mysore	6,040 (8·4)	967 (1·3)	437 (0·6)	1,905 (2·7)		71,676
Orissa	1,841 (6·8)	970 (3·6)	259 (1·0)	428 (1·5)		27,202
Punjab	4,832 (6·1)	2,023 (2·5)	386 (0·5)	983 (1·2)	423 (0·5)	79,830
Rajasthan	1,911 (4·7)	1,372 (3·4)	180 (0·4)	1,101 (2·7)		40,591
Uttar Pradesh	5,596 (1·7)	27,029 (8·1)	864 (0·4)	5,230 (1·5)	6,247 (1·8)	334,122
West Bengal	4,199 (2·3)	594 (0·3)	153 (0·1)	3,778 (2·1)	363 (0·2)	179,446
Delhi	2,161 (7·1)			705 (2·3)	35 (0·1)	30,431
Total	61,742 (4·0)	44,228 (2·9)	5,711 (0·4)	32,000 (2·1)	9,227 (0·6)	1,528,227

Includes enrollment in Intermediate Boards.　　　Source: *University Development in India*, University Grants Commission.

CONSTITUTION OF THE NATIONAL BOARD OF CHRISTIAN HIGHER EDUCATION

Preamble

The Constitution of a National Board of Christian Higher Education was recommended by the ISS-FERES Consultation of 150 principals of Christian colleges in India held at Tambaram, Madras, from 30 December 1966 to 5 January 1967, at which the following resolution was unanimously passed:

> 'This consultation strongly recommends the formation of a federation between the Xavier Board of Higher Education in India and the Christian Colleges Association to be established on the initiative of the National Christian Council of India.'

I. *Name*

The Federation shall be called the 'National Board of Christian Higher Education in India'.

II. *Aims and Functions*

The Board's aims and functions shall be:

1. to foster moral and spiritual values and to promote Christian ideals in education;
2. to co-ordinate the work of Christian colleges in India at the national, regional and local levels;
3. to promote mutual help and support;
4. to collect and circulate useful and worthwhile information;
5. to publish a journal;
6. to arrange for meetings and seminars;
7. to act as an employment exchange for teachers wanting to serve in Christian institutions;
8. to arrange for the exchange of staff and students between Christian colleges;
9. to initiate and assist special educational projects in colleges under its purview;
10. to study national issues bearing upon education and offer practical suggestions;
11. to serve as a channel through which Christian colleges can contribute to the formation of a national educational policy;
12. to interpret to the public the role of Christian colleges in national development;
13. to represent member institutions before Government and other agencies;

14. to collaborate wherever possible with other institutions and associations concerned with higher learning.

III. *Membership*

The Board's membership shall be twofold: executive and associate.

1. The following shall be the executive members:
   (a) The President, the two Vice-Presidents, the General Secretary and the Joint Secretary.
   (b) Five members nominated by the Xavier Board of Higher Education and five by the Christian Colleges Association.
   (c) Not more than three members, if any, co-opted by the executive members.
2. The following shall be Associate members: All principals of Christian institutions of higher learning in India which are affiliated to the federating organizations mentioned above, viz.: the Xavier Board of Higher Education in India and the Christian Colleges Association.
3. In the subsequent articles, the words 'The Board' shall include executive members only and the words 'The Colleges' shall refer to the institutions mentioned in III 2.

IV. *Appointment of Office-bearers and Members*

1. The Board shall be reconstituted every three years on the occasion of a Conference of the Principals of the Colleges; provided, however, that the term of office of the General Secretary will be as defined by IV 4.
2. The office of the President will be held alternately by the nominee of each of the two federating organizations for a term of three years.
3. Each of the federating organizations will nominate one Vice-President and five other members for each three-year term.
4. The General Secretary shall be a salaried official appointed by the Board on such terms and conditions as the Board shall determine.
5. The Joint Secretary, who shall work in an honorary capacity, shall be named for a three-year term by the Board.

V. *Vacancies*

Vacancies occurring in the post of General Secretary and Joint Secretary shall be filled by the Board itself. Vacancies among other members shall be filled by the federating organization to which the previous incumbent belonged.

VI. *Duties*

1. The Board's duties shall be to carry out the aims set forth in II, to watch over the interests of the colleges; to carry out the directions given to it by the Conference of Principals; to frame the annual budget and raise funds; to represent the colleges before the public, governments, universities, etc.; to lay down the policy of the Secretariat and to direct its work.

2. The President shall preside at all meetings of the Board and meetings of the Principals or Staffs of Colleges called by the Board. He shall ordinarily represent the Board before the public, governments, universities, etc. He shall also guide the Secretary in his work.

3. The Vice-Presidents shall represent the President whenever necessary and, in his absence, one of them shall be elected by the other members of the Board to preside at meetings of the Board or of Principals or Staffs of Colleges.

4. The General Secretary shall be in charge of the Board's Secretariat and shall be entitled to incur the expenses necessary for its ordinary administration, within budgetary provisions.

5. The Joint Secretary shall assist the General Secretary as and when needed.

VII. *Powers*

The Board shall be empowered:

1. to recommend to the colleges, through the Secretariat, policies to be followed, measures to be adopted and steps to be taken in pursuance of its aims and objects.

2. to make representations, carry on correspondence, issue public statements, in the interests and on behalf of the colleges.

VIII. *Meetings*

1. *Board*

  (*a*) The Board shall meet at least once a year, and as often as decided by the President or requisitioned by at least five members.

  (*b*) Six members of the Board shall form a 'quorum'.

  (*c*) Members of the Board attending a meeting called by the Board shall be paid first-class rail fare to and fro, plus Rs 15 per day of travel or meeting.

2. *Regional*

  (*a*) The Board shall endeavour to constitute regional groups of Christian colleges with a convener for each group, so that Regional Meetings may be held at least once a year, to discuss common problems pertaining to the region.

  (*b*) Regional groups of colleges shall be entitled, through their convener, to claim from the Secretariat payment up to a maximum of Rs 20 per college per year (subject to a minimum of Rs 150 per region) for their common expenses in accordance with the aims and objects of the Board.

  (*c*) All members of the Board belonging to a region shall be entitled to attend the Regional Meetings of that region.

  (*d*) Members of the Board, not belonging to the region, may also be invited by the convener.

  (*e*) At the convener's request, the President, or a member of the Board deputed by him, may preside over Regional Meetings.

3. *General*

    (*a*) A Conference of the Principals of the Colleges or their deputies shall be held every three years, and other General Meetings as often as the Board shall think fit.

    (*b*) Members of the Board other than principals shall also be entitled to attend.

    (*c*) Conferences of the members of the teaching staffs, hostel wardens, administrative staffs of all or some of the colleges may be held from time to time at the discretion of the Board. All members of the Board and all principals of the respective colleges shall be entitled to attend such conferences.

IX. *Resolutions*

Resolutions shall ordinarily be passed by a simple majority at duly convened meetings of the Board and at General Meetings. But resolutions passed by a circular signed by not less than two-thirds of the members of the Board shall have the same authority as if they had been passed at duly convened Board Meetings.

X. *Committees*

1. The Board shall appoint three committees, each consisting of five members, three of whom shall be members of the Board, including the General Secretary. These committees shall be called the ' Committee on Academic Affairs', the ' Committee on Moral and Spiritual Affairs and Student Welfare' and the ' Financial and General Administrative Committee'.

2. The committees shall study matters within their scope, in order to assist the General Secretary, the Board, in general, and the Conference of Principals or Staff, with expert opinion and advice.

3. The committees shall work by correspondence and shall meet at the General Secretary's discretion. The conveners shall have the power to invite others to meetings of the committees where necessary. For such meetings T.A. and D.A. shall be paid as under VIII 1 (c), to all who attend.

XI. *Secretariat*

1. The Board's Secretariat shall be located at Delhi.

2. The Secretariat shall:

    (*a*) keep all records and accounts;

    (*b*) make, under the Board's direction, all necessary arrangements for the Conferences and other General Meetings of Principals or Staffs of Colleges referred to under VIII 3 (a) and (c) ;

    (*c*) supply to the colleges all possible information regarding qualified teachers available, scholarships in India and abroad for Indian students, details concerning National or International Academic Congresses and any other matter likely to be useful to the colleges ;

(*d*) give to the colleges, or obtain for them, as far as possible, any expert advice that may be required by them;

(*e*) bring about, whenever necessary, under the Board's direction, such co-ordination of activities of the colleges as the common good may require;

(*f*) in general carry out the Board's aims and functions and provide such assistance and guidance to the colleges as may be beneficial to them;

(*g*) operate the bank account and keep audited statements.

XII. *Finances*

1. The funds of the Board shall be obtained from the colleges affiliated to the two federating organizations and from such other sources as may be available.

2. The rates of subscription for the colleges shall be as follows:
   (*a*) Colleges with 1,500 students or more   Rs 200 per year
   (*b*) Colleges with 800 students or more and less than 1,500 students   Rs 150 per year
   (*c*) Colleges with 250 students or more and less than 800 students   Rs 100 per year
   (*d*) Colleges with under 250 students   Rs 50 per year

3. These subscriptions shall be collected from all colleges by the Secretariat of the Board before 31 March of every financial year.

4. The Board's funds shall be deposited in a bank account to be operated by the General Secretary who will circulate to the members of the Board an Audited Statement of Accounts on or before 1 June of each year, and also present the same to the Annual Meeting of the Board. The financial year will be deemed to run from 1 April to 31 March.

5. The Budget shall be framed at the Annual Meeting of the Board to be held between July and December of each year.

6. The President, however, shall have power to sanction unbudgeted expenditure not exceeding Rs 2,000 in any financial year for any purpose which in his opinion falls within the aims and functions laid down in II.

7. The Annual Budget and Statement of Accounts shall be circulated to the principals of the colleges and their comments, if any, shall be transmitted by the General Secretary to the members of the Board for their information and guidance.

The Triennial Conference of Principals shall have power to review the financial policies and administration of the Board.

XIII. *Amendments*

Amendments to this Constitution shall require not less than a two-thirds majority of the principals or their deputies and members of the Board present and voting at a Conference or other General Meetings.

APPENDIX 7

THEOLOGICAL SCHOOLS IN INDIA (1956)

Name	Location	Full-time faculty	Part-time faculty	Theology students	Non-theology students	Denominational support
Theological Colleges affiliated with Serampore Senate						
Serampore College	Serampore	8		25	2	Baptists, etc.
United Theological College	Bangalore	8	6	30	14	Church of South India, etc.
Leonard Theological College	Jabalpur	11	2	64	20	Methodists, etc.
Bishop's College	Calcutta	4		22		CIIPBC[1]
Gurukul Theological College	Madras	4		11		Lutheran
Subtotal: 5		35	8	152	36	
Theological Schools affiliated with Serampore Senate						
Union Theological Seminary	Bareilly	8	3	26		Methodists, English Baptists, etc.
Tamilnad Theological College	Tirumaraiyur	5	4	30		Church of South India
Gujerat United School of Theology	Ahmedabad	4		9	4	Irish Presbyterian, etc.
Kerala United Theological Seminary	Trivandrum	4	4	16		Church of South India
North India United Theological College	Saharanpur	8	4	23		United Church of Northern India, etc.
Mar Thoma Theological Seminary	Kottayam	1	4	9		Mar Thoma Syrian Church
Lutheran Theological College	Ranchi	3		30		Lutheran
Basel Mission Theological Seminary	Mangalore	3	5	10		Basel Evangelical Mission, etc.
Lutherigi Theological Seminary	Rajahmundry	9	3	23	20	Amer. Evan. Luth. Church, etc.
Andhra United Theological College	Dornakal	4	4	14	9	Church of South India, etc.
Baptist Theological Seminary	Kakinada	11	2	25	6	Canadian Baptist
United Theological College of Western India	Poona	5	5	22		Scottish Presbyterian, etc.
Cherta Theological College	Cherrapunji	3	3	14	18	Welsh Presbyterian, etc.
Union Kanarese Seminary	Tumkur	3	3	9		Church of South India, etc.
Union Theological College	Indore	3	2	4	6	Church of Scotland, etc.
Subtotal: 15		74	46	264	63	

21

APPENDIX 7 (continued)

Name	Location	Full-time faculty	Part-time faculty	Theology students	Non-theology students	Denominational support
Theological Schools not affiliated with Serampore Senate						
Union Biblical Seminary	Yeotmal	10	6	59	13	Free Methodist, etc.
Assam Baptist Theological Seminary	Jorhat	8	7	40		American Baptist
Theological Seminary	Kotapud	6	3	17	30	Lutheran (German)
Christian Training College	Cuttack	2	4	14		Baptist (English and Canadian)
Andhra Baptist Theological Seminary	Ramapatnam	4	3	12	19	American Baptist
Allahabad Bible Seminary	Allahabad	3	5	15	2	Oriental Mission Society
Santal Theological Seminary	Benagaria	6	1	20		Lutheran (Danish)
United Theological School	Calcutta	2	3	—[2]	7	CIPBC[1]
Karnataka Bible Seminary	Gadag	2	2	21		Oriental Mission Society
Concordia Seminary	Nagercoil	3	1	25	8	Missouri Synod (Lutheran)
Nimasarai Bengali Divinity School	Old Malda	2	1	8 ?		Lutheran (Danish)
Tamil Evan. Luth. Seminary	Tranquebar	2	3	15	10	Tamil Evan. Luth. Synod
Subtotal: 12		50	39	246	89	
Total: 32		159	93	662	188	

[1] Church of India, Pakistan, Burma and Ceylon (Anglican). [2] No theological students in ministerial courses offered.

SOURCE: Allen, Yorke, *A Seminary Survey*, pp. 94-5.

QUESTIONNAIRES USED IN THE STUDY

I. STUDENTS

STUDENT PROFILE
Do not write your name anywhere on this sheet

1. College ....
2. For what Degree (P.U.C., B.Sc., M.A., etc.)?....................................
3. Main subject of study (e.g. Education, Medicine, Economics, Physics etc.) ....
4. Years you have been at this college so far.....................................
5. Sex ....
6. Age..
7. Religion (including denomination, if Christian).............................
8. From which State do you come?..
9. Mother tongue..
10. Father's occupation..
11. Family income per year...
12. Number of brothers..
13. Number of sisters...
14. Position in family...
15. Population of your home town/village (approximate)...........................
16. Its approximate distance from college ....
17. Do you belong to the Scheduled Caste?...
    or Backward Community?..
18. Class in Secondary School Exam: (if any)......................................
19. Where do you live during college? Hostel/Home/Other arrangement
    ....
20. Did you have choice in selecting your hostel room-mates?...................
21. What kind of hostel room do you have?
    Single..........................Double............................
    Triple...........................4 or more in a room.........................
22. Are you now receiving any financial aid for your studies?

	Yes	*No*
Scholarship		
Fee concession		
Other		

23. If yes, how much are you receiving per year (amount per year)?

....

24. What percentage of your total expenses at college does the scholarship cover?...

25. Where does this aid come from? Please mark ×.

Government	
College administration	
Religious institutions	
Funds from community (like educational trusts etc.)	
Private funds	
Other	

Have you been able to buy your text books? All...............................
Some...None...

26. Rank in order of importance your reasons for attending this college. I am attending this college, because: (e.g. put 1, 2, 3, 4, etc., against each in order of importance)

It has the best reputation	
It is the only one I could get into	
It is near my home	
It is not expensive	
My family wanted me to join	
My friends were going here	
It is a good college for getting a good education	
It is a good college for getting a good job	
It offers the course I wanted	
Other	

27. Has the college come up to your expectations? Yes............No............
28. If not, in what ways have you been disappointed?

....
....
....
....
....
....
....
....
....
....
....
....

29. What percentage of your classes do you attend per week?....................
....

30. The best things about this college are the following: Rank 1 to 5 only in order of importance.

	Rank
Good academic standard	
Fellowship with students and staff	
Good job-training	
The values it stands for	
Superior facilities and living conditions	
Quality of the teachers and staff	
The extracurricular program	
Its active involvement in vital issues of India	
Its concern for the individual student	
Character training which it imparts	
Moderate fees	
Other	

31. How many hours per week do you spend in the following ways?

Classroom	
Laboratory	
Study (preparation)	
Library	
Tutorials or special classes	
Extracurricular (including sports and N.C.C.)	
Transportation (to college and back home)	
Relaxation, general reading	
Other	

32. Is the college library open at convenient times for you to use it?
....

33. How many books do you borrow from the library in a month?...........

34. Do you participate in the 'religious' program of the college?
Yes...No...

35. If so, how? Mark ×.

	Yes	No
Chapel attendance		
Assisting chapel program		
Evangelistic program		
Study and prayer groups		
Drama/choir and other program		
Other		

36. Have you studied, or do you plan to study (mark ×):

	Yes	No
Hindi		
An Indian language other than mother tongue		
A foreign language		

37. Do you feel that political parties and other groups are distracting students on certain national issues?..

38. Which political group or groups are most active in your area?............
....

39. How often do you meet teachers for discussion of academic questions? Mark ×.

Very often	Often	Occasionally	Never

40. How often do you meet teachers for discussion of personal problems? Mark ×.
Very often.................Often................Occasionally...........Never............

41. It is often said that Indian students have little contact with their teachers! Is this true at your college? Yes.........................No.....................

42. If so, why?
....

....

....

43. Do you feel that teachers have been really interested in listening to you and helping you?
....

....

44. Are you allowed to discuss points concerning your studies in class? Mark ×.
Frequently.........................Occasionally........................Never....................

45. How many hours per week do you spend reading subject-matter (reference books, etc.) not prescribed in your syllabus?
....

46. On what basis did you vote in the last student elections? Mark ×.

Personalities	
National issues	
Living and working conditions at the college	
Student Union/Government policy	
Other (specify)	

47. What four or five things do your student friends talk about most?

....

....

....

....

....

....

....

48. What are the three most pressing problems students face?

....

....

....

....

....

....

49. What kind of a job would you like? (Rank 1, 2, 3, 4, 5 etc. in order of preference.) And what are your chances of obtaining it ? (Very Good, Good, Poor.)

	Rank	Very Good	Good	Poor
Government administration				
Government service				
College teaching				
School teaching				
Professional (Medicine, Engineering, Law, etc.)				
Research				
Business executive				
Private business				
Church work				
Social welfare work				
Agriculture				
Industry				
Other (specify) e.g. Military				

II. STAFF

QUESTIONNAIRE
FOR COLLEGE STAFF

1. Age...............Sex...............Religion (with denomination).........................
2. Your father's occupation.........................Mother tongue.........................
3. Which state do you come from?...
4. College in which you are teaching?...
5. Teaching experience at this college...................Elsewhere....................
6. Are you a graduate of a Christian college?...
7. Are you a graduate of this college?...
8. What is the highest degree you have taken?...
9. What is the subject you teach? ....
10. What is your teaching rank?...
11. Have you studied outside India?...
12. For what degrees?...................................Where?...................................
13. How do you apportion your time (indicate in hours per week) and what would be the ideal?

	Yours	*Ideal*
Teaching and laboratory/ Tutorial		
Administration		
Preparation for classes		
Research		
Extracurricular		
Social service		
Recreation		
Other (specify if you wish)		

14. Have you ever taken a 'refresher' course in connection with your teaching? ....
    When?.........................For how long?...
15. Did the college assist in this with 'leave'?...
    ... with financial assistance?...........................
    ... in other ways?...........................

16. What posts on staff committees have you held in the past three years?
....
....

17. What do you hold now?..

18. What newspapers do you read regularly?...

19. How many books do you buy per year?..

20. How many books do you own?..

21. How many journals are there in the college library in your subject?
....

22. How many books (approximation) in the college library are there in your subject?..

23. How many times a month do you speak outside the college, on an average?..

24. To which organizations?...

25. Of the total number of students taught by you, what percentage is from the following:
Inter/P.U.C.............% B.A./B.Sc.............% Post-graduate............%

26. How many have you in your tutorial group?...

27. How often do you advise students on personal and vocational questions? ....

	Frequently	Occasionally	Hardly ever
Personal			
Vocational			

28. Do students visit you at home? Frequently ....Occasionally ....
Seldom ....Never...................

29. For how many days have you had to take leave in the last academic year?
Due to illness............................Social obligations..............................
Academic........................Personal.......................Other........................

30. Does the college attract the best students in the area?............................

31. Why or why not?..
....

32. In your opinion what are the seven best colleges in India today?

....
....
....
....
....
....
....

33. What are the most important reasons for your choice?

....
....
....
....

34. Have you read a part or the whole of the Education Commission (Kothari) Report?..
....

35. What changes would you suggest for the improvement of Higher Education in India? Be specific (e.g. control of syllabuses and text-books by the teachers; partial or complete internal assessment; freedom of teachers to set and value examinations of their own students etc.)

....
....
....
....
....
....
....
....
....
....

36. In what specific ways can your college, or the staff of your college, help in bringing about these changes?

....
....

37. What are the 'aims and objects' of the college?..
....

Does the college consciously act on them in the day-to-day life of the college? ....
....

Are you in agreement with these aims?...

Why or why not?..
....

38. Does the fact that the college is sponsored by a Christian organization strengthen it as an institution? Yes..............................No..........................

39. Do you think that the preferential treatment of Christians in your college is strong, normal or weak with regard to the following? Please mark ×.

	Strong	Normal	Weak
Recruitment and promotion of staff			
Admission of students			
Formation of governing body			
Financial assistance to staff and students for study			
Facilities for living etc., for students and staff			

40. Is the religious program at the college in any way objectionable to you? ....

41. Is this program really useful for staff and students? ....

42. Are you actively involved in the religious service activities of the college? Please mark ×.

By attending religious services	
As Staff Advisor of AICUF, SCM etc.	
By planning religious programs and services	
By sharing in social service programs organized in the college	
Any other ways	

43. Without additional expendirure could the college be significantly improved by better organization of existing resources?
....
....

44. Do you consciously strive to make your teaching relevant to the problems of society and the nation, as well as of the students?
....

45. Rank in order of importance (e.g. 1, 2, 3, 4, 5) the functions of a college:

Getting students through their examinations	
National and social service	
Character building	
Leadership training	
The nurture of the individual	
Other	

46. List in order of importance, the qualities of a good teacher:

1. ....
2. ....
3. ....
4. ....
5. ....

47. Do you have departmental discussion groups, or staff discussion groups in your college? ....

48. What percentage of these discussions did you attend last year? ....

49. Did you contribute by way of reading papers, leading discussions?
....
....

50. Has your department started new courses in the past five years?
....
....

51. What changes have been attempted in the department (teaching methods, texts, addition to curriculum, etc.), and with what success?
....
....

52. What percentage of your classes are:

Lectures	
Seminars and discussions	
Lab work/field/or outdoor work	

53. How old are the textbooks and syllabuses in your subjects? Please mark ×

    0–5 years old (   ); 6–10 years old (   ); 11–15 years old (   ); 16–20 years old (   ); over 21 years (   ).

54. Do you encourage extra reading outside the syllabus?..........................

55. With what success and response from students?..........................

56. Can anything be done to improve their response?..........................

57. In what way do you make your class-teaching distinctive?..................

58. What are the 5 most important reasons for the continuation and development of Christian colleges? Rank in order of importance, e.g. 1, 2, 3, 4, 5.

To provide a Christian environment and teach Christian social values	
To provide personnel for the institutional work of the churches	
To impart personal values and qualities (self-discipline) not sufficiently emphasized in other institutions	
To provide educational facilities for Christians and other groups not normally covered by Government	
To provide a sense of community and fellowship	
To promote education of high quality for evangelistic purposes	
To innovate and experiment in new fields and methods	
To maintain a strong 'private sector' in education, to counter-balance governmental control	
Other (specify)	

III. GRADUATES

QUESTIONNAIRE
FOR UNIVERSITY GRADUATES
(Average answering time : 30 minutes)

1. Name of the college you attended...
2. The degrees you received and from where..................................
3. The year of your first graduation..
4. Your major subject of study (Econ., Eng., etc.)..........................
5. Your present age..................Sex................Married..................
6. Number of children..
7. Your religion (with denomination, if Christian) ....
8. Do you consider yourself a member of a caste? Yes.........No...........
9. If so, which caste?..
10. Your home state..
11. Father's occupation (previous or present)................................
12. Present place of residence..
13. Your present occupation..
14. How long have you worked at it?...
15. Is it directly related to your college training? Yes.........No...........
16. Were you unemployed after graduation? Yes................No..............
    If yes, for how long?..
17. Have you changed the kind of work that you have done since graduation? Yes.........................No...
    If so, how many times?...
18. What is your present income per month?...................................
19. How do you feel about your present employment? Mark relevant items × :

I like it, because it suits my training and interests	
I think it makes a good contribution to others	
I am bored, but there is nothing else better available	
I am hoping for a change soon	
A job is a job and one shouldn't expect much from it	

20. Please give a general idea (in percentages) of your expenditure under the following heads :

Food and clothing	
Housing	
Transport and travel	
Miscellaneous	
Savings	
Other	

21. Have you travelled outside India? Yes....................No................
22. For how long have you travelled outside India?.............................
23. What foreign countries have you visited?.............................
24. Mark × the newspapers which you read regularly :

The Indian Express	
The Hindu	
The Mail	
The Statesman	
Blitz	
The Times of India	
The Hindustan Times	
Amrita Bazar Patrika	
Vernacular newspapers	
Other	

25. How many books have you read in the last year? ....

26. Please name three of the most impressive books you have read during last year.

....

....

....

27. Do you have a copy of an Indian *Year Book* for any of the past four years? Yes..................................No...

28. What magazines do you read regularly?

....

....

29. Indicate × your reading interests.

	Very interested	*Moderately interested*	*Little or no interest*
Thrillers			
Books about India			
Travel books			
Fiction			
History & social science			
Professional books			
Literature			
Current events (e.g. politics, social problems)			
Religion and culture			
Other			

30. Have you stood for election at any time? Yes....................No...............

31. If so, to which of the following (mark ×):

Municipal Council	
District Board	
State Legislature	
Central Legislature	

32. Were you successful? Yes.............................. No.............................

33. Which political party did you vote for in the state elections?

	1961	*1964*
D.M.K.		
Congress		
Swatantra		
Communist		
P.S.P.		
Other		
Didn't vote		

4. Have you been imprisoned for political reasons? Yes............No...........

35. Do you belong to a service club or association? Have you held an office in such a club?

Name of Club or Association	Office
....	....
....	....
....	....
....	....

36. What are the five most important internal problems facing India today?

   Please rank : 1 = most important; 2 = second most important; etc.

Caste and communalism	
Spiritual and moral decline in public life	
Dependance on foreign aid	
Population growth	
Illiteracy	
Lack of productive industry	
Weakness of democratic institutions	
Other	

37. Do you consider yourself :

A believer in a Divine Being	
An agnostic	
An atheist	

38. What moral-ethical values do you think most important in society? Please rank :

Charity	
Participation in religious ceremonies	
Upright living	
Service to others	
Helping family members	
Other	

39. How would you spend a free evening? Rank 1-3.

Visit friends	
Read or listen to music	
Take your family out	
Go to the cinema	
Go to a coffee shop or restaurant	
Attend lectures or functions	
Visit the 'club' or watch sporting events	
Other	

40. What do you think your college has given you? Rank 1-5.

A good job	
Ethical values	
Self-discipline	
Life-long and valuable friendships	
Knowledge and information	
Self-reliance and self-respect	
Associations with distinguished teachers	
A sense of social responsibility	
Other	
Nothing really significant	

41. What are the keys to Indian development? Mark × relevant items.

Nation-wide literacy	
More spiritual and moral values in public life	
More efficient action by Government	
More free enterprise	
More big industry	
More national self-reliance and less dependance on foreign aid	
Other	
Problems are too vast to have an opinion	
Never think much about it	

42. How many hours on the average, per day, do you spend on the following?

At work	
Travel to and from work	
Civic and social service	
Study	
General relaxation, reading, music etc.	
Other	

43. Whose opinions do you rely on most, when making a major decision in your life?   Please rank :

Parents	
Wife or Husband	
Brother/Sister	
Former teacher	
Religious leader	
Family friend	
Own judgement	
Other	

44. How often in the past three years, have you been on your former college campus? Mark ×.
    Never   *Once or twice*   *Several times*   *Frequently*

45. Are you in contact with your former college friends? Mark ×.
    Never   *From time to time*   *Now and then*   *Quite often*

46. Are you in correspondence with any of your former teachers? Mark ×.
    Never   *From time to time*   *Now and then*   *Quite often*

47. With how many of these teachers are you in frequent contact?

48. If you wish to make further comments on whether or not your college has influenced your life, please add comments below. This is entirely optional.

NOTES

I

A NOTE ON THE CHRISTIAN COMMUNITY IN INDIA

1. Nicolas Zernov, *The Christian East*, Delhi, Madras, Lahore: S.P.C.K., 1956, p. 100.
2. ibid., p. 101.
3. ibid., p. 104.
4. ibid., pp. 104–5.
5. ibid., pp. 112–13.
6. Kenneth S. Latourette, *Christianity in a Revolutionary Age*, London: Eyre and Spottiswoode, III, 1961, p. 403.
7. ibid., p. 403.
8. *The Catholic Directory of India*, Bombay: The Examiner Press, 1964. My own totals.
9. Bishop Thomas Pothacamury, *The Church in Independent India*, Bombay: The Examiner Press, 1961, p. 136.
10. ibid., p. 146.
11. Latourette, op. cit., p. 407.
12. In Sigfrid Estborn, *The Church among Tamils and Telegus*, Nagpur: National Christian Council, 1961, p. 19.
13. Kaj Baago, *A History of the National Christian Council of India: 1914–64*, Nagpur: National Christian Council, 1965.
14. Kenneth S. Latourette, *Christianity in a Revolutionary Age*, London: Eyre and Spottiswoode, V, 1963, pp. 317 ff.
15. These totals were compiled from the figures in the *Christian Handbook of India*, Nagpur: National Christian Council, 1959, pp. xvi–xix.
16. Church of South India, *Renewal and Advance*, Madras: Christian Literature Society, 1964, Table II, no pagination.
17. ibid., p. 10.
18. Latourette, V, op. cit., pp. 317–18.
19. *Census of India, 1961*, Volume I, Part II C (i) 'Social and Cultural Tables,' pp. 484–5.
20. Kaj Baago, 'Religions in India (1961 census),' *International Review of Missions*, LIII, 210 (April 1964), pp. 169–72.
21. Estborn, op. cit., p. 20.
22. ibid., p. 20.
23. S. D'Souza, 'Some Demographic Characteristics of Christianity in India,' *Social Compass*, XIII, 5–6 (1966), p. 417.
24. Baago, 'Religions in India,' p. 171.
25. D'Souza, op. cit., p. 416.

26. Government of India, Ministry of Information and Broadcasting, *India, 1966,* New Delhi: Government of India Press, 1967, p. 19.
27. D'Souza, op. cit., p. 420.
28. ibid., p. 420.
29. ibid., p. 421.
30. Latourette, V, op. cit., p. 309.
31. Reference is in D'Souza, op. cit., p. 423. *The Mysore Population Study,* Department of Economic and Social Affairs of the U.N., New York, 1961; and J. N. Sinha, ' Differential Fertility and Family Limitation in an Urban Community of Uttar Pradesh,' *Population Studies,* XI, 2 (November 1957), pp. 157–69.
32. Estborn, op. cit., pp. 33–4.
33. Ernest Campbell, *The Church in the Punjab,* Nagpur: National Christian Council, 1961, p. 98.
34. ibid., pp. 97–9.
35. ibid., p. 11.
36. Barbara Boal, ' The Church in the Kond Hills,' in Victor Hayward (editor), *The Church as Christian Community,* London: Lutterworth Press, 1966, p. 275.
37. ibid., p. 275.
38. There is an attempt to describe the Christian socio-economic position based on Census figures in Anthony Parel, ' The Present Position of the Church in India,' *World Justice,* VI, 4 (June 1965), pp. 441–61.
39. James Alter and Herbert Jai Singh, *The Church in Delhi,* Lucknow: Lucknow Publishing House, 1961, *passim.*
40. ibid., p. 84.
41. Campbell, op. cit., p. 37.
42. ibid., p. 77.
43. Baago, *A History,* op. cit., p. 76.
44. *Plan of Church Union in North India and Pakistan,* Madras: Christian Literature Society, Fourth revised edition, 1965, pp. iii–vii.

II

UNIVERSITY EDUCATION IN INDIA

1. Inter-University Board, *Universities' Handbook,* New Delhi: Inter-University Board, 1964, Chapter 1.
2. London University itself soon afterward became a teaching university, but Indian universities did not shift until about 50 years later. There are basically three kinds of institutions in Indian universities today. There are teaching departments of the university itself, constituent colleges which are an integral part of the university itself, and affiliated colleges which are dependent on the university for syllabii, examinations, conferring of degrees and certain standards, but which are

administered independently. David Moses, ' Christian Colleges in the Universities of India,' *Missionary Research Library Occasional Bulletin*, VI, 4 (27 May 1955), p. 2.

3. Beatrice Lamb, *India, a World in Transition*, New York: Praeger, p. 180.

4. T. N. Siqueira, *Modern Indian Education*, Calcutta: Oxford University Press, 1960, p. 77.

5. Aubrey Zellner, *Education in India*, New York: Bookman Associates, 1951, p. 113.

6. Siqueira, op. cit., p. 80.

7. ibid., p. 82.

8. A. D. Lindsay (chairman), *Report of the Commission on Christian Higher Education in India*, London: Oxford University Press, 1931.

9. Chapter IX of the Report is the most important concentration of recommendations. Others are scattered throughout.

10. For two volumes on this consultation, see Richard and Nancy Dickinson, *Directory of Christian Colleges in India*, Madras: Christian Literature Society, 1966; and Richard Dickinson and S. P. Appasamy (editors), *The Christian College and National Development*, Madras: Christian Literature Society, 1967.

11. Frank Wilson (editor), *Report of Survey of Twenty-Eight Schools and Colleges Related to the United Church of Northern India*, New York: United Presbyterian Church in the USA, 1962.

12. Government of India, Ministry of Education, *Report of the Committee of Members of Parliament on Higher Education*, New Delhi: Government of India Press, 1964.

13. (Sri Prakasa Report), *Religious and Moral Instruction*, New Delhi: Government of India Press, 1960.

14. Education Commission, *Education and National Development*, New Delhi: Government of India Press, 1966.

15. J. P. Naik, *Educational Planning in India*, New Delhi: Allied Publishers, 1965, pp. 1–14. *passim*.

16. Robert Gaudino, *The Indian University*, Bombay: Popular Prakashan, 1965; and Edward Shils, ' Indian Students: Rather Sadhus than Philistines,' *Encounter*, 1961. Taken from Reprint.

17. See Tables 32 and 33.

18. J. P. Naik, ' The Role and Problems of Private Enterprise in Education,' in Richard Dickinson and S. P. Appasamy (editors), op. cit., pp. 123–6.

III

THE DEVELOPMENT SETTING

1. *India, 1966*, op. cit., p. 168.

2. ibid., p. 169.

3. ibid., p. 169.
4. ibid., p. 172.
5. ibid., pp. 174–6.
6. ibid., p. 9.
7. ibid., p. 180.
8. ibid., p. 181.
9. *Le Monde*, 30 May 1967, p. 5, columns 5 and 6.
10. Naik, *Educational Planning in India*, op. cit., pp. 32–3.
11. UNESCO, *Long Term Projections for Education in India*, Bangkok: UNESCO Regional Office for Education in Asia, 1965, p. 39.
12. Education Commission Report, p. 470.
13. Naik, *Educational Planning in India*, op. cit., p. 53.
14. This statement of purpose was modified at the New Delhi Assembly, 1961 to read ' to express the ecumenical solidarity of the churches and through mutual aid to strengthen them in their life and mission, and especially in their service to the world around them, and to provide facilities by which the churches may serve men and women in acute human need everywhere, especially orphaned peoples, including refugees of all categories.' Division of Inter-Church Aid, Refugee and World Service, 'A Statement of the Aim, Functions, Facilities and Procedures of its Programme and Project Listing,' Geneva: World Council of Churches, 1964, p. 3.
15. Marcel Herle (director), *Les Eglises Chretiennes' et la Decolonisation*, Paris: Librairie Armand Colin, 1967 (Cahiers de la Foundation Nationale des Sciences Politiques); Stephen Neill, *A History of Christian Missions*, Harmondsworth, Middlesex: Penguin Books, 1964. See especially Chapter 13 and conclusion, pp. 510–78.
16. See, for example, Frederick Harbison and C. A. Myers, *Human Resources, Education and Economic Growth*, New York: McGraw Hill, 1963; T. W. Schultz, 'Capital Formation by Education,' *Journal of Political Economy*, LXVII (1960); T. W. Schultz, *Education and Economic Growth*, Chicago: University of Chicago, 1960 (mimeographed); M. Debeauvais, 'The Concept of Human Capital,' *International Social Service Journal*, XIV, 4(1962); Odd Aukrust, 'Investment and Economic Growth,' *Productivity Measurement Review*, 16 (February 1959); E. F. Denison, 'Measuring the Contribution of Education (And the Residual) to Economic Growth,' *The Residual Factor and Economic Growth*, Paris: O.E.C.D., 1964.
17. H. M. Phillips, 'Education and Development,' in *Economic and Social Aspects of Educational Planning*, Paris: UNESCO, 1964, pp. 15–57.
18. ibid., p. 54–5.
19. Philip Foster, 'The Vocational School Fallacy in Development Planning,' in C. A. Anderson and M. J. Bowman (editors), *Education and Economic Development*, Chicago: Aldine Publishing Company, 1965, pp. 142–66.

20. C. T. Kurien, *Our Five Year Plans*, Bangalore: Christian Institute for the Study of Religion and Society, 1966, p. 158.
21. ibid., p. 159.
22. ibid., p. 161.
23. ibid., p. 162.
24. ibid., p. 162.
25. Education Commission Report, pp. 1–2.
26. ibid., p. 5.
27. ibid., p. 5.
28. Herbert De Souza and T. Mathias, 'Views of the Xavier Board of Higher Education in India, and the Jesuit Educational Association (India) on the Recommendations made by the Education Commission,' Gamdi-Anand: Anand Press, 1966.
29. ibid., pp. 1–3.

IV

PROFILE OF INDIAN CHRISTIAN COLLEGES

1. Education Commission Report, p. 112.
2. Despite crowding and much complaining about lack of facilities, little has been done to rationalize the use of existing facilities. An 'efficiency study' would show sizeable gaps in the use of much equipment, suggesting that what is often needed is not more additions, but doubling up. It may be that in some instances additional students could be accommodated without new buildings.
3. Gaudino, op. cit.
4. Particularly in 'attitudinal' questions it is important to refer to the actual wording of the questions in Appendix 6 — especially since some of the phrases used in the tables are abbreviated for convenience.
5. Unfortunately there was not enough control in the administration of the questionnaire, and we may have attracted the more critical respondees. Therefore, we constantly re-iterate the limitations of this particular sample group.
6. 92% of the expenditures for scholarships on the national level come from Central and State Governments. Education Commission Report, p. 122.

V

ASPECTS OF CHRISTIAN COLLEGES' INVOLVEMENT IN DEVELOPMENT

1. Philip Jacob, *Changing Values in College*, New York: Harper and Brothers, 1957.

2. Manning Patillo and Donald MacKenzie, *Church Sponsored Higher Education in the United States*, (Report of the Danforth Commission), Washington, D.C.: American Council on Education, 1966.

3. Fr. Theo Mathias, Notes for the second meeting of the Executive of the National Board for Christian Higher Education in India, Loyola College, Madras, 26–28 January 1968.

4. John B. Carman, 'The Place of the Study of World Religions in the University.' Speech at Lady Doak College, 17 November 1966. Typed manuscript.

5. A. P. Barnabas and Subhash Mehta, *Caste in Changing India*, New Delhi: Indian Institute of Public Administration, 1965; and Lloyd and Susanne Rudolph, 'The Political Role of India's Caste Associations,' *Pacific Affairs*, XXXIII, 1 (March 1960), pp. 5–22.

6. Madras Christian College (staff), *Developing a College in a Developing Country (Summary of a Ten Year Plan of Development)*, Madras: Thompson and Company, 1966.

7. S. K. Hulbe, 'The Social Mission of the College,' in Dickinson and Appasamy, op. cit., pp. 158–9.

8. S. K. Hulbe and T. Barnabas, *New Horizons in University Education*, (Progress Report on the Rural Life Development and Research Project at Ahmednagar College), Ahmednagar: R. B. Hiray, 1965, p. 5.

9. ibid., pp. 5–7.

10. The Minute of Supplementation was written by Sri Gopalaswami.

11. See especially Chapter VII and the Minute of Supplementation.

12. Education Commission Report, Supplement, pp. 543–5.

13. ibid., pp. 549–50.

14. Education Commission Report, Summary, p. 646.

15. Paul D. Devanandan and M. M. Thomas (editors), *Christian Participation in Nation Building*, Bangalore: The National Christian Council of India and The Christian Institute for the Study of Religion and Society, 1960.

VI

GENERAL ASSESSMENT OF PERFORMANCE

1. Education Commission Report, p. 313.

2. ibid., p. 401.

3. ibid., p. 478.

4. ibid., p. 283.

5. ibid., p. 310.

6. ibid., p. 649.

7. A. R. Kamat and A. G. Deshmukh, *Wastage in College Education*, London: Asia Publishing House, 1963, *passim*.

TOWARDS THE FUTURE

1. Pothacamury, op. cit., p. 27.
2. Education Commission Report, p. 446.
3. ibid., p. 446.
4. Charles Riddle (chairman), *Guidance Needs of College Students*, Delhi: All India Educational and Vocational Guidance Association, 1965, pp. 28–9.
5. J. Edward Dirks, 'A College Self-Study: Issues and Methods,' and ' Self-analysis as a Means of Educational Reform,' in Dickinson and Appasamy, op. cit., 195–210 and pp. 211–20.

BIBLIOGRAPHY

Abel, M., 'University Education and National Integration,' *National Christian Council Review*, LXXXIII, 3 (March 1963), pp. 116–21.

Adiseshiah, Malcolm S., ' Education and Development,' in *Restless Nations: A Study of World Tensions and Development*, New York : Dodd, Mead and Company, 1962, pp. 148–62.

Airan, J. W., 'A Christian Academic Community,' *National Christian Council Review*, LXXX, 10 (October 1960), pp. 364–72.

Airan, J. W., *The Role of Christian Colleges in India Today*, Bombay : Wilson College, 1960.

Airan, J. W., ' The Purpose of the Christian College,' *National Christian Council Review*, XLI, 1 (January 1963), pp. 68–75.

Airan, J. W., 'A Re-examination of the Mission of the Church,' *Christian Education*, XIII, 2nd quarter (June 1963), pp. 33–9.

Airan, J. W., *College Administration: A Proposal*, Bombay : Asia Publishing House, 1965.

Airan, J. W., Barnabas, T., and Shah, A. B. (editors), *Climbing a Wall of Glass*, Bombay : P. C. Manaktala and Sons, Private, Limited, 1965.

Allen, Yorke, *A Seminary Survey*, New York : Harper and Brothers, 1960.

All-India Association of Training Colleges in India, *Report of the Study Group on Education of Secondary Teachers in India*, (Baroda, March 1964), Mysore : Mysore Printing and Publishing House, 1964.

Alter, James and Jai Singh, Herbert, *The Church in Delhi*, Lucknow : Lucknow Publishing House, 1961.

American Church Union, *Christianity in India (Anglican)*, New York : American Church Publication, 1955.

American Council of Voluntary Agencies for Foreign Service, *The Role of Voluntary Agencies in Technical Assistance*, New York : American Council of Voluntary Agencies, 1953.

Anderson, C. Arnold and Bowman, Mary-Jean (editors), *Education and Economic Development*, Chicago : Aldine Publishing Company, 1965.

Anderson, George and Whitehead, Henry, *Christian Education in India*, London : Macmillan and Company, Limited, 1932.

Andhra Loyola College, *College Students of the Krishna District* ('A Socio-Economic Study '), Vijayawada : Andhra-Loyola College Planning Forum, 1963.

Appasamy, A. J., *Christian Task in Independent India*, London : S.P.C.K., 1951.

Appasamy, S. P., 'Approach to Tribal Communities Today,' *Religion and Society*, VIII, 3 (October 1961). This is the theme for this issue of the journal.

Appasamy, S. P., 'The Christian Colleges in the Life and Witness of the Church in India,' *National Christian Council Review*, LXXXVI, 10 (October 1966), pp. 402–14.

Arsenian, S., 'Change in Evaluative Attitudes during Four Years of College,' *Journal of Applied Psychology*, Volume 27 (1943), pp. 233–49.

Asirvatham, Eddy, *Christianity in the Indian Crucible*, Calcutta: YMCA Publishing House, 1957.

Baago, Kaj, 'Religions in India (1961 Census),' *International Review of Missions*, LIII, 210 (April 1964), pp. 169–72.

Baago, Kaj, *A History of the National Christian Council of India, 1914–64*, Nagpur: National Christian Council of India, 1965.

Barnabas, A. P. and Mehta, Subhash, *Caste in Changing India*, New Delhi: Indian Institute of Public Administration, 1965.

Barnabas, T. and Hulbe, S. K., 'The University and the Rural Community,' in *Climbing a Wall of Glass* (J. W. Airan, T. Barnabas and A. B. Shah, editors), Bombay: Manaktala, 1965, pp. 86–101.

Bathgate, K., 'Christian Participation in the Rural Development of India,' *International Review of Missions*, 52 (July 1963), pp. 289–99.

Bender, Richard, 'Academic Community and Christian Community,' *Religion in Life*, XXIX, 2 (Spring 1960), pp. 252–62.

Bhargava, G. S., 'The Indian Intellectual: A Survey, Ambivalence is Nearly Universal,' *The New Leader* (29 May 1956).

Bhatty, E. C., 'The Economic Background of the Christian Community in the United Provinces,' *National Christian Council Review*, LVIII, 9 (September 1938), pp. 493–505.

Bhatty, E. C., 'The Church's Contribution to Social Development in India,' *National Christian Council Review*, LXXXI, 4 (April 1961), pp. 136–45.

Boeschenstein, Harold, *et alii., The University in World Affairs*, New York: The Ford Foundation, 1960.

Braisted, Paul, *Indian Nationalism and the Christian Colleges*, New York: Association Press, 1935.

Brembeck, Cole S. and Weidner, Edward W., *Education and Development in India and Pakistan: A Select and Annotated Bibliography*, East Lansing, Michigan: Michigan State University Press, 1963.

Campbell, Ernest, *The Church in the Punjab*, Nagpur: National Christian Council of India, 1961.

Carman, John B., 'Present Encounters between Christianity and Hinduism in India,' *Review and Expositor*, 58 (1961), pp. 67–90.

Carman, John B., *The Catholic Directory of India*, Bombay: The Examiner Press, 1964.

Carman, John B., 'The Place of the Study of World Religions in the University.' Speech at Lady Doak College, Madurai, South India, 17 November 1966. Typed manuscript.

Cattell, E. L., 'Christian Impact on India,' *International Review of Missions*, 51 (April 1962), pp. 153-62.

Chamberlain, Ronald, 'The Asia Christian Colleges Association, (An Account of Aims and Programme),' *National Christian Council Review*, LVXXVII, 5 (May 1957), pp. 215-20.

Chandi, P. T., 'The Christian Educational Programme in Relation to National Development,' *National Christian Council Review*, LXXVI, 3 (March 1956), pp. 99-102.

Chandi, P. T., 'Christian University Teachers' Conference,' *National Christian Council Review*, LXXVII, 4 (April 1957), pp. 155-8.

Chandrakant, L. S., *Technical Education in India Today*, New Delhi: Government of India Press, 1963.

Chetsingh, Ranjit, 'The Isolation of the Church from the Life of the Nation,' *National Christian Council Review*, LVIII, 8 (January 1938), pp. 6-13.

Chetsingh, Ranjit, *The Christian Handbook of India*, Nagpur: National Christian Council of India, 1959.

Chetsingh, Ranjit, 'The Church of Christ and the Christian Community in India,' *Religion and Society*, X, 4 (December 1963). This is the theme for this issue of the journal.

Church of South India, *Renewal and Advance*, (Report of the Church of South India Commission on Integration and Joint Action), Madras: The Christian Literature Society, 1964.

Cole, Arthur, 'The Relation of Missionary Activity to Economic Development,' *Economic Development and Cultural Change*, IX, 2 (January 1961), pp. 120-7.

Coleman, I. S. (editor), *Education and Political Development*, Princeton: Princeton University Press, 1965.

Coombs, Philip, 'Programming Higher Education within the Framework of National Development Plans.' Paper for meeting on 'Higher Education and Latin American Development,' Inter-American Development Bank, Asuncion, Paraguay, April 1965.

Cormack, Margaret, *She Who Rides a Peacock*, London: Asia Publishing House, 1961.

Council of Serampore College, *The Story of Serampore and Its College*, Calcutta: Baptist Mission Press, 1960.

Curle, Adam, *Educational Strategy for Developing Countries*, London: Tavistock Publications, Limited, 1963.

Devanandan, Paul D., 'Caste, the Christian, and the Nation in India Today,' *Ecumenical Review*, IX, 3 (April 1959), pp. 268-81.

Devanandan, Paul D., and Thomas, M. M. (editors), *Christian Participation in Nation Building*, Bangalore: National Christian Council of India and Christian Institute for the Study of Religion and Society, 1960.

Devanesen, Chandran, 'The Role of the Affiliated Colleges,' *The Education Quarterly*, (January 1967), pp. 88–90.

Dickinson, Richard and Appasamy, S. P. (editors), *The Christian College and National Development*, Madras: Christian Literature Society, 1967.

Dickinson, Richard and Dickinson, Nancy, *Directory of Christian Colleges in India*, Madras: Christian Literature Society, 1966.

Dirks, J. Edward, 'Crucial Problems of Indian Higher Education,' in *Climbing a Wall of Glass* (J. W. Airan, T. Barnabas and A. B. Shah, editors), Bombay: Manaktala, 1965, pp. 42–55.

Doescher, Waldemar, *The Church College in Today's Culture*, Minneapolis: Augsburg Publishing House, 1963.

Eddy, Edward, 'Education of Christians in India,' *The East and the West*, (January 1924), pp. 76–85.

Education Commission, *Education and National Development*, (Report of the Education Commission 1964–6), New Delhi: Government of India Press, 1966.

Education Commission, 'Education et développement,' *Revue Tiers-Monde*, VI, 1965. This is the theme of this issue of the journal.

Education Commission, 'Educational Trends in India,' (Consultation Findings), *Religion and Society*, XII, 2 (June 1965), pp. 108–19.

Education Commission, 'Education's Role in Modernizing Developing Societies: India,' *The Christian Scholar*, XLVIII, 2 (Summer 1965).

Embree, Ainslie T., 'The Distinctive Contribution of the Christian Colleges in India,' 1947. Typed manuscript.

Estborn, Sigfrid, *Our Village Christians*, Madras: Christian Literature Society, 1959.

Estborn, Sigfrid, *The Church among Tamils and Telegus*, Nagpur: National Christian Council of India, 1961.

Firth, C. B., *An Introduction to Indian Church History*, Madras: Christian Literature Society, 1961.

Foster, Philip, 'The Vocational School Fallacy in Development Planning,' in *Education and Economic Development*, (C. A. Anderson and M-J. Bowman, editors), Chicago: Aldine Publishing Company, 1965, pp. 142–66.

Gardiner, T., *Our Indian Colleges*, Edinburgh: Foreign Mission Committee, 1946.

Gaudino, Robert, *The Indian University*, Bombay : Popular Prakashan, 1965.

Government of India, *Census of India, 1961*, New Delhi : Government of India Press, I, 1962.

Government of India, *Census of India, 1961*, I, Part II C (i), (' Social and Cultural Tables '), New Delhi : Government of India Press, 1965.

Government of India, Ministry of Education, *Scholarships for Study Abroad and at Home*, New Delhi : Government of India Press, First edition, 1959; Fourth edition, 1964.

Government of India, Ministry of Education, ' Report on the University Grants Commission,' New Delhi : University Grants Commission, 1960.

Government of India, Ministry of Education, *Review of Education in India (1947–61)*, New Delhi : Government of India Press, 1961.

Government of India, Ministry of Education, *Report of the Committee of Members of Parliament on Higher Education*, New Delhi : Government of India Press, 1964.

Government of India, Ministry of Education, *Education in the States, 1963–4: A Statistical Survey*, New Delhi : Government of India Press, 1965.

Government of India, Ministry of Information and Broadcasting, *India — 1966*, New Delhi : Government of India Press, 1967.

Government of India, Ministry of Labour and Employment, *Employment Survey of the Alumni of Delhi University*, New Delhi : Government of India Press, 1962.

Government of India, Ministry of Labour and Employment, *University Curricula and Occupational Performance — Part II*, New Delhi : Government of India Press, 1964.

Government of India, National Council of Educational Research and Training, *Educational Expenditure in India*, New Delhi : Government of India Press, 1965.

Government of India, National Council of Educational Research and Training, *Educational Opportunities in India*, New Delhi : Government of India Press, 1965.

Government of India, National Council of Educational Research and Training, *Financial Assistance to Students in India, 1950–1 to 1960–1*, New Delhi : Government of India Press, 1965.

Government of India, Planning Commission, *Third Five Year Plan*, New Delhi : Government of India Press, 1961.

Government of India, Planning Commission, *The Third Plan: Mid-Term Appraisal*, New Delhi : Government of India Press, 1963.

Government of India, Planning Commission, *Memorandum on the Fourth Five Year Plan*, New Delhi : Government of India Press, 1964.

Griffith, Alison (editor), *The Role of American Higher Education in Relation to Developing Areas*, Washington D.C. : American Council on Education, 1961.

358 THE CHRISTIAN COLLEGE IN DEVELOPING INDIA

Growths, H. M., *Education and Economic Growth,* Washington D.C.: National Education Association, 1961.

Gupta, Moti Lal, *Problems of Unemployment in India.* Dissertation in 1955, but no other information available.

Harbison, Frederick, and Myers, Charles, *Human Resources, Education and Economic Growth,* New York: McGraw-Hill Book Company, Inc., 1963.

Harbison, Frederick, and Myers, Charles, *Man-power and Education,* New York: McGraw-Hill Book Company, Inc., 1965.

Hart, Henry, *Campus India,* (An Appraisal of American College Programs in India), East Lansing: Michigan State University Press, 1961.

Hayden, Howard (director), *Higher Education and Development in South-east Asia,* Paris: UNESCO, 1967.

Heimsath, Charles, *Indian Nationalism and Hindu Social Reform,* Princeton: Princeton University Press, 1964.

Hesburgh, T. M., 'The Cultural and Educational Aspects of Development,' Paris: International Federation of Catholic Universities, 1964.

Hogg, Alfred, ' The Function of the Christian College,' *International Review of Missions,* (January 1934), pp. 110–19.

Hoselitz, Bert, *Investment in Education and Its Political Impact in Developing Countries,* New York: Social Science Research Council, 1960.

Hulbe, S. K., and Barnabas, T., *New Horizons in University Education,* (Progress Report on the Rural Life Development and Research Project at Ahmednagar College), Ahmednagar: R. B. Hiray, 1965.

Iglehart, Charles, *International Christian University,* Tokyo: International Christian University, 1964.

Institute of Applied Man-power Research, *Fact Book on Man-power,* New Delhi: Government of India Press, Part II, 1964.

Institute of Applied Man-power Research, *Educated Persons in India, 1960–1 to 1975–6,* New Delhi: Government of India Press, 1965.

International Association of Universities, *University Education and Public Service,* Paris: International Universities Bureau, 1959.

Inter-University Board of India and Ceylon, *Universities' Handbook,* New Delhi: Inter-University Board, 1964.

Jacob, Korula, 'Government of India and Entry of Missionaries,' *International Review of Missions,* 47 (October 1958), pp. 410–16.

Jacob, Philip, *Changing Values in College,* New York: Harper and Brothers, 1957.

Jester, David, ' Basic Considerations in Founding a College in Nigeria.' Ph.D. from Teachers College, Columbia University, 1959.

Jones, W. Paul, ' Toward a Contemporary Theological Understanding of the Christian College,' *The Journal of Religion*, XLIII, 3 (July 1962), pp. 185–202.

Kabir, Humayun, *Education in New India*, London: George Allen and Unwin, Limited, 1956.

Kabir, Humayun, ' National Integration in India,' *Education Quarterly*, (Autumn 1961), pp. 229–34.

Kamat, A. R. and Deshmukh, A. G., *Wastage in College Education*, London: Asia Publishing House, 1963.

Kapp, Karl, ' Report of the Conference of Heads of Universities,' (Karachi University, 25 January to 1 February 1961). Sponsored by the Southeast Treaty Organization.

Kapp, Karl, *Hindu Culture, Economic Development and Economic Planning in India*, Bombay and New York: Asia Publishing House, 1963.

Karat, G. R., ' The Student Christian Movement in India Today,' *National Christian Council Review*, LXXXII, 10 (October 1962), pp. 369–73.

Kiano, G., 'At What Points Can Christianity Make a Difference to Political and Economic Development in Africa? ' *Background Information for Church and Society* (mimeographed), Geneva: World Council of Churches, (November 1959), pp. 9–14.

King, Earl (editor), *Christian Education Today and Tomorrow in South Asia*, Lucknow: Lucknow Publishing House, 1947.

Koilpillai, J. Victor, ' Koinonia and Caste within the Church,' *National Christian Council Review*, LXXVII, 11 (November 1958), pp. 459–70.

Koilpillai, J. Victor, ' Journalism Education at Hislop College,' *National Christian Council Review*, LXXXII, 4 (April 1962), pp. 162–6.

Krishnaya, G. S., ' Education for National Unity,' *National Christian Council Review*, LVIII, 4 (April 1938), pp. 186–93.

Kurien, C. T., *Our Five Year Plans*, Bangalore: Christian Institute for the Study of Religion and Society, 1966.

Lacy, Creighton, *The Conscience of India*, New York: Holt, Rinehart and Winston, 1965.

Langdon, John, ' The Sri Prakasa Report,' *National Christian Council Review*, LXXXI, 1 (January 1961), pp. 17–25.

Latourette, Kenneth S., *Christianity in a Revolutionary Age*, London: Eyre and Spottiswoode (Publishers), Limited, III, 1961.

Latourette, Kenneth S., *Christianity in a Revolutionary Age*, London: Eyre and Spottiswoode (Publishers), Limited, V, 1963.

Lewis, W. A., ' Education and Economic Development.' Information Document Number 4, Conference on Education and Economic and

Social Development in Latin America, at Santiago, Chile, March, 1962.

Lindsay, A. D. (Chairman), *Report of the Commission on Christian Higher Education in India*, London: Oxford University Press, 1931.

McKenzie, John (editor), 'Higher Education,' in *The Christian Task in India*, London: Macmillan and Company, Limited, 1929, pp. 85–102.

Macphail, J. R., *Future of the Indian University*, Calcutta: YMCA Publishing House, 1963.

Macphail, J. R., 'The Christian Colleges in India Today,' *The International Review of Missions*, LIII, 210 (April 1964), pp. 162–8.

Macphail, J. R., *Reflections from a Christian College*, Madras: The Christian Literature Society, 1966.

Madras Christian College (staff), *Re-thinking Our Role (Role of a Christian College in India Today)*, Bangalore: Christian Institute for the Study of Religion and Society, 1964.

Madras Christian College (staff), *Developing a College in a Developing Country (Summary of a Ten Year Plan of Development)*, Madras: Thompson and Company, Private, Limited, 1966.

Mathai, Samuel, 'Our Academic Standards,' *Christian Education*, XIII, First Quarter (March 1963), pp. 51–7.

Mathur, P. N., 'Cultural Roots and the Modern University,' in *Climbing a Wall of Glass* (J. W. Airan, T. Barnabas and A. B. Shah, editors), Bombay: Manaktala, 1965, pp. 55–70.

Mayhew, Arthur, *The Education of India*, London: Faber and Gwyer, 1928.

Mayhew, Arthur, 'The Meaning of Christian Service in a World of Rapid Change,' *Religion and Society*, VIII, 1 (April 1961). This is the theme for this issue of the journal.

Mehok, William, 'Jesuit Man-power in India.' Unpublished paper, 1966, in process of publication.

Mellenbaum, W., 'Urban Unemployment in India,' *Pacific Affairs*, (June 1957), pp. 138–50.

Methodist Church in Southern Asia, *Christian Education Today and Tomorrow*, Lucknow: Lucknow Publishing House, 1946.

Mishra, Vikas, *Hinduism and Economic Growth*, London: Oxford University Press, 1962.

Moses, David, 'Christian Colleges in the Universities of India,' *Missionary Research Library Occasional Bulletin*, VI, 4 (May 1955).

Moses, David, 'The Nature and Functions of Christian Colleges and Universities in Asia Today,' *Silliman Journal*, XII, 4 (Fourth Quarter, 1965), pp. 393–411.

Motwani, Kewal, *Integration: A Programme of Education*, Madras: Ganesh and Company, Private, Limited, 1962.

Mudaliar, Chandra, 'State and Religion in India, (A Study of the 'Secular State' in India)'. Paper presented at the Fifth Colloquim on the Sociology of Protestantism, Sigtuna, Sweden, April 1965.

Mukerji, S. N., 'The Role of Higher Education in the Rural Development in Free India.' 1954 Ph.D. dissertation at Columbia University, New York City.

Muthyalu, Y., 'Caste in the Church,' *National Christian Council Review*, LVIII, 3, pp. 145–9.

Naik, J. P., 'The Role of Private Enterprise in Education,' New Delhi, 1965, processed. Background paper prepared for the Education Commission, 1964–6.

Naik, J. P., *Educational Planning in India*, New Delhi: Allied Publishers, Private, Limited, 1965.

Namikam, Rajah, *Missionary Collegiate Education in the Presidency of Madras*, Lancaster, Pennsylvania: Conestoga Publishing Company, 1929.

Natarajan, S. A., *A Century of Social Reform in India*, Bombay: Asia Publishing House, 1959.

National Christian Council, Executive Committee, 'Basic Education — A Call to the Churches,' *National Christian Council Review*, LXXVII, 4 (April 1957), pp. 171–3.

National Christian Council, 'The Role of the Missionary in India Today,' (Report of a Consultation), *National Christian Council Review*, LXXXI, 12 (December 1961), pp. 435–42.

National Christian Council, 'Proceedings of a Joint Meeting of the Central Board of Christian Higher Education and Principals of Christian Colleges,' (Nagpur, February 1963), Kottayam: CMS Press, 1963.

Oomnan, Philip, *The Christian Church in Social and Economic Action in India*, Calcutta: Baptist Mission Press, 1938.

Orr, Clara (compiler), *Directory of Christian Colleges*, (Asia, Africa, Middle East, the Pacific, Latin America and the Caribbean), New York: Missionary Research Library, 1961.

Pakynstein, E. H., 'Christians in India,' *National Christian Council Review*, LXXXIII, 9 (September 1963), pp. 349–50.

Pande, G. C., 'The State and Higher Education: Some Suggestions,' in *Climbing a Wall of Glass*, (J. W. Airan, T. Barnabas and A. B. Shah, editors), Bombay: Manaktala, 1965, pp. 167ff.

Parel, Anthony, 'The Present Position of the Church in India,' *World Justice*, VI, 4 (June 1965), pp. 441–61.

Patillo, Manning and MacKenzie, Donald, *Church Sponsored Higher Education in the United States*, (Report of the Danforth Commission), Washington, D.C.: American Council on Education, 1966.

Patonm William, *Alexander Duff*, London: SCM Press, 1923.

Patton, Leslie Karr, *The Purpose of Church-Related Colleges*, New York: Teachers College, Columbia University, 1940.

Philip, Puthenveetre, *Christian Church and Society and Economic Action in India*, Calcutta: Baptist Mission Press, 1938.

Phillips, H. M., 'Education as a Basic Factor in Economic and Social Development,' *UNESCO Conference of African States*, (Addis Ababa, 1961), Paris: UNESCO, 1961, pp. 97–106.

Phillips, H. M., 'Education and Development,' *Economic and Social Aspects of Educational Planning*, Paris: UNESCO, 1964, pp. 15–57.

Pickett, J. Waskom, *Christian Mass Movements in India*, New York: The Abingdon Press, 1933.

Pickett, J. Waskom, *Plan of Church Union in North India and Pakistan*, Madras: Christian Literature Society, Fourth revised edition, 1965.

Pothacamury, Thomas, *The Church in Independent India*, Bombay: The Examiner Press, 1961.

Quequiner, M., ' L'Inde et les missionaires étrangers,' *Etudes*, April 1958. Pagination not available.

Raichur, Sunder, 'Religion and Public Education in India.' Ph.D. dissertation, Boston University, 1949.

Raju, S. P., 'Church Statistics and Their Evaluation,' *National Christian Council Review*, LXXVIII, 1 (January 1958), pp. 20–36.

Raju, S. P., *A Master Plan of National Strategy*, Bangalore: Bible Society of India and Ceylon, 1962.

Rallia, Ram, ' The Caste System and Its Influence on the Christian Church in India,' *National Christian Council Review*, LVIII, 11 (November 1938), pp. 603–14.

Ramm, Bernhard, *The Christian College in the Twentieth Century*, Grand Rapids, Michigan: William B. Eerdmans Publishing Company, 1963.

Raymond, L. J., ' Emotional Integration: Fostering an All-India Perspective,' *Clergy Monthly Supplement*, 6 (Summer 1962), pp. 89–102.

Reddick, Olive (editor), *Handbook of Indian Universities*, New Delhi: Allied Publishers, Private, Limited, 1963.

Reddick, Olive (editor), ' Rediscovery of the Tribal Personality in the Context of Church and Nation,' *Religion and Society*, IX, 4, (December 1962). This is the theme for this issue of the journal.

Rego, V., ' Enseignement nouveuax en Inde,' *Questions Scolaires aux Missions*, Louvain: Desclee de Brouwer, Museum Lessianum, 32 (1954), pp. 168–81.

Revelle, Roger, ' Reconstruction of Higher Education.' Paper prepared for the Education Commission, November 1965.

Riddle, Charles (chairman), *Guidance Needs of College Students*, Delhi: All India Educational and Vocational Guidance Association, 1965.

Robbins, Lord, *Higher Education Report*, London: Her Majesty's Stationery Office, 1963.

Rudolph, Lloyd and Rudolph, Susanne, 'The Political Role of India's Caste Associations,' *Pacific Affairs*, XXXIII, 1 (March 1960), pp. 5–22.

Ryan, F., 'The Caste System and Social Education,' *Social Action*, X, 11 (November 1960), pp. 469–78.

Ryerson, Charles, ' Students, the Tamil Renascence, and the Church,' *The Christian Scholar*, XLVII, 2 (Summer 1965), pp. 121–4.

Scott, David, 'The Theological Foundations of the Christian College,' *National Christian Council Review*, LXXXIII, 4 (April 1963), pp. 160–70.

Scott, Roland, *Social Ethics in Modern Hinduism*, Calcutta: YMCA Publishing House, c. 1958.

Shea, Thomas, 'Barriers to Economic Development in Traditional Societies: Malabar, a Case Study,' *The Journal of Economic History*, 19 (1959), pp. 504–22.

Shah, A. B. (editor), *Higher Education in India*, Bombay, Calcutta, New Delhi, Madras: Lalvani Publishing House, 1967.

Shils, Edward, ' Intellectuals in the Political Development of New States,' *World Politics*, 12 (April 1960), pp. 329–68.

Shils, Edward, ' Indian Students: Rather Sadhus than Philistines.' Reprint from *Encounter*, 1961.

Shils, Edward, *The Intellectual between Tradition and Modernity*, The Hague: Mouton and Company, 1961.

Shipstone, Eva, ' Basic Concerns in Christian Higher Education,' *Christian Education*, XIII, 1 (March 1963), pp. 58–64.

Shridevi, Pati, ' The Development of Women's Higher Education in India.' Ph.D. dissertation, Columbia University, 1954.

Shrimali, K. L., *Education in Changing India*, London: Asia Publishing House, 1965.

(Sri Prakasa Report), *Religious and Moral Instruction*, New Delhi: Government of India Press, 1960.

Singh, Amar K., *Indian Students in Britain*, London: Asia Publishing House, 1963.

Singh, Ram, ' Living Conditions of College Students,' *National Christian Council Review*, LXXV, 3 and 4 (3 March 1955 and 4 April 1955), pp. 111–20 and 164–73.

Sinha, D. P., *The Educational Policy of the East India Company in Bengal to 1854*, Calcutta: publisher unknown, 1964.

Siqueira, T. N., *Modern Indian Education*, Calcutta: Oxford University Press, 1960.

Smith, Donald E., *India as a Secular State*, London: Oxford University Press, 1963.

De Souza, H. A., and Mathias, T. A., ' Views of the Xavier Board of Higher Education in India, and the Jesuit Educational Association (India) on the Recommendations made by the Education Commission,' Gamdi-Anand: Anand Press, 1966. For private circulation only.

Stanford Research Institute, *Toward Strategies of Education*, Menlo Park, California: Stanford Research Institute, 1961.

Taylor, H. J., ' Examinations as a Creative Aid in University Education,' in *Climbing a Wall of Glass* (J. W. Airan, T. Barnabas and A. B. Shah, editors), Bombay: Manaktala, 1965, pp. 101–15.

Taylor, W. L., *Reflections on the Economic Role of Education in Underdeveloped Countries*, London: Oxford University Press, 1964.

Taylor, W. S., ' Religious and Social Beliefs of Students in Certain Christian Colleges,' *National Christian Council Review*, LVIII, 10 (October 1938), pp. 563–73.

Thomas, M. M., ' The Christian College in Asia Today,' *The Christian Scholar* (Autumn 1956), p. 193.

Thomas, M. M. (editor), *The Idea of a Responsible University in Asia Today*, (The Asian University Teachers' Consultation, Bandung, 1951), Geneva : The World's Student Christian Federation, 1954.

UNESCO, *Report on the Regional Meeting of Representatives of Asian Member States on Primary and Compulsory Education*, (Karachi, 1959-60), Paris: UNESCO, 1960.

UNESCO, *Final Report: Conference of African States on the Development of Education in Africa, Addis Ababa, 15-25 May 1961*, Paris: UNESCO, 1961.

UNESCO, *Final Report: Meeting of Ministers of Education of African Countries Participating in the Implementation of the Addis Ababa Plan*, Paris: UNESCO, 1962.

UNESCO, *Rapport Final: Conference sur l'education et le developement economique et social en Amerique Latine, Santiago du Chili, 5-19 Mars 1962*, Paris: UNESCO, 1964.

UNESCO, *Economic and Social Aspects of Educational Planning*, Paris: UNESCO, 1964.

UNESCO, *Long Term Projections for Education in India*, (Report of the UNESCO Regional Advisory Team for Educational Planning in Asia), Bangkok: UNESCO Regional Office for Education in Asia, 1965.

UNESCO, and International Association of Universities, *Higher Education and Development in South-east Asia*, (Summary Report and Conclusions), Paris : UNESCO, 1965.

University Grants Commission, *Report on the Examination Reform*, New Delhi: University Grants Commission, 1962.

University Grants Commission, *Handbook of Universities in India, 1963*, New Delhi: University Grants Commission, 1964.

University Grants Commission, *Teachers' Hostels*, New Delhi: University Grants Commission, 1964.

University Grants Commission, *Development Programmes Sponsored by the University Grants Commission*, New Delhi: University Grants Commission, 1964.

University Grants Commission, *Summer Institutes*, New Delhi: University Grants Commission and National Council of Educational Research and Training, 1965.

University Grants Commission, *University and College Libraries*, New Delhi: University Grants Commission, 1965.

University Grants Commission, *Report of the Committee on Residential Accommodation for Students and Teachers*, New Delhi: University Grants Commission, 1965.

University Grants Commission, *Report on Standards of University Education*, New Delhi: University Grants Commission, 1965.

University Grants Commission, *Sociology in Indian Universities*, New Delhi: University Grants Commission, 1966.

University Grants Commission, *University Development in India*, (Basic Facts and Figures), New Delhi: University Grants Commission, 1966.

University Grants Commission, *Some Facts and Figures*, New Delhi: University Grants Commission, 1966.

Useem, John and Useem, Ruth, *The Western Education Man in India*, New York: Dryden Press, 1955.

Walsh, W., ' University Problems: The University in India,' *Twentieth Century*, 168 (August 1960), pp. 154–63.

Walter, Gladys, ' Education for Girls in India under the Methodist Church.' Ph.D. dissertation, Teachers College, Columbia University, 1950.

Webster, Douglas, *What is the Church of South India?* London: The Highway Press, 1954.

Webster, John, 'An Experiment in General Education at Baring Union Christian College,' *The Christian Scholar*, XLVII, 2 (Summer 1965), pp. 125–30.

Wicke, Myron, *The Church-Related College*, Washington: Center for Applied Research in Education, 1964.

Wilson College (staff), *Thoughts on Indian Education*, Bombay: Wilson College, 1961–2.

Wilson College (staff), *The Role of University Education in National Integration*, Bombay: Wilson College, 1963 or 1964.

Wilson College (staff), *The Roots and the Wings*, (A Discussion on Indian Culture), Bombay: Wilson College, 1965.

Wilson, Frank (editor), *Report of Survey of Twenty-Eight Schools and Colleges Related to the United Church of Northern India*, New York: United Presbyterian Church in the USA, 1962.

Wilson, Frank (editor), ' Aims and Objectives of Liberal Education in a Developing Country,' in *Climbing a Wall of Glass* (J. W. Airan, T. Barnabas and A. B. Shah, editors), Bombay: Manaktala, 1965, pp. 16–26.

Xavier Board of Higher Education in India, *Xavier Board of Higher Education in India, 1962–4*, Mangalore: St. Aloysius' College Press, 1964. For private circulation only.

Xavier Board of Higher Education in India, *XASS Directory of Catholic Secondary and Secondary Training Schools in India, 1964*, Bombay: Louis Printing Press, 1964.

Zellner, Aubrey, *Education in India*, New York: Bookman Associates, 1951.

Zernov, Nicolas, *The Christian East*, Delhi, Madras, Lahore: S.P.C.K., 1956.

INDEX